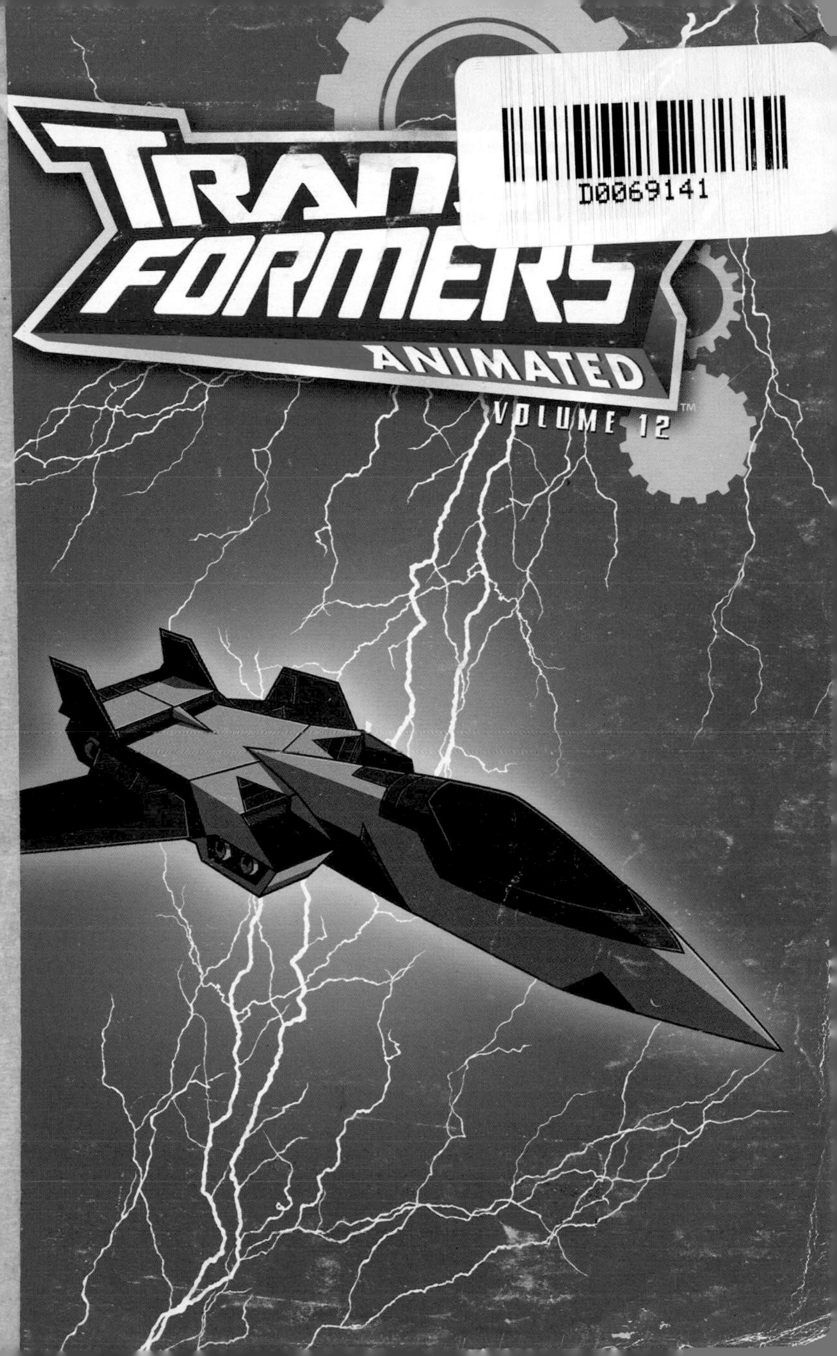
FORMERS
ANIMATED
VOLUME 12™

BLACK FRIDAY
WRITTEN BY:
RICH FOGEL

SARI, NO ONE'S HOME
WRITTEN BY:
TODD CASEY

ADAPTATION BY:
ZACHARY RAU

EDITS BY:
JUSTIN EISINGER

LETTERS AND DESIGN BY:
TOM B. LONG

ISBN: 978-1-60010-556-2
12 11 10 9 1 2 3 4 5

Licensed by:

Special thanks to Hasbro's Aaron Archer, Michael Kelly,
Amie Lozanski, Val Roca, Ed Lane, Michael Provost,
Erin Hillman, Samantha Lomow, and Michael Verrecchia
for their invaluable assistance.

IDW Publishing is:
Operations:
Ted Adams, Chief Executive Officer
Greg Goldstein, Chief Operating Officer
Matthew Ruzicka, CPA, Chief Financial Officer
Alan Payne, VP of Sales
Lorelei Bunjes, Dir. of Digital Services

AnnaMaria White, Marketing & PR Manager
Marci Hubbard, Executive Assistant
Alonzo Simon, Shipping Manager
Angela Loggins, Staff Accountant

Editorial:
Chris Ryall, Publisher/Editor-in-Chief
Scott Dunbier, Editor, Special Projects
Andy Schmidt, Senior Editor
Justin Eisinger, Editor
Kris Oprisko, Editor/Foreign Lic.

Denton J. Tipton, Editor
Tom Waltz, Editor
Mariah Huehner, Associate Editor
Carlos Guzman, Editorial Assistant

Design:
Robbie Robbins, EVP/Sr. Graphic Artist
Neil Uyetake, Art Director
Chris Mowry, Graphic Artist

Amauri Osorio, Graphic Artist
Gilberto Lazcano, Production Assistant

To discuss this issue of *Transformers*, or join
the IDW Insiders, or to check out exclusive Web
offers, visit our site:

www.IDWPUBLISHING.com

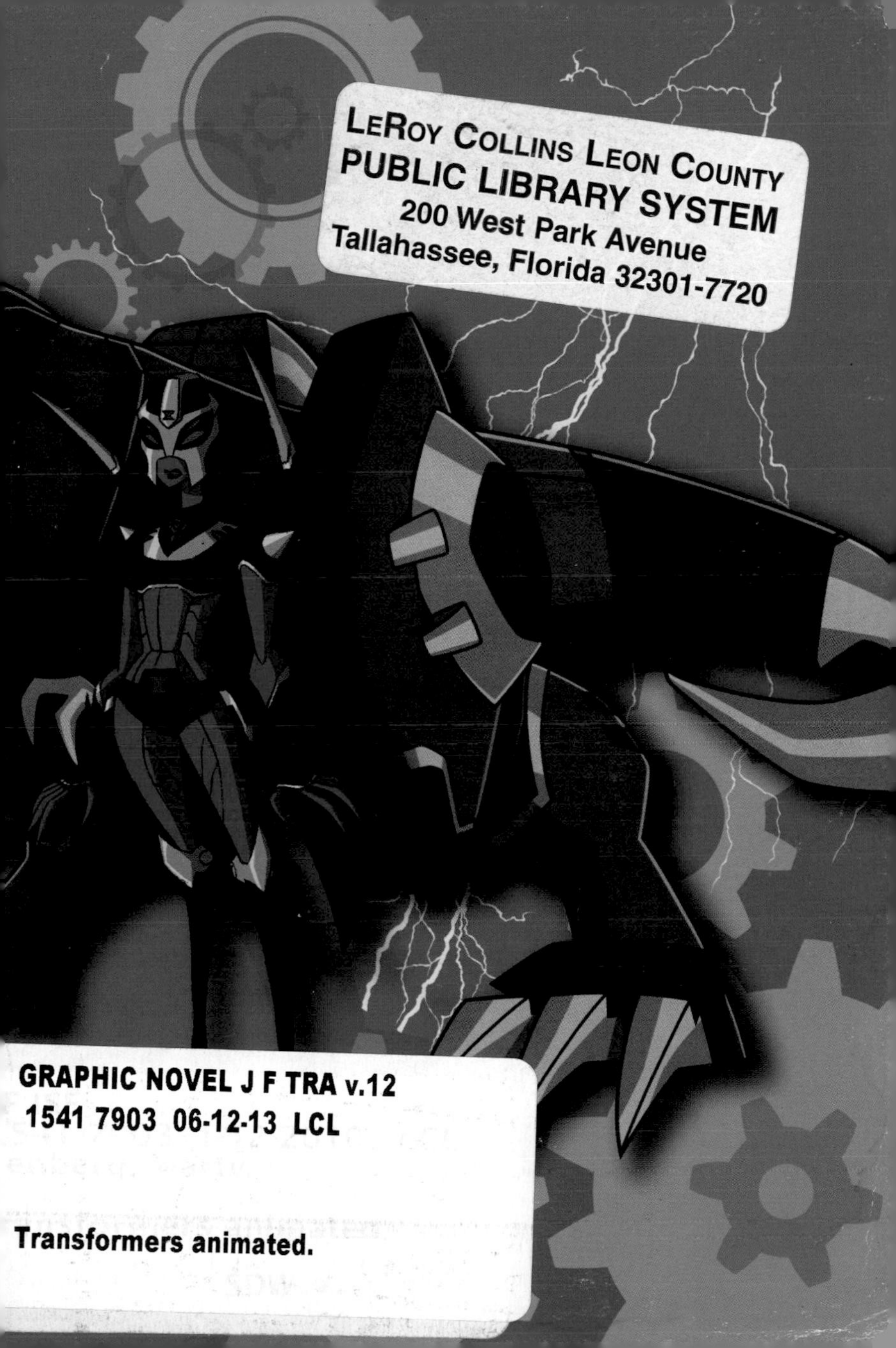

Roll Call

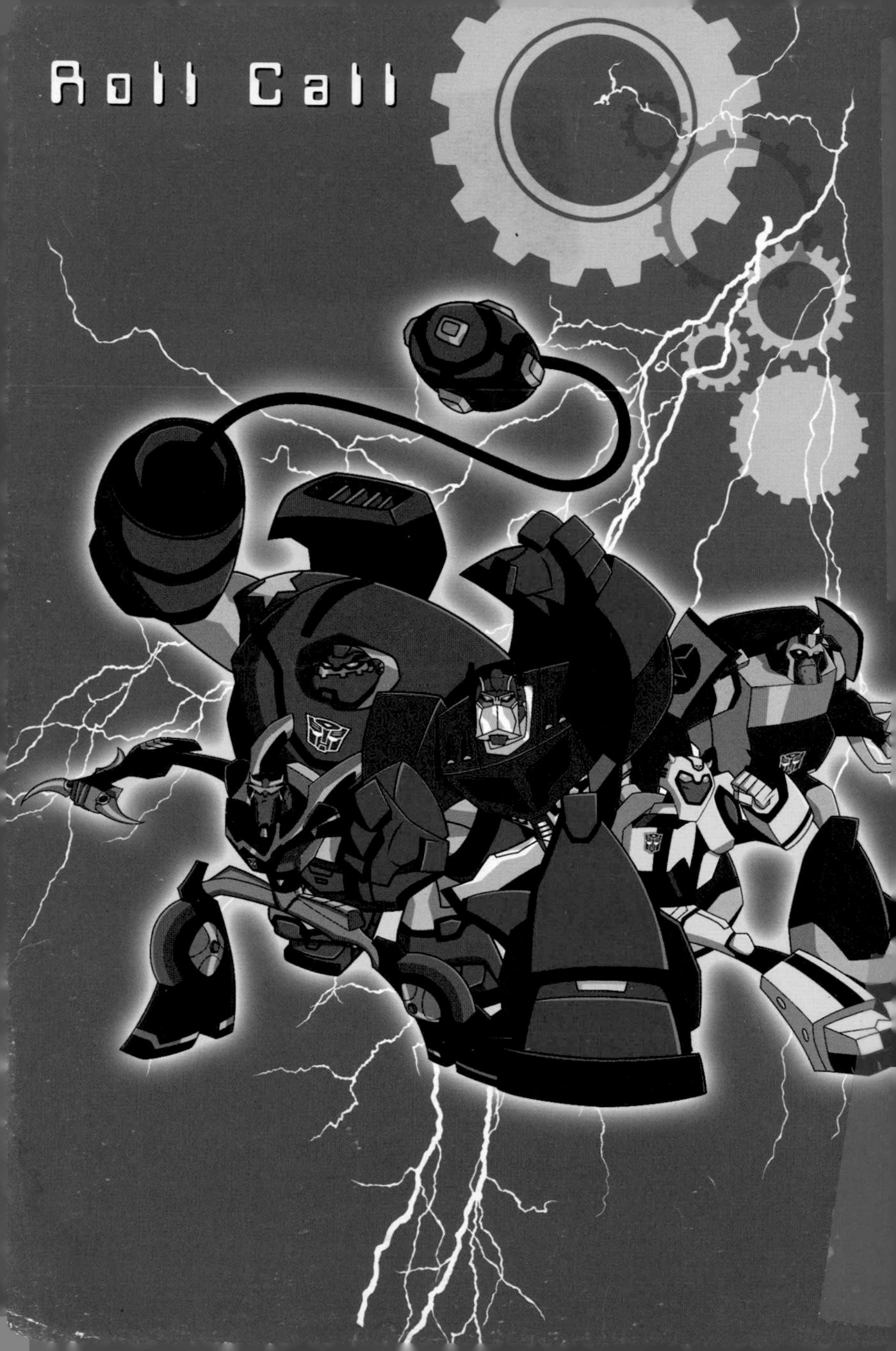

Optimus Prime

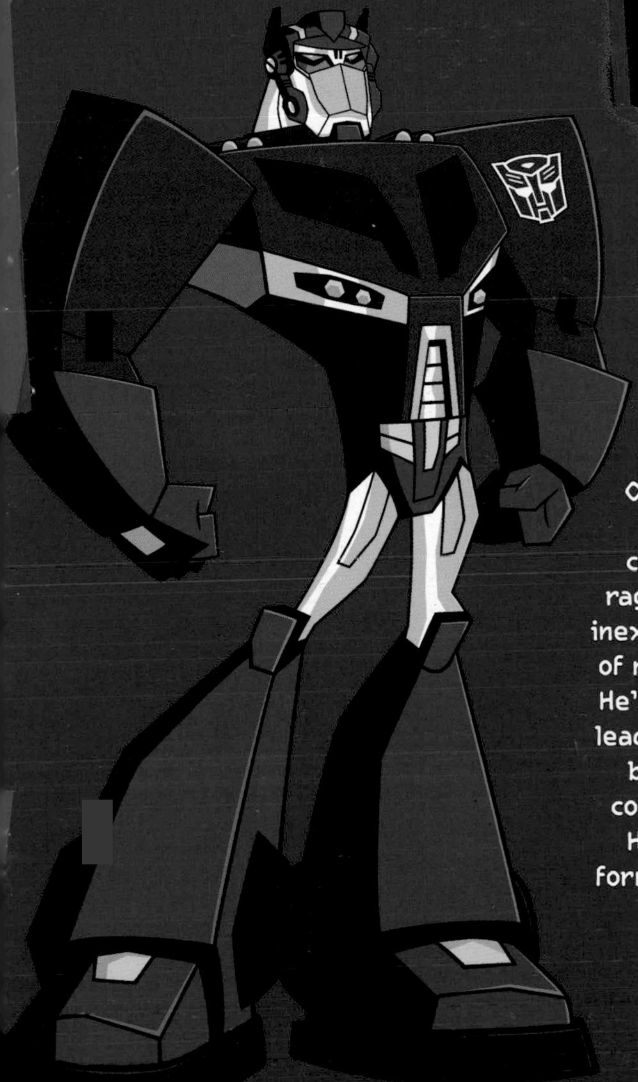

OPTIMUS PRIME
is the young
commander of a
ragtag and largely
inexperienced group
of misfit AUTOBOTS.
He's not the kind of
leader who needs to
bark orders to
command respect.
His mechanized
form is a fire truck.

Ratchet

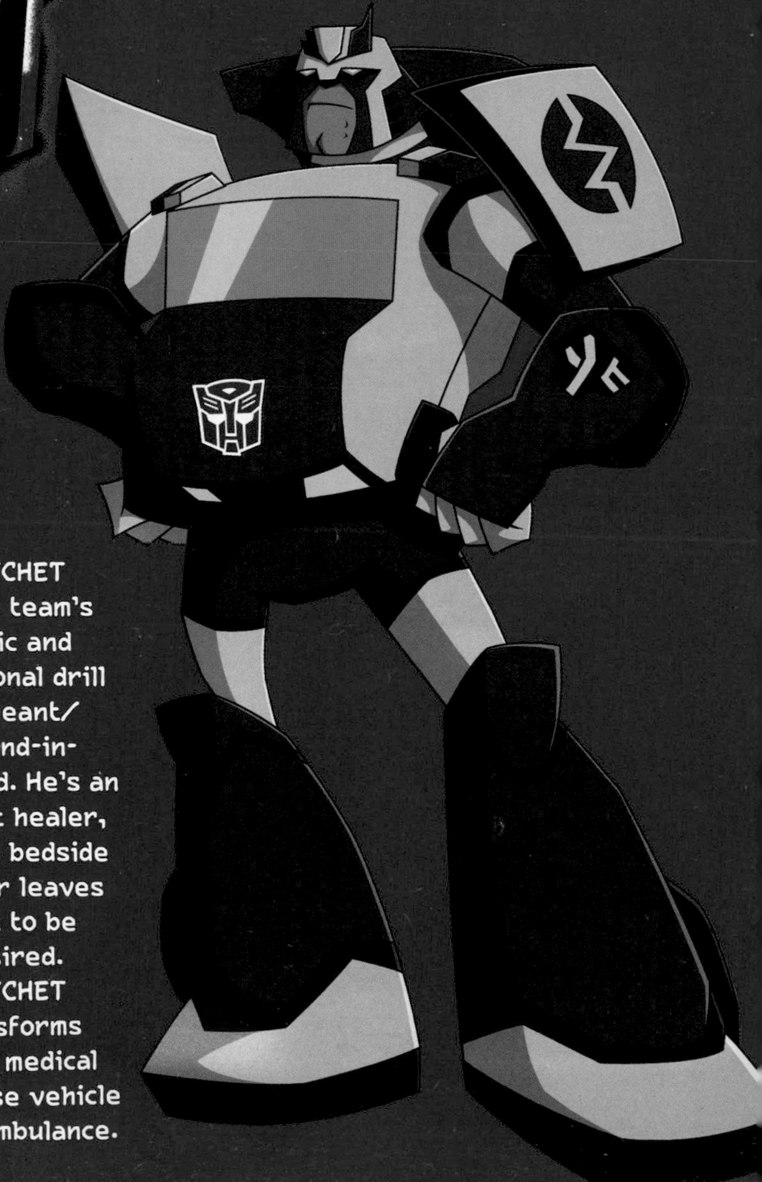

RATCHET is the team's medic and occasional drill sergeant/ second-in-command. He's an expert healer, but his bedside manner leaves a lot to be desired. RATCHET transforms into a medical response vehicle or an ambulance.

Bulkhead

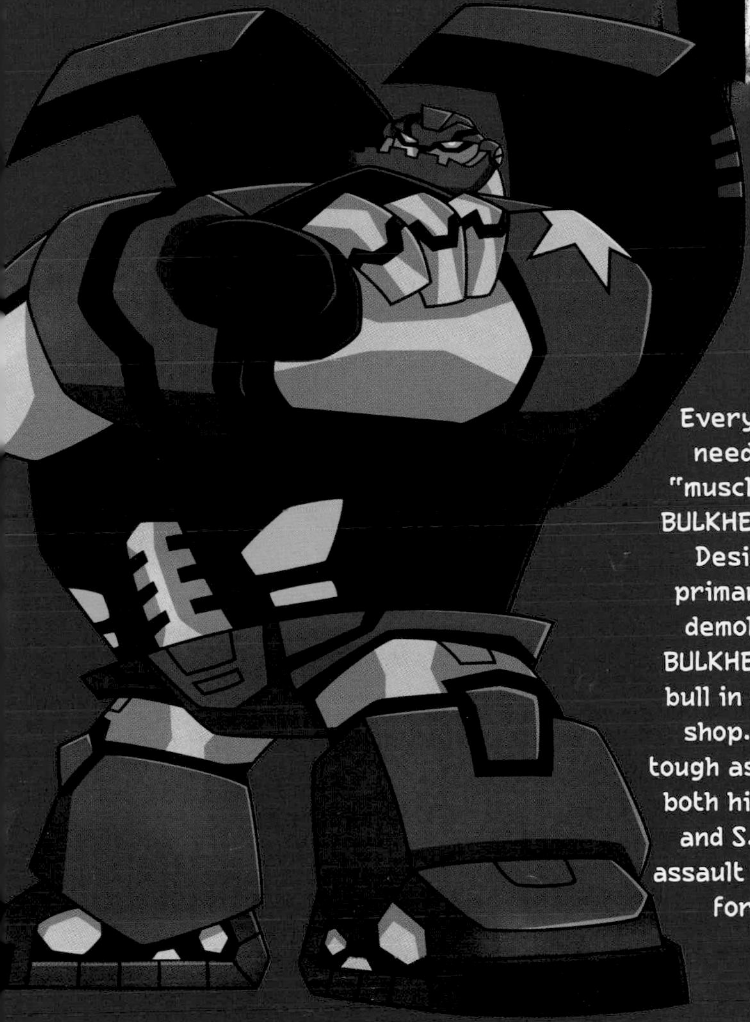

Every team needs its "muscle" and BULKHEAD is it. Designed primarily for demolition, BULKHEAD is a bull in a china shop. He is tough as nails in both his robot and S.W.A.T. assault cruiser forms.

Bumblebee

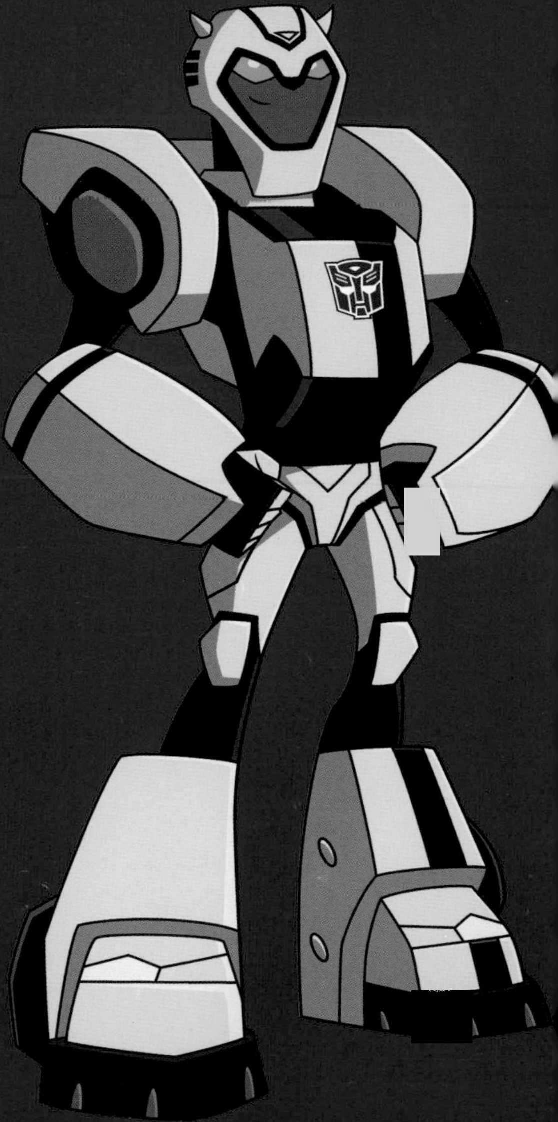

BUMBLEBEE is the "kid" of the team, easily the youngest and least mature of the AUTOBOTS. He's a bit of a show off, always acting on impulse and rarely considering the consequences. But, he looks awesome in his undercover police cruiser form.

Prowl

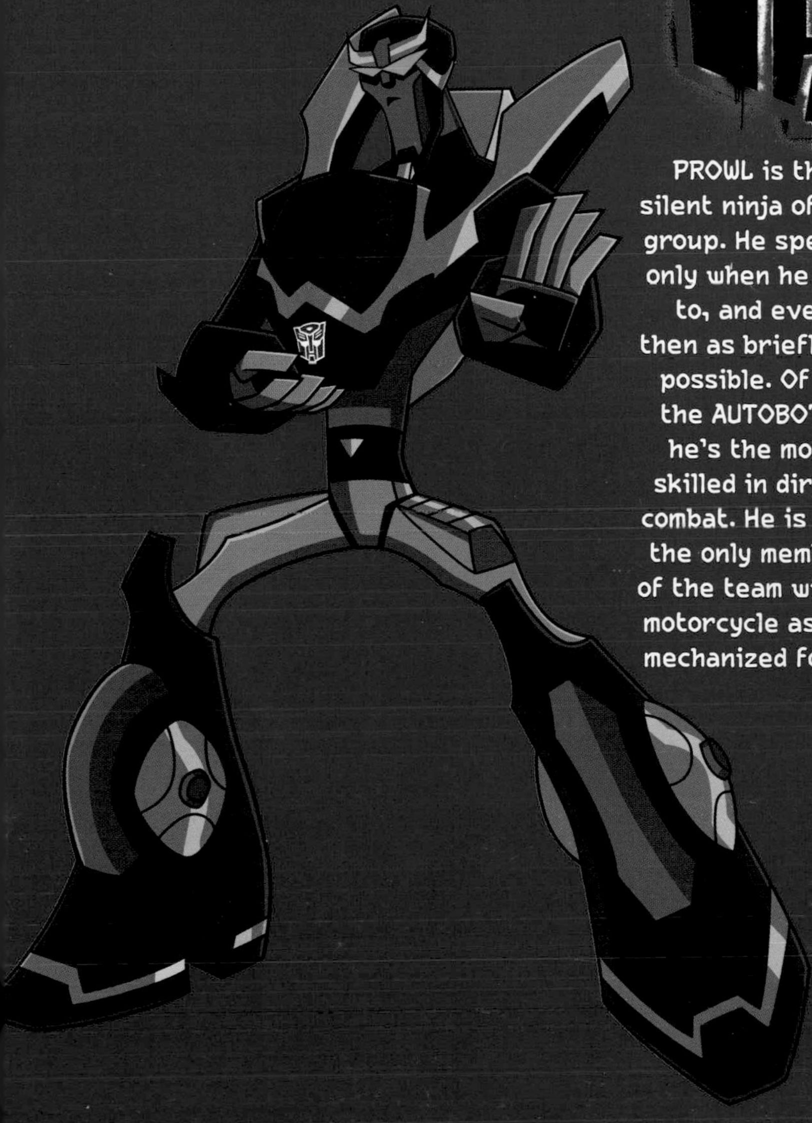

PROWL is the silent ninja of the group. He speaks only when he has to, and even then as briefly as possible. Of all the AUTOBOTS, he's the most skilled in direct combat. He is also the only member of the team with a motorcycle as his mechanized form.

Sari

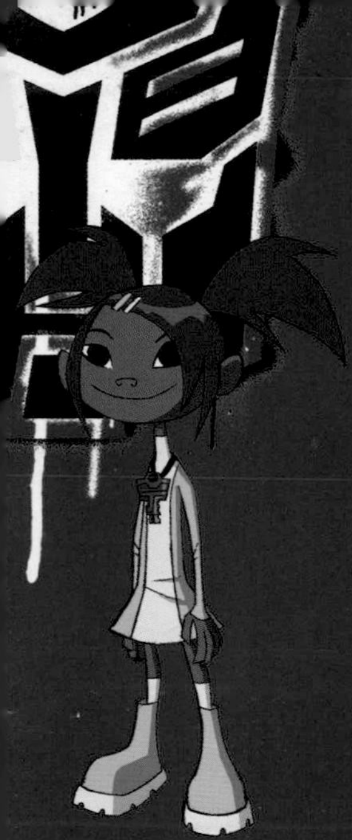

SARI is the adopted daughter of Professor Sumdac. Call it an accident or call it destiny, but the AllSpark projected part of itself onto her in the form of a key. Wearing it on a chain around her neck, SARI can use the key to absorb the AllSpark energy and store it like a battery, providing an emergency power supply and healing source for the AUTOBOTS in battle. It also provides her with an almost psychic connection to the AUTOBOTS.

Professor Sumdac

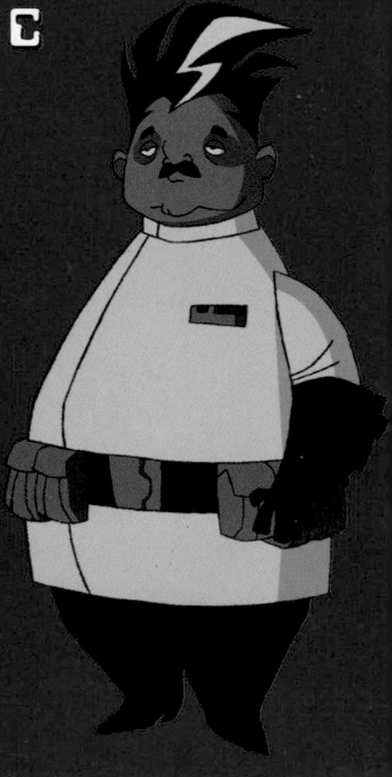

One night in the late 21st Century, the young SUMDAC thought he saw a falling star cascade into his back field, but it was something much better. It was the smoldering, non-functioning remains of the head of an alien robot, MEGATRON. In the decades that passed while the AUTOBOTS slumbered in stasis at the bottom of Lake Erie, SUMDAC was able to reverse engineer the Cybertronian technology within MEGATRON and usher in the Automatronic Revolution of the 22nd Century.

Captain Fanzone

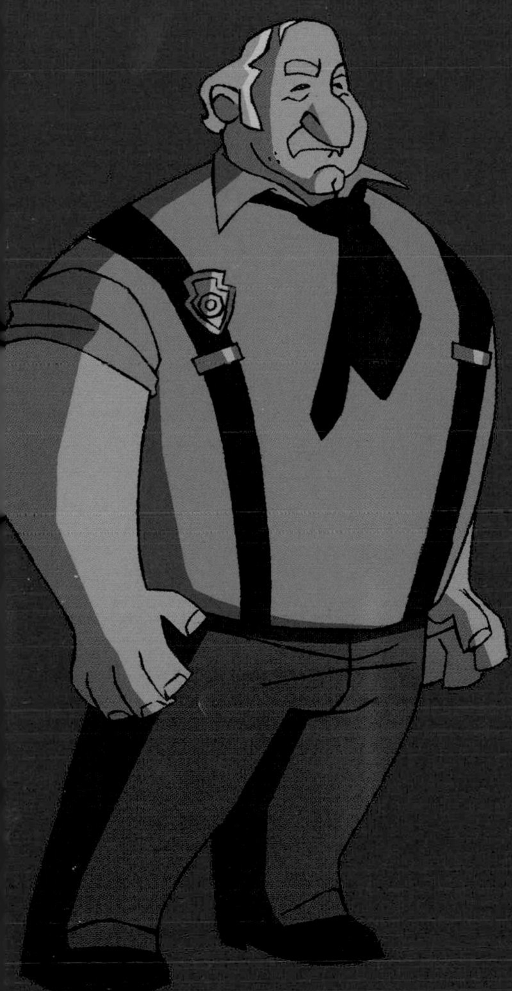

CAPTAIN FANZONE
is not an AUTOBOT,
but a police detective
whose car was
scanned to become
the vehicle mode for
BUMBLEBEE. He's a
harried, overworked,
but basically good and
honest cop, albeit
one whose day is
perpetually ruined by
one of those "giant
walking toasters."

Megatron

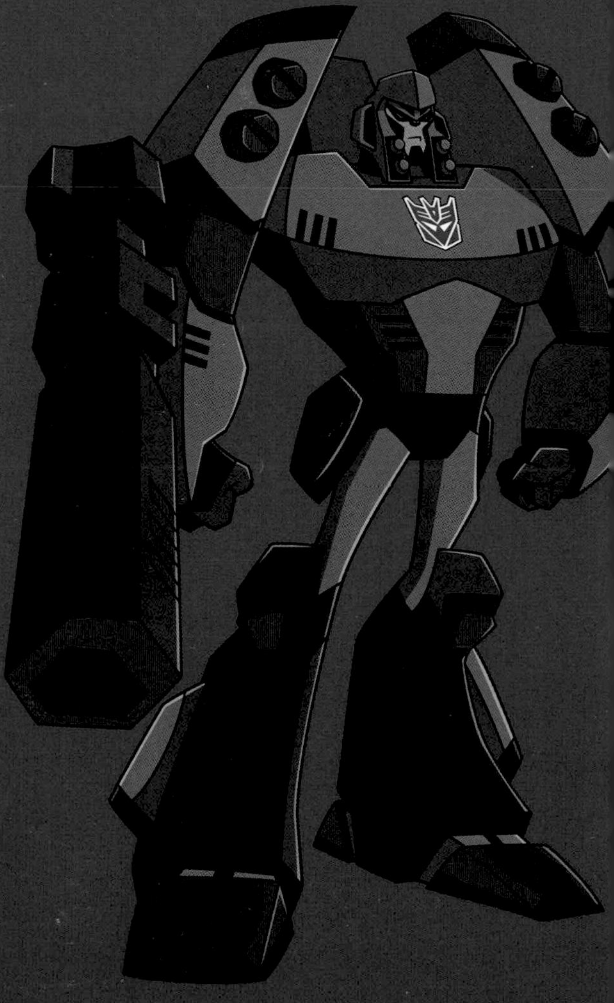

MEGATRON has the zeal of a fanatic and demands the unquestioning loyalty of those who serve under him. He sees the DECEPTICONS as an oppressed race suffering under the tyranny of the AUTOBOTS.

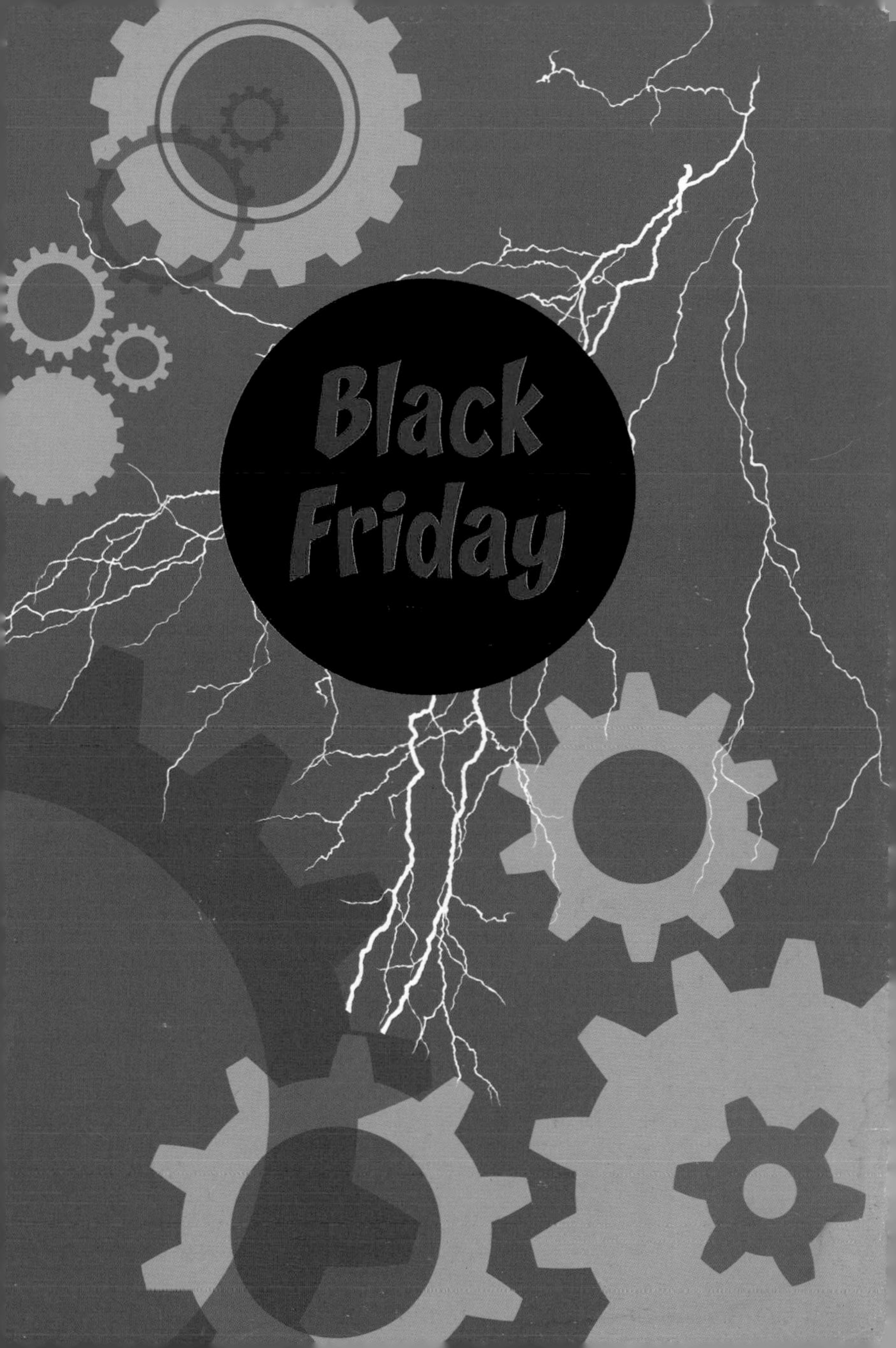
Black
Friday

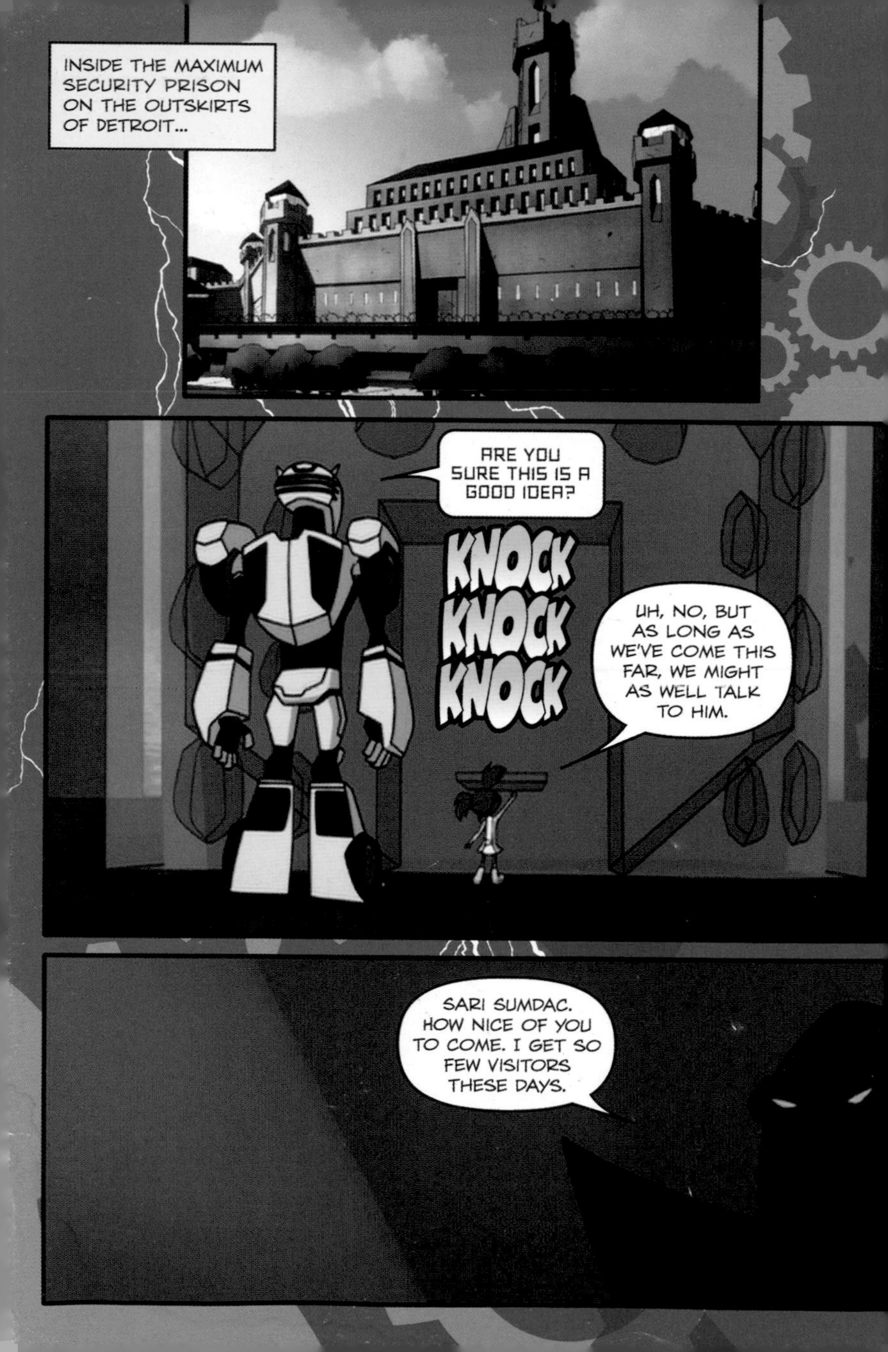
INSIDE THE MAXIMUM SECURITY PRISON ON THE OUTSKIRTS OF DETROIT...
ARE YOU SURE THIS IS A GOOD IDEA?
KNOCK KNOCK KNOCK
UH, NO, BUT AS LONG AS WE'VE COME THIS FAR, WE MIGHT AS WELL TALK TO HIM.
SARI SUMDAC. HOW NICE OF YOU TO COME. I GET SO FEW VISITORS THESE DAYS.

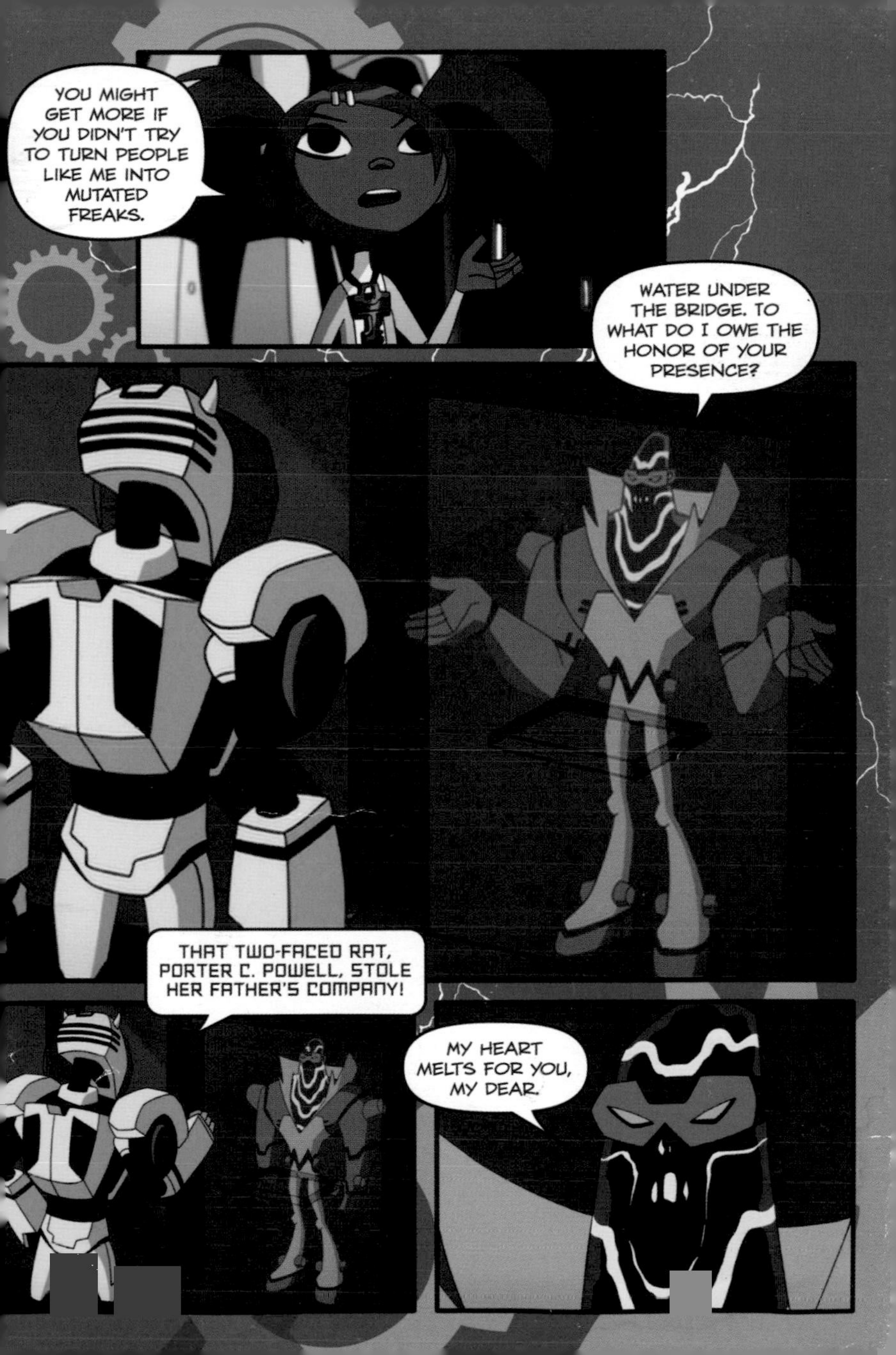
YOU MIGHT GET MORE IF YOU DIDN'T TRY TO TURN PEOPLE LIKE ME INTO MUTATED FREAKS.
WATER UNDER THE BRIDGE. TO WHAT DO I OWE THE HONOR OF YOUR PRESENCE?
THAT TWO-FACED RAT, PORTER C. POWELL, STOLE HER FATHER'S COMPANY!
MY HEART MELTS FOR YOU, MY DEAR.

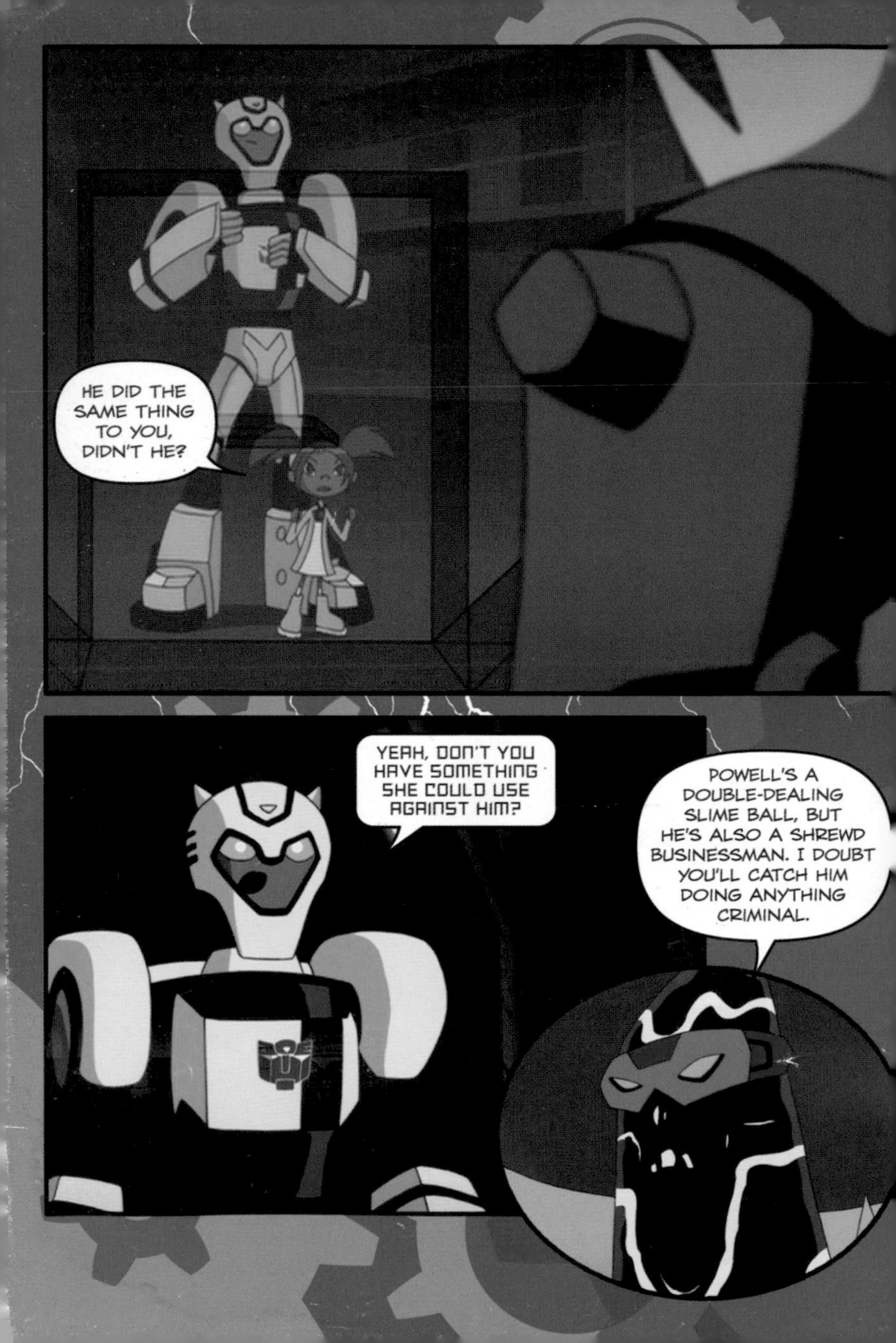
HE DID THE SAME THING TO YOU, DIDN'T HE?
YEAH, DON'T YOU HAVE SOMETHING SHE COULD USE AGAINST HIM?
POWELL'S A DOUBLE-DEALING SLIME BALL, BUT HE'S ALSO A SHREWD BUSINESSMAN. I DOUBT YOU'LL CATCH HIM DOING ANYTHING CRIMINAL.

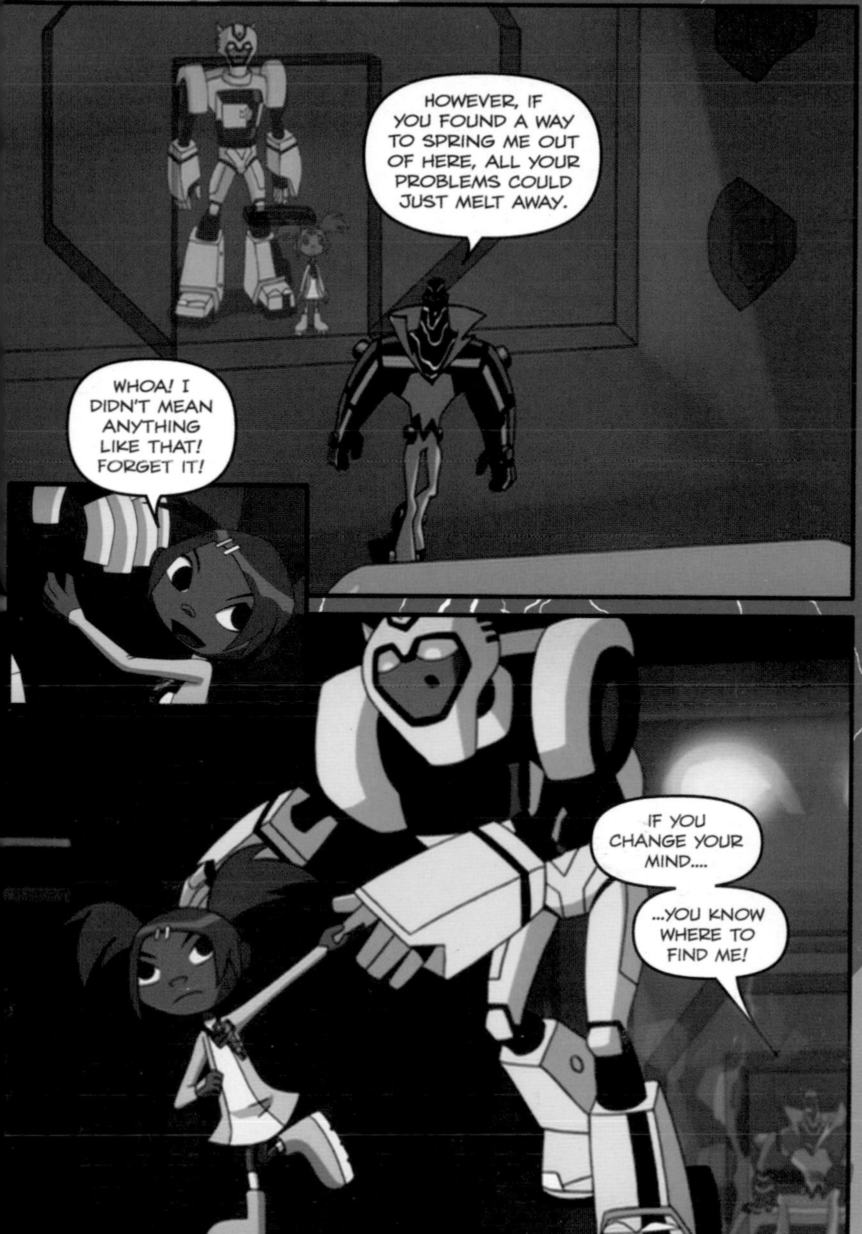
HOWEVER, IF YOU FOUND A WAY TO SPRING ME OUT OF HERE, ALL YOUR PROBLEMS COULD JUST MELT AWAY.
WHOA! I DIDN'T MEAN ANYTHING LIKE THAT! FORGET IT!
IF YOU CHANGE YOUR MIND....
...YOU KNOW WHERE TO FIND ME!

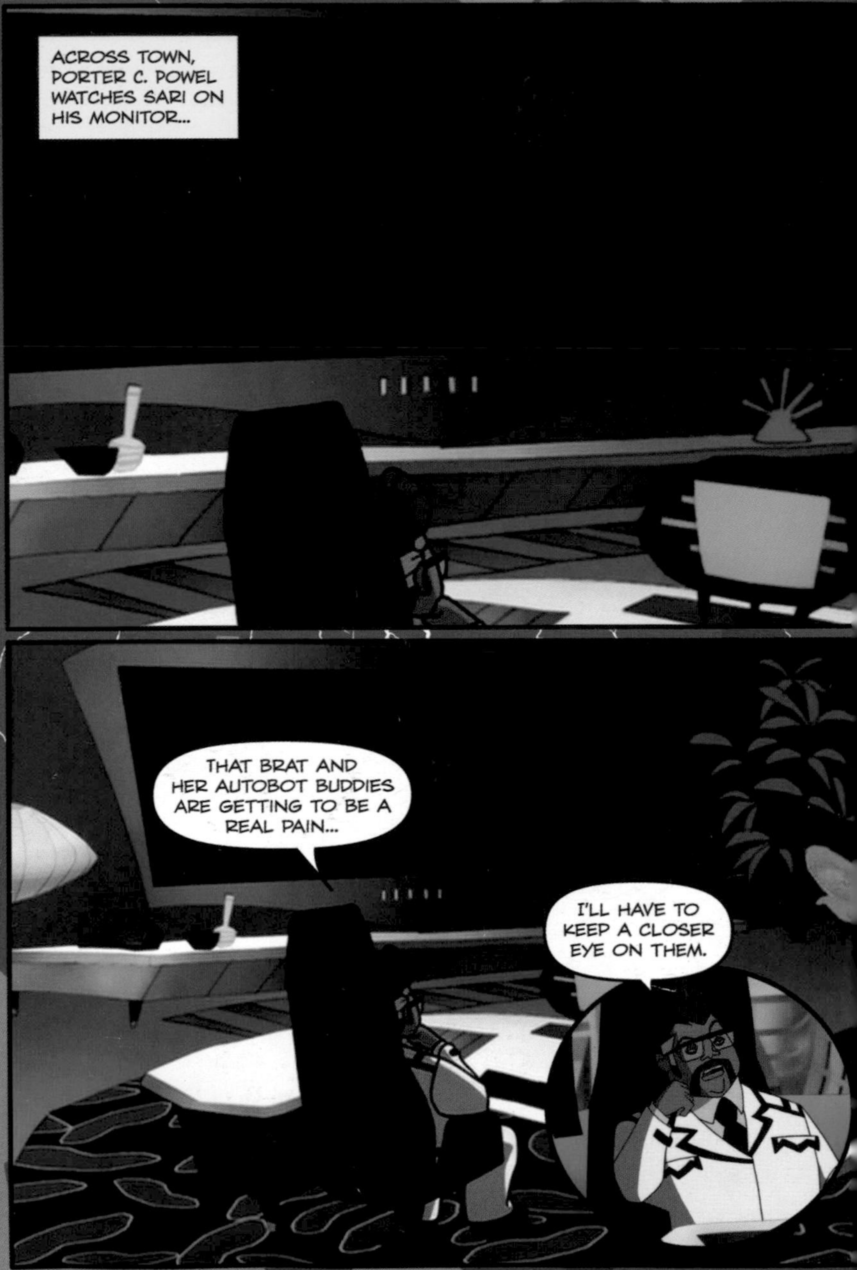
ACROSS TOWN, PORTER C. POWEL WATCHES SARI ON HIS MONITOR...
THAT BRAT AND HER AUTOBOT BUDDIES ARE GETTING TO BE A REAL PAIN...
I'LL HAVE TO KEEP A CLOSER EYE ON THEM.

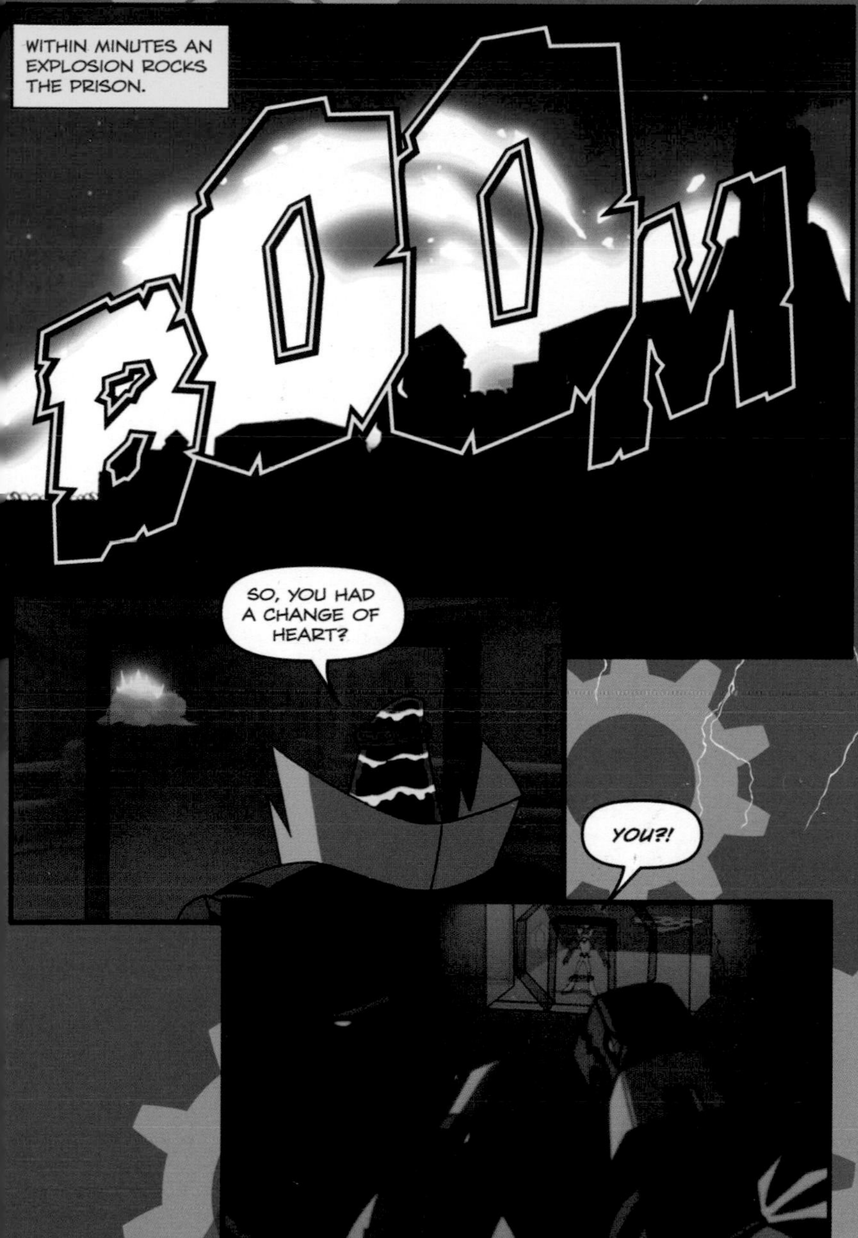
WITHIN MINUTES AN EXPLOSION ROCKS THE PRISON.
BOOM
SO, YOU HAD A CHANGE OF HEART?
YOU?!

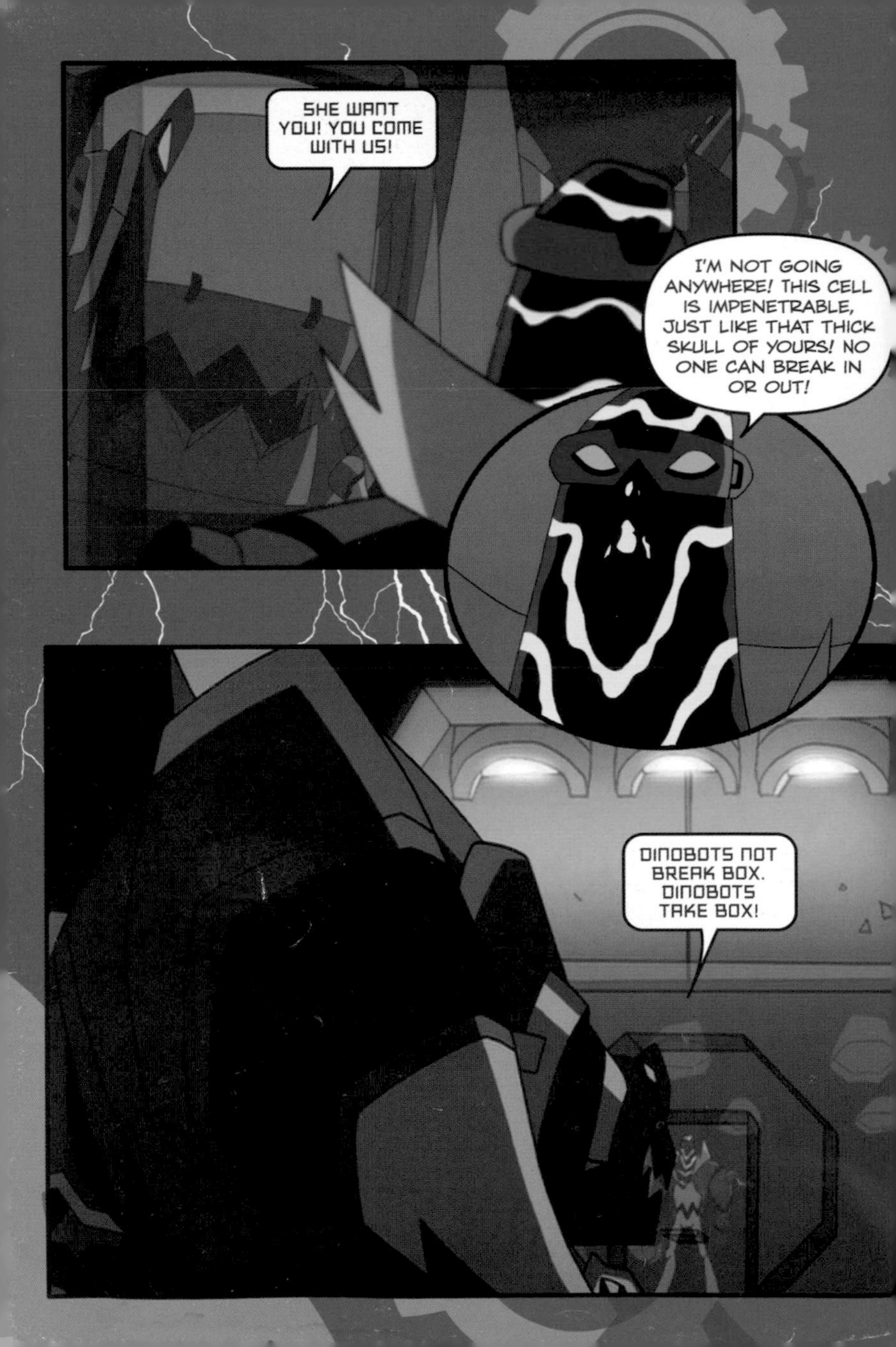
SHE WANT YOU! YOU COME WITH US!
I'M NOT GOING ANYWHERE! THIS CELL IS IMPENETRABLE, JUST LIKE THAT THICK SKULL OF YOURS! NO ONE CAN BREAK IN OR OUT!
DINOBOTS NOT BREAK BOX. DINOBOTS TAKE BOX!

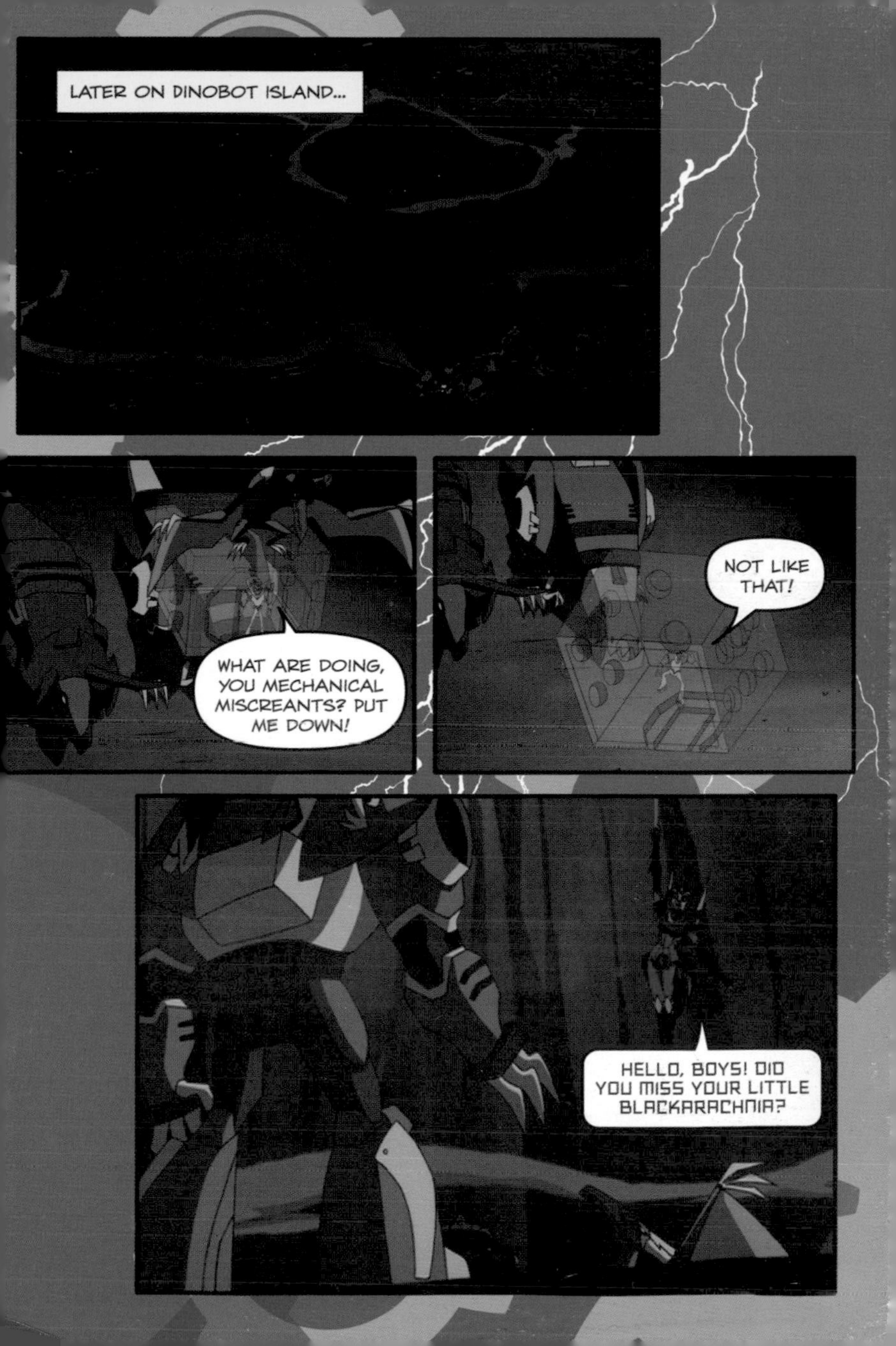
LATER ON DINOBOT ISLAND...
WHAT ARE DOING, YOU MECHANICAL MISCREANTS? PUT ME DOWN!
NOT LIKE THAT!
HELLO, BOYS! DID YOU MISS YOUR LITTLE BLACKARACHNIA?

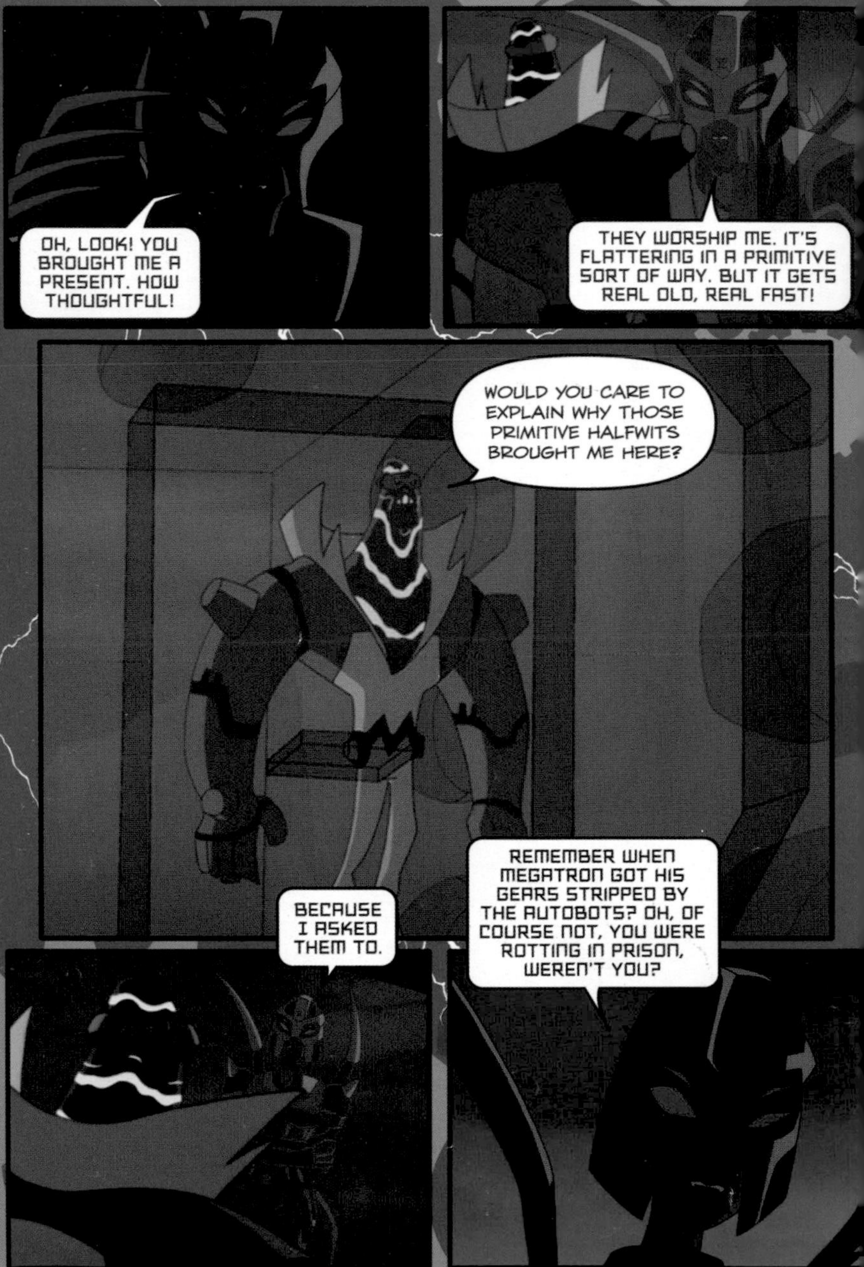
OH, LOOK! YOU BROUGHT ME A PRESENT. HOW THOUGHTFUL!
THEY WORSHIP ME. IT'S FLATTERING IN A PRIMITIVE SORT OF WAY. BUT IT GETS REAL OLD, REAL FAST!
WOULD YOU CARE TO EXPLAIN WHY THOSE PRIMITIVE HALFWITS BROUGHT ME HERE?
BECAUSE I ASKED THEM TO.
REMEMBER WHEN MEGATRON GOT HIS GEARS STRIPPED BY THE AUTOBOTS? OH, OF COURSE NOT, YOU WERE ROTTING IN PRISON, WEREN'T YOU?

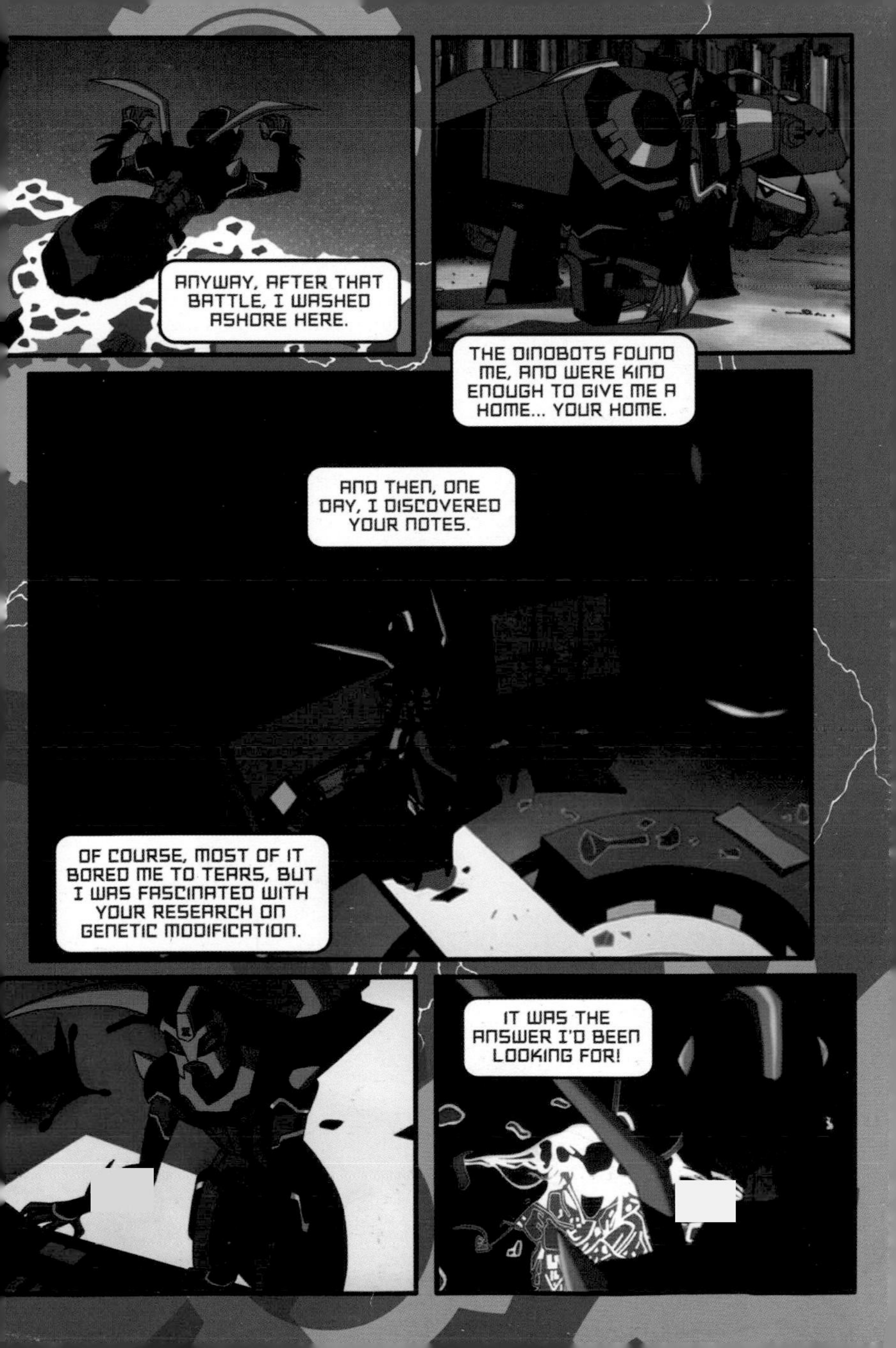
ANYWAY, AFTER THAT BATTLE, I WASHED ASHORE HERE.
THE DINOBOTS FOUND ME, AND WERE KIND ENOUGH TO GIVE ME A HOME... YOUR HOME.
AND THEN, ONE DAY, I DISCOVERED YOUR NOTES.
OF COURSE, MOST OF IT BORED ME TO TEARS, BUT I WAS FASCINATED WITH YOUR RESEARCH ON GENETIC MODIFICATION.
IT WAS THE ANSWER I'D BEEN LOOKING FOR!

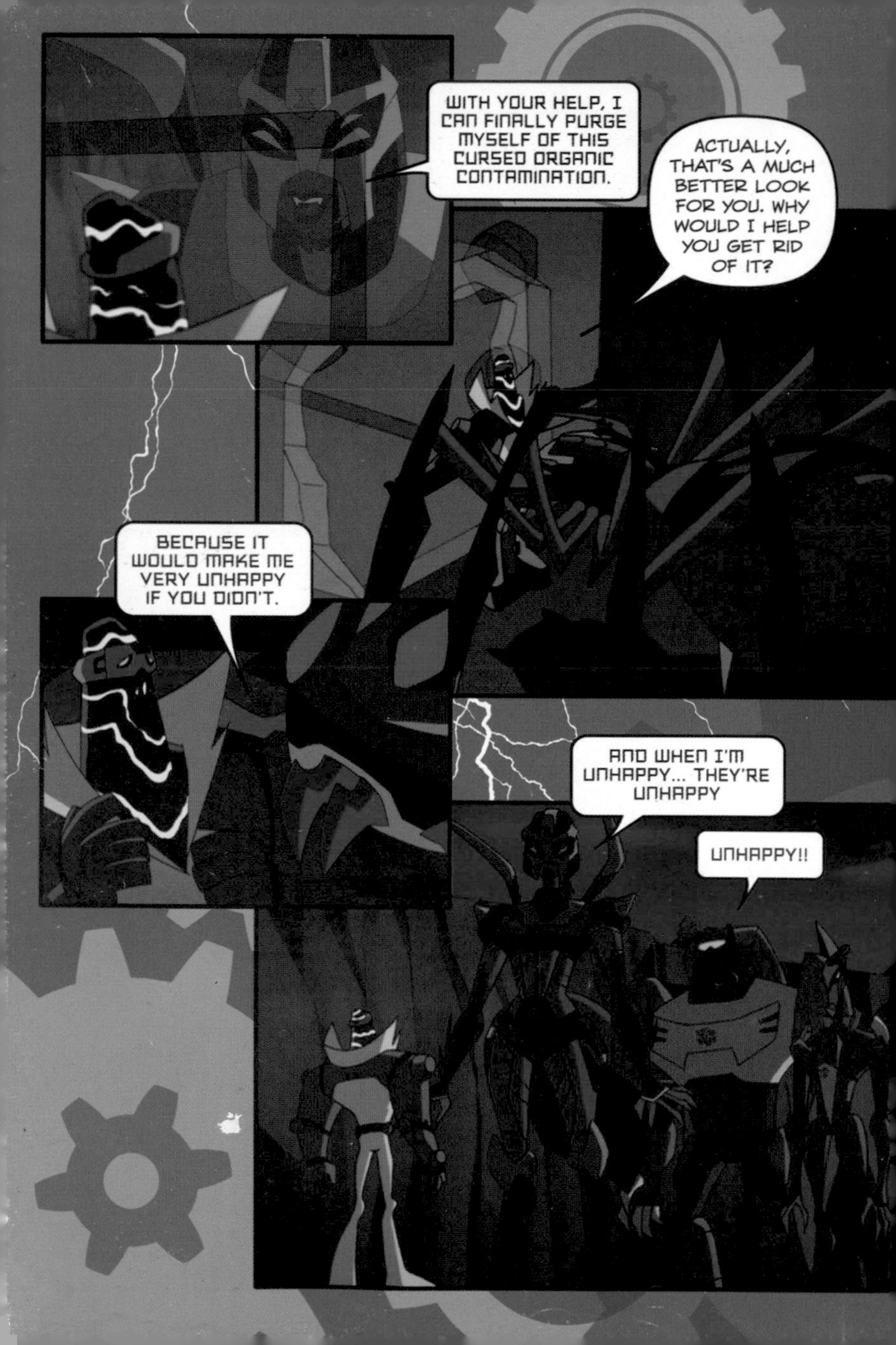
WITH YOUR HELP, I CAN FINALLY PURGE MYSELF OF THIS CURSED ORGANIC CONTAMINATION.
ACTUALLY, THAT'S A MUCH BETTER LOOK FOR YOU. WHY WOULD I HELP YOU GET RID OF IT?
BECAUSE IT WOULD MAKE ME VERY UNHAPPY IF YOU DIDN'T.
AND WHEN I'M UNHAPPY... THEY'RE UNHAPPY
UNHAPPY!!

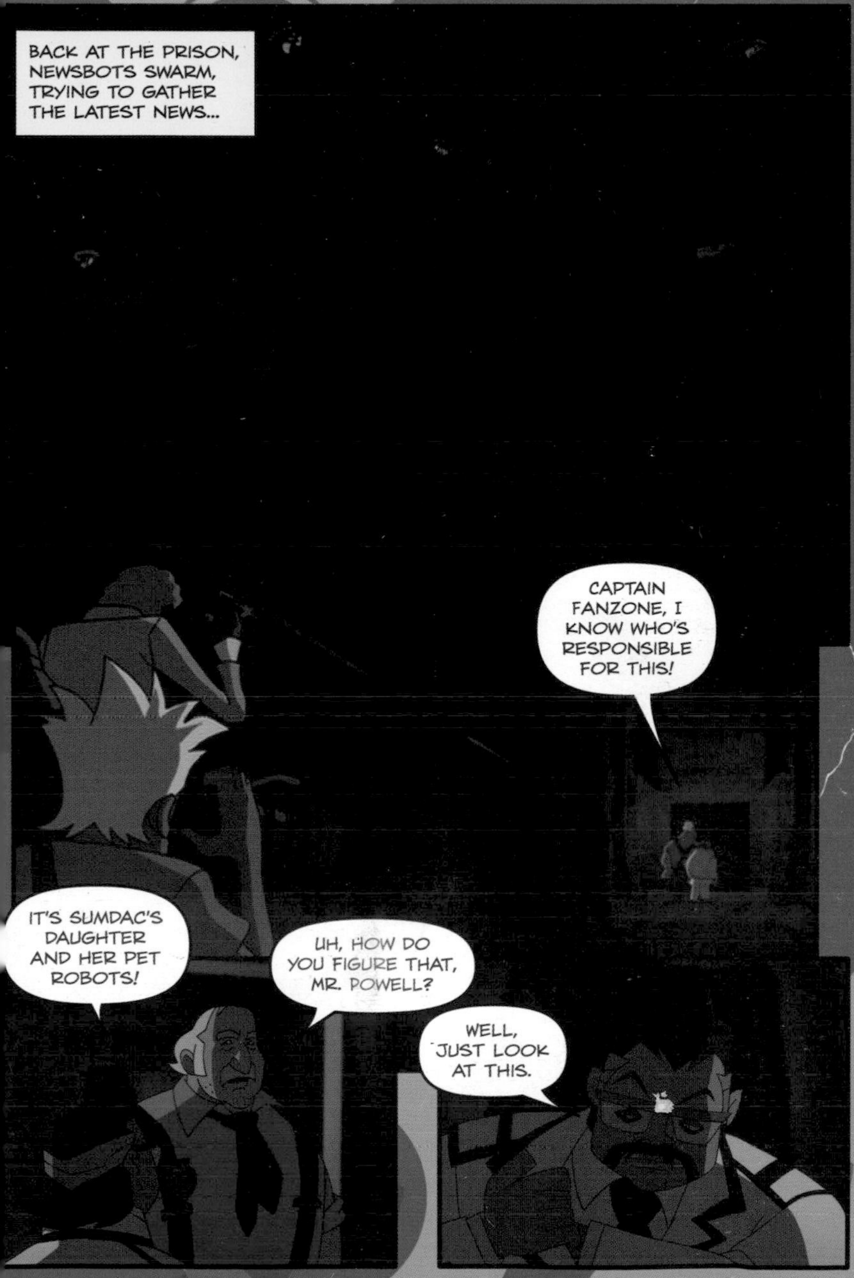
BACK AT THE PRISON, NEWSBOTS SWARM, TRYING TO GATHER THE LATEST NEWS...
CAPTAIN FANZONE, I KNOW WHO'S RESPONSIBLE FOR THIS!
IT'S SUMDAC'S DAUGHTER AND HER PET ROBOTS!
UH, HOW DO YOU FIGURE THAT, MR. POWELL?
WELL, JUST LOOK AT THIS.

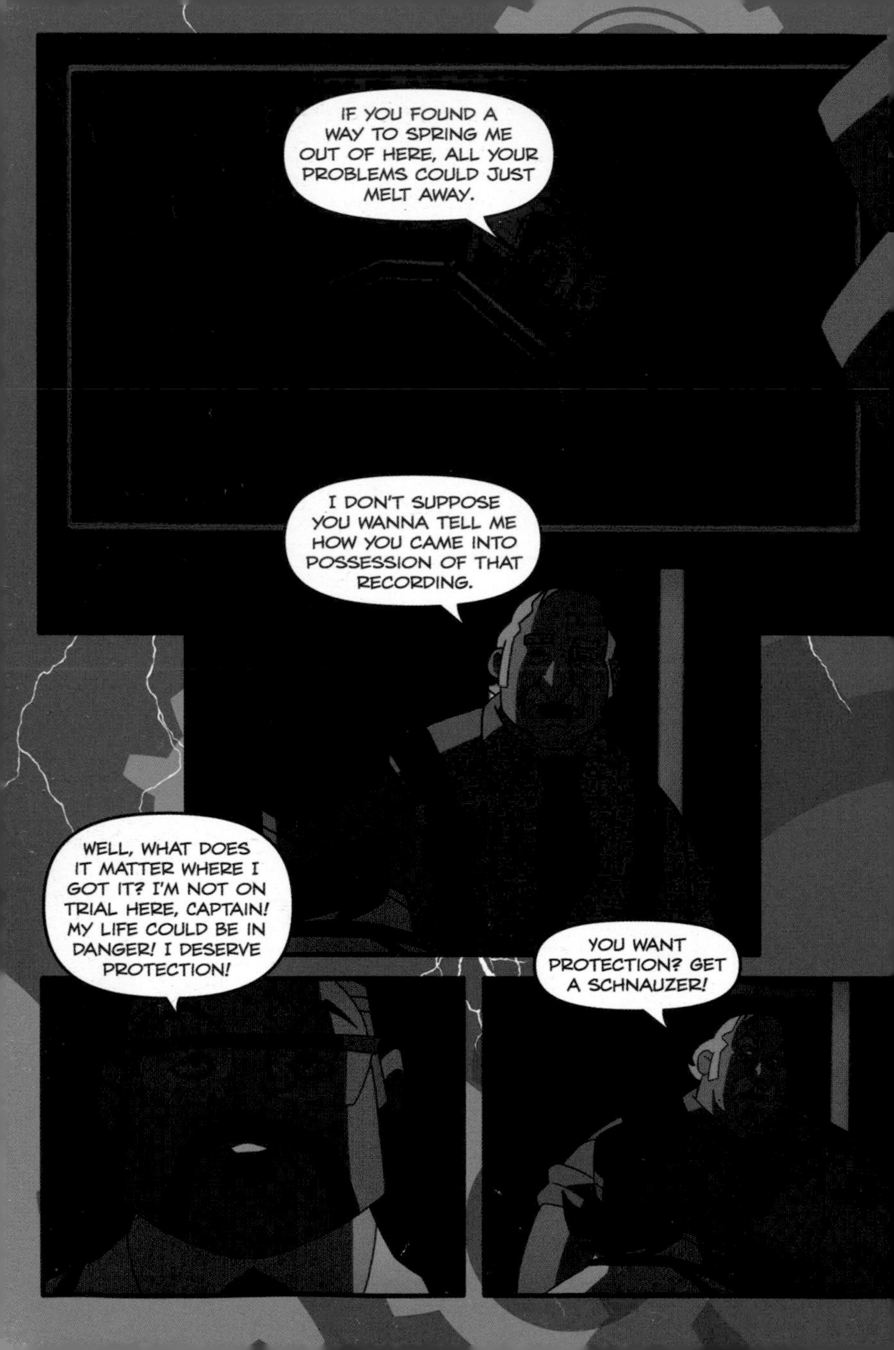
IF YOU FOUND A WAY TO SPRING ME OUT OF HERE, ALL YOUR PROBLEMS COULD JUST MELT AWAY.
I DON'T SUPPOSE YOU WANNA TELL ME HOW YOU CAME INTO POSSESSION OF THAT RECORDING.
WELL, WHAT DOES IT MATTER WHERE I GOT IT? I'M NOT ON TRIAL HERE, CAPTAIN! MY LIFE COULD BE IN DANGER! I DESERVE PROTECTION!
YOU WANT PROTECTION? GET A SCHNAUZER!

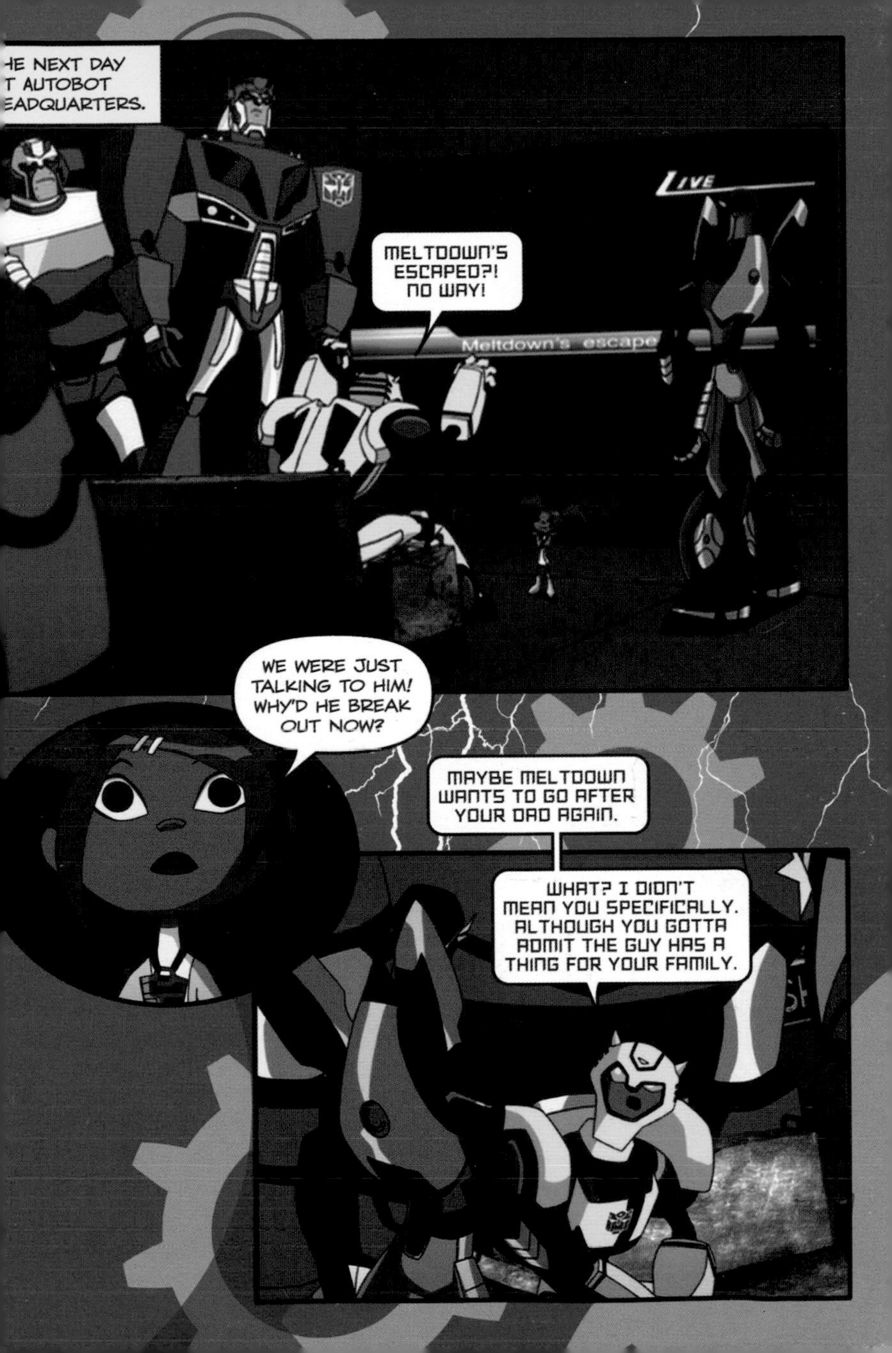
HE NEXT DAY
T AUTOBOT
EADQUARTERS.
LIVE
Meltdown's escape
MELTDOWN'S ESCAPED?! NO WAY!
WE WERE JUST TALKING TO HIM! WHY'D HE BREAK OUT NOW?
MAYBE MELTDOWN WANTS TO GO AFTER YOUR DAD AGAIN.
WHAT? I DIDN'T MEAN YOU SPECIFICALLY. ALTHOUGH YOU GOTTA ADMIT THE GUY HAS A THING FOR YOUR FAMILY.

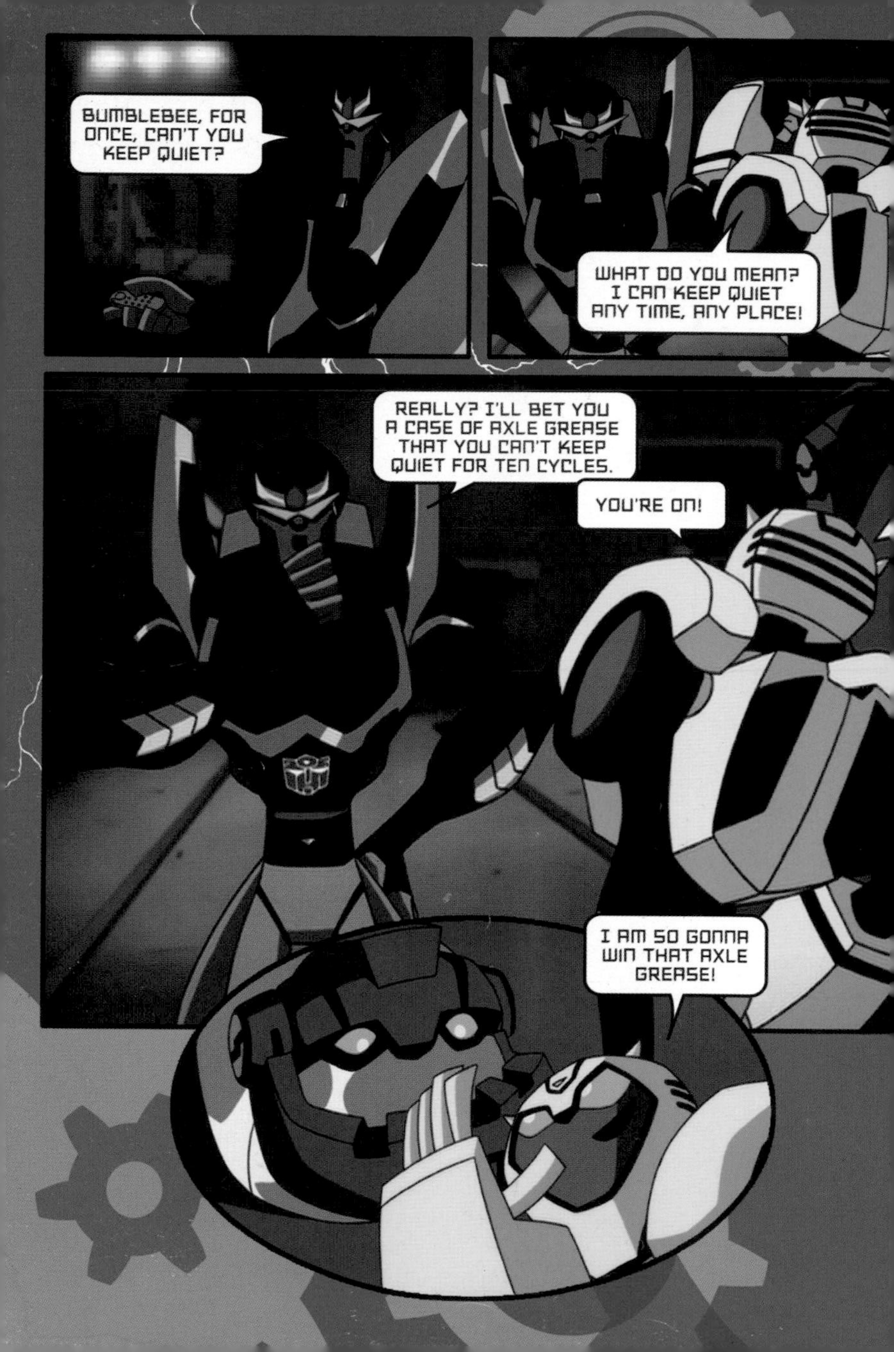
BUMBLEBEE, FOR ONCE, CAN'T YOU KEEP QUIET?
WHAT DO YOU MEAN? I CAN KEEP QUIET ANY TIME, ANY PLACE!
REALLY? I'LL BET YOU A CASE OF AXLE GREASE THAT YOU CAN'T KEEP QUIET FOR TEN CYCLES.
YOU'RE ON!
I AM SO GONNA WIN THAT AXLE GREASE!

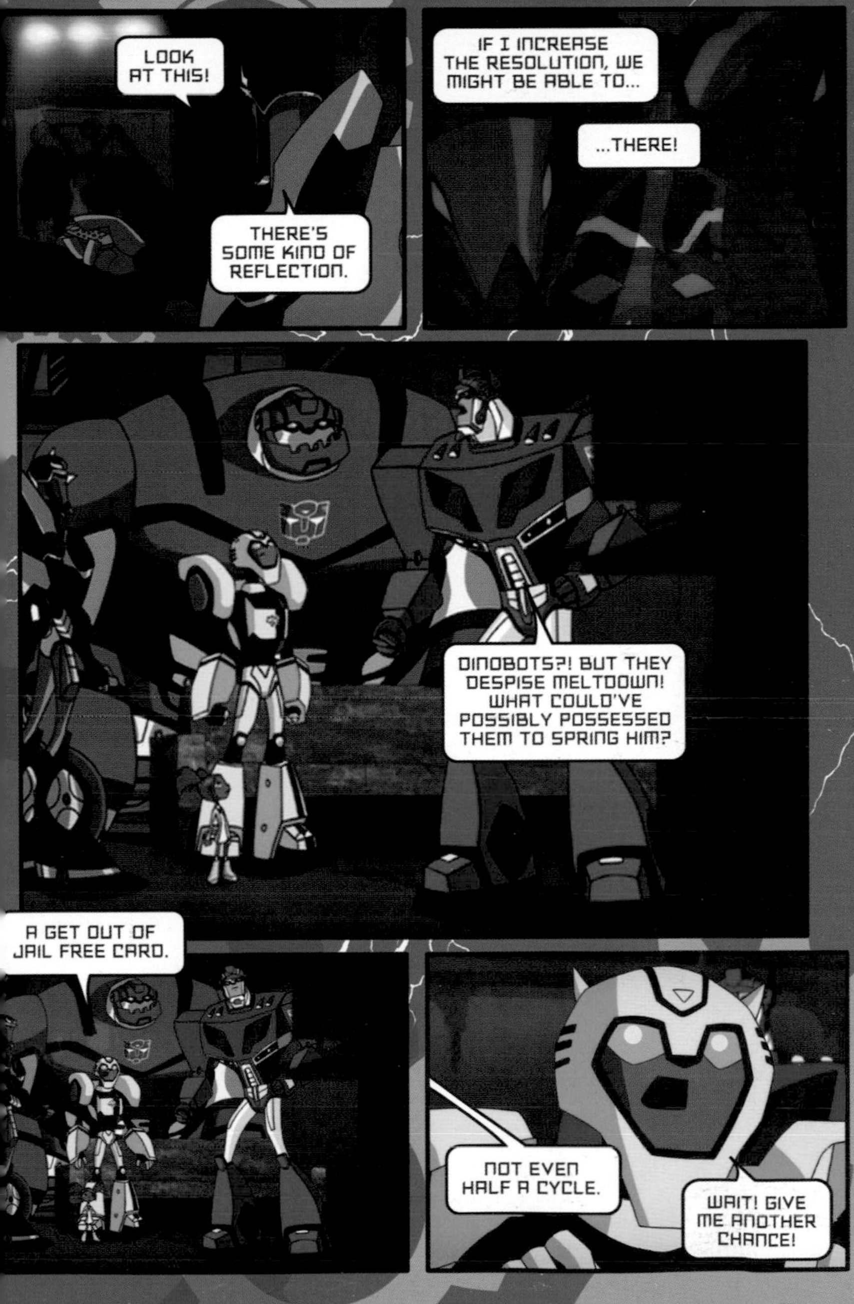
LOOK AT THIS!
THERE'S SOME KIND OF REFLECTION.
IF I INCREASE THE RESOLUTION, WE MIGHT BE ABLE TO...
...THERE!
DINOBOTS?! BUT THEY DESPISE MELTDOWN! WHAT COULD'VE POSSIBLY POSSESSED THEM TO SPRING HIM?
A GET OUT OF JAIL FREE CARD.
NOT EVEN HALF A CYCLE.
WAIT! GIVE ME ANOTHER CHANCE!

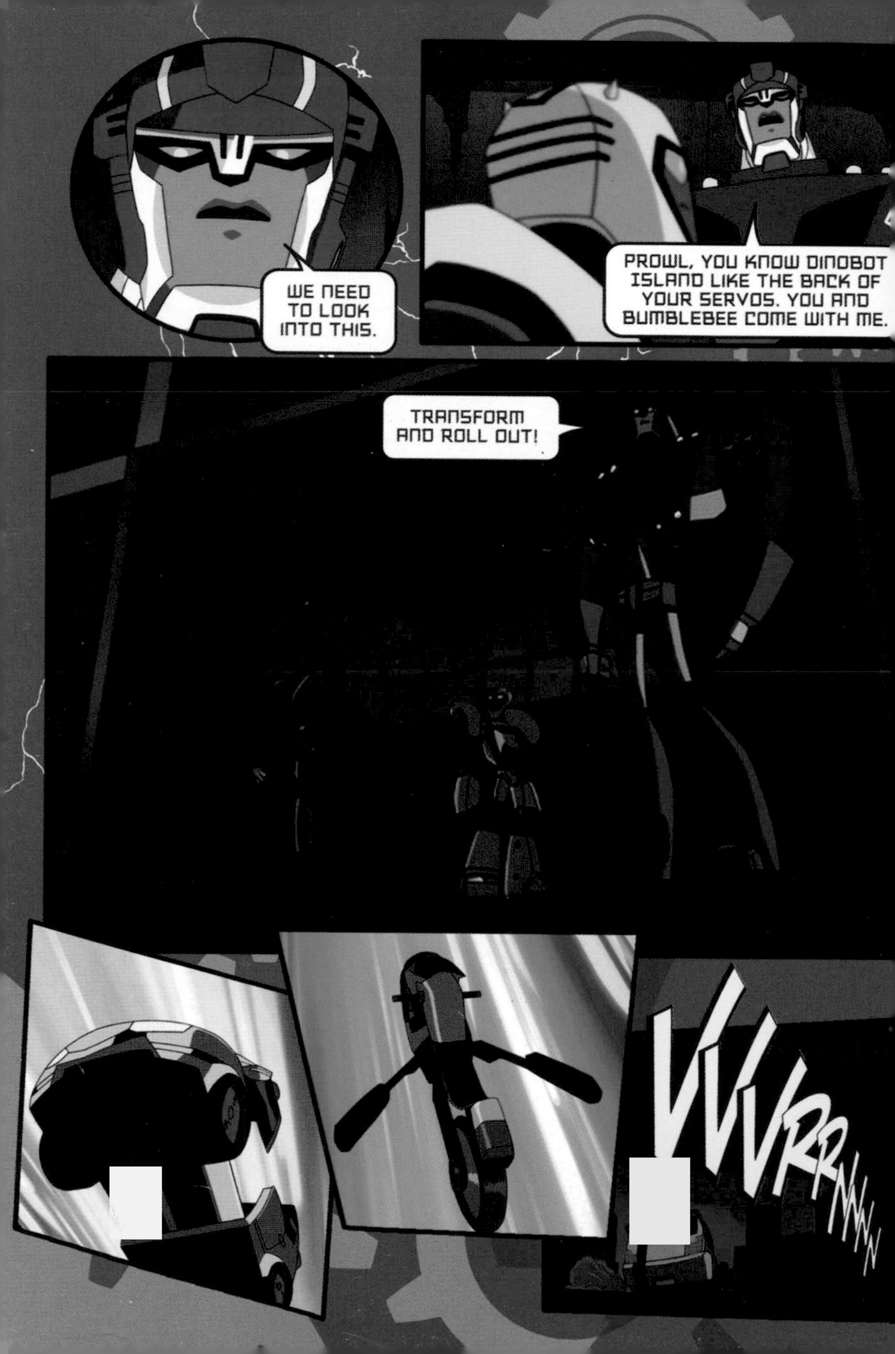
WE NEED TO LOOK INTO THIS.
PROWL, YOU KNOW DINOBOT ISLAND LIKE THE BACK OF YOUR SERVOS. YOU AND BUMBLEBEE COME WITH ME.
TRANSFORM AND ROLL OUT!
VVVRRNNNN

A SHORT TIME LATER, THE AUTOBOTS REACH DINOBOT ISLAND.

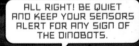

ALL RIGHT! BE QUIET AND KEEP YOUR SENSORS ALERT FOR ANY SIGN OF THE DINOBOTS.

I'M ALREADY BEING QUIET. DIDN'T YOU NOTICE?

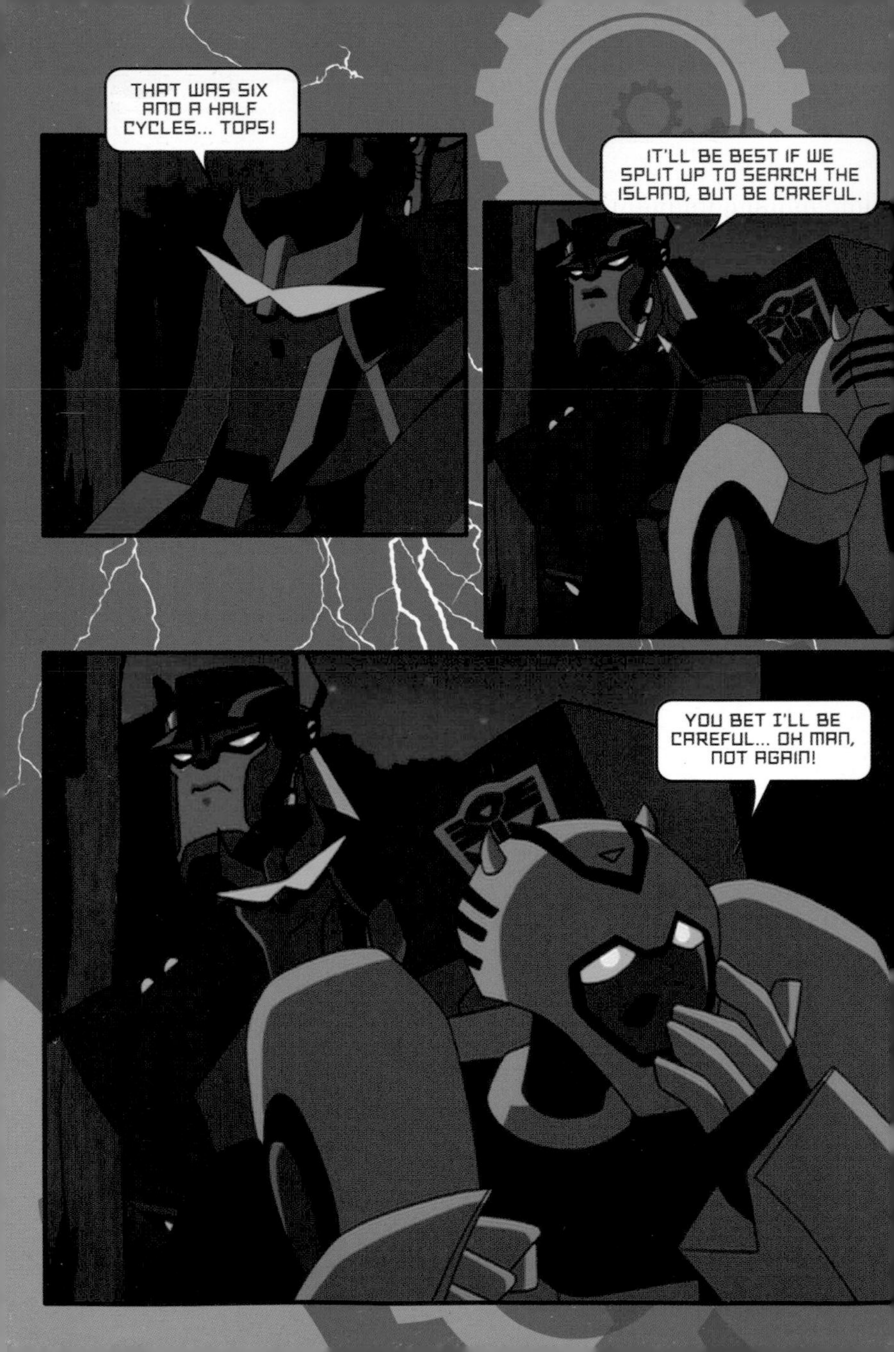
THAT WAS SIX AND A HALF CYCLES... TOPS!
IT'LL BE BEST IF WE SPLIT UP TO SEARCH THE ISLAND, BUT BE CAREFUL.
YOU BET I'LL BE CAREFUL... OH MAN, NOT AGAIN!

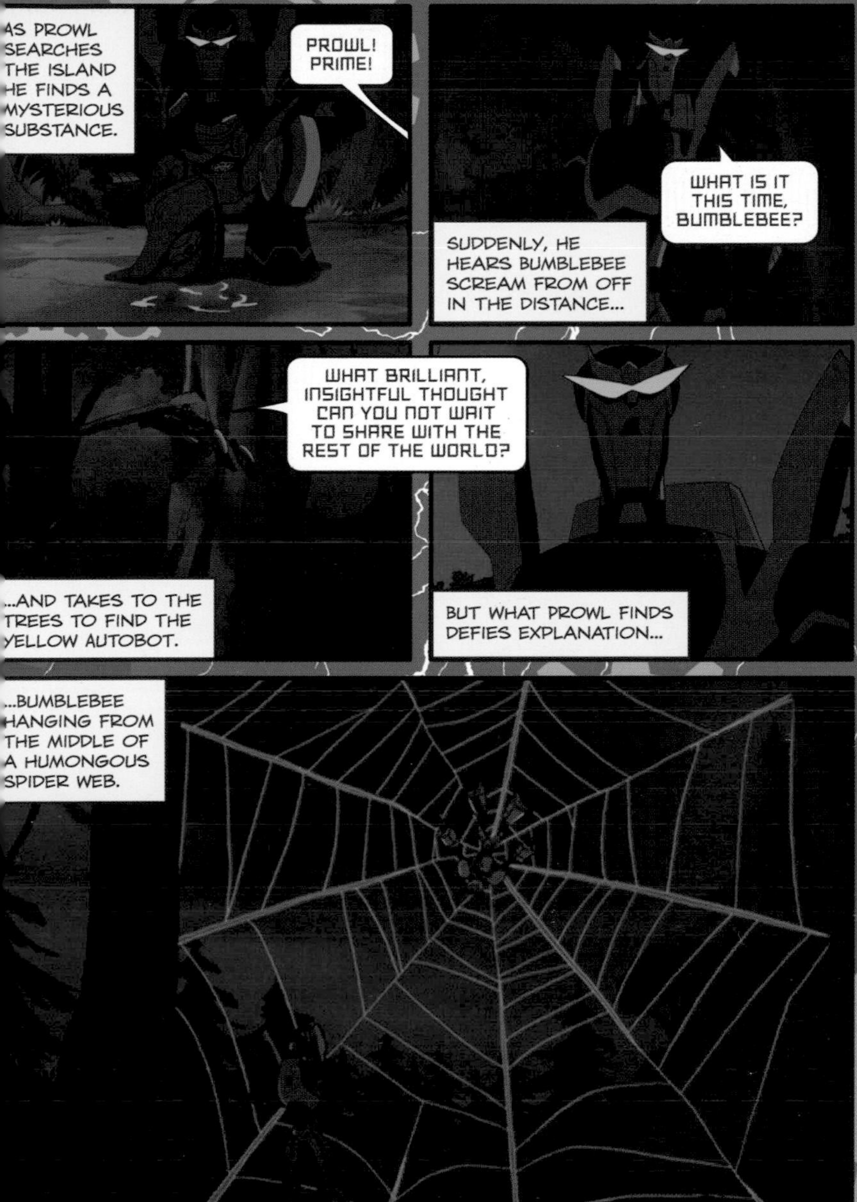
AS PROWL SEARCHES THE ISLAND HE FINDS A MYSTERIOUS SUBSTANCE.
PROWL! PRIME!
WHAT IS IT THIS TIME, BUMBLEBEE?
SUDDENLY, HE HEARS BUMBLEBEE SCREAM FROM OFF IN THE DISTANCE...
WHAT BRILLIANT, INSIGHTFUL THOUGHT CAN YOU NOT WAIT TO SHARE WITH THE REST OF THE WORLD?
...AND TAKES TO THE TREES TO FIND THE YELLOW AUTOBOT.
BUT WHAT PROWL FINDS DEFIES EXPLANATION...
...BUMBLEBEE HANGING FROM THE MIDDLE OF A HUMONGOUS SPIDER WEB.

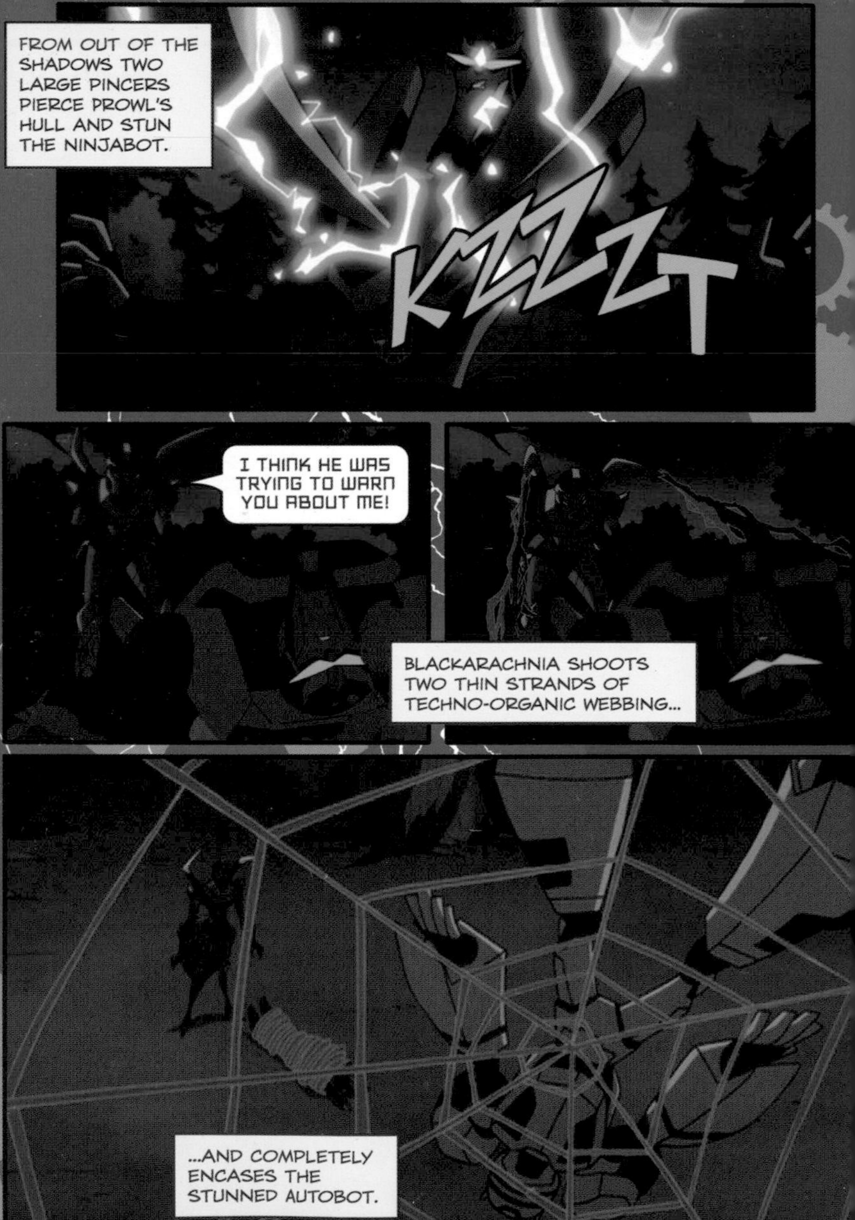

FROM OUT OF THE SHADOWS TWO LARGE PINCERS PIERCE PROWL'S HULL AND STUN THE NINJABOT.
KZZZZT
I THINK HE WAS TRYING TO WARN YOU ABOUT ME!
BLACKARACHNIA SHOOTS TWO THIN STRANDS OF TECHNO-ORGANIC WEBBING...
...AND COMPLETELY ENCASES THE STUNNED AUTOBOT.

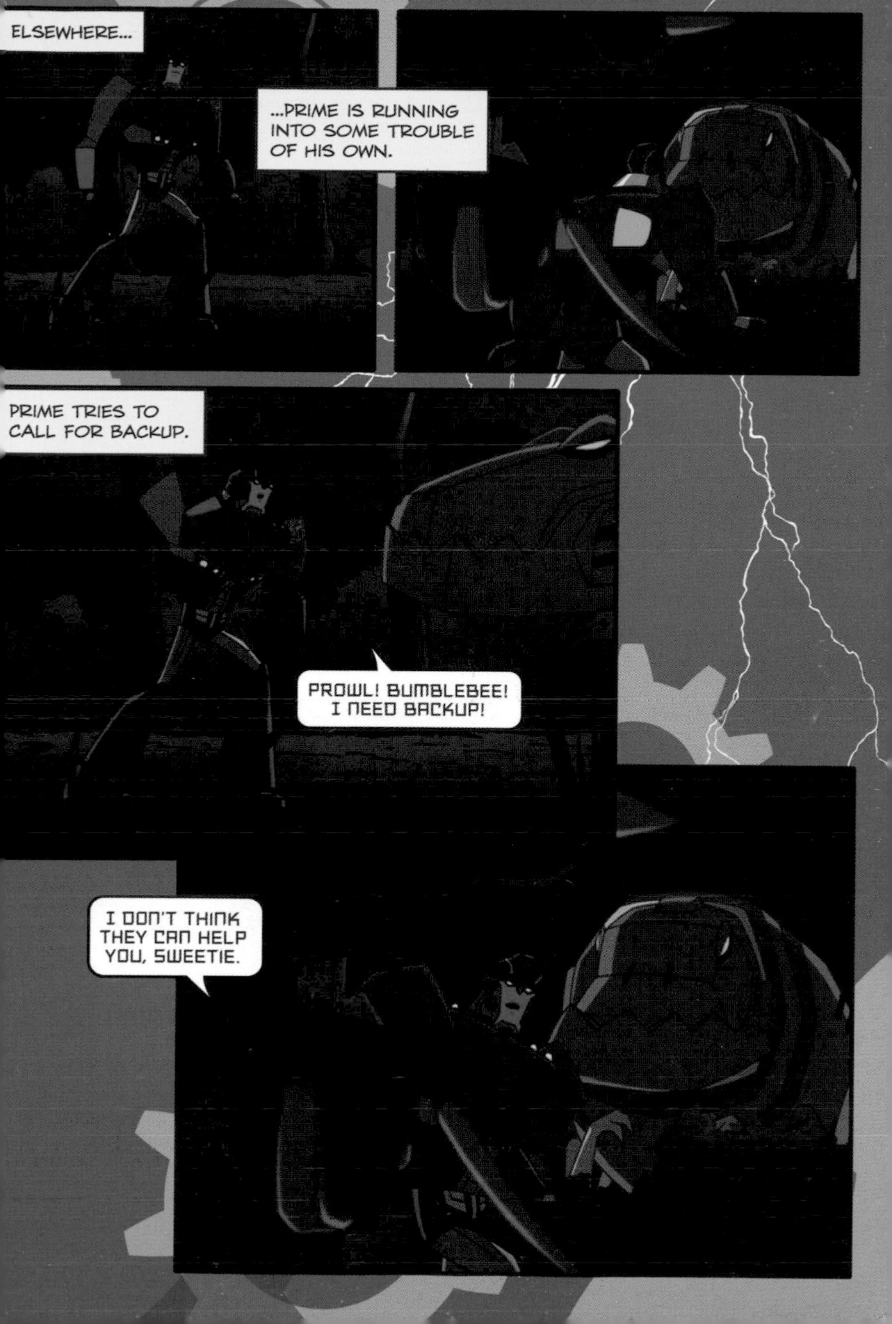
ELSEWHERE...
...PRIME IS RUNNING INTO SOME TROUBLE OF HIS OWN.
PRIME TRIES TO CALL FOR BACKUP.
PROWL! BUMBLEBEE! I NEED BACKUP!
I DON'T THINK THEY CAN HELP YOU, SWEETIE.

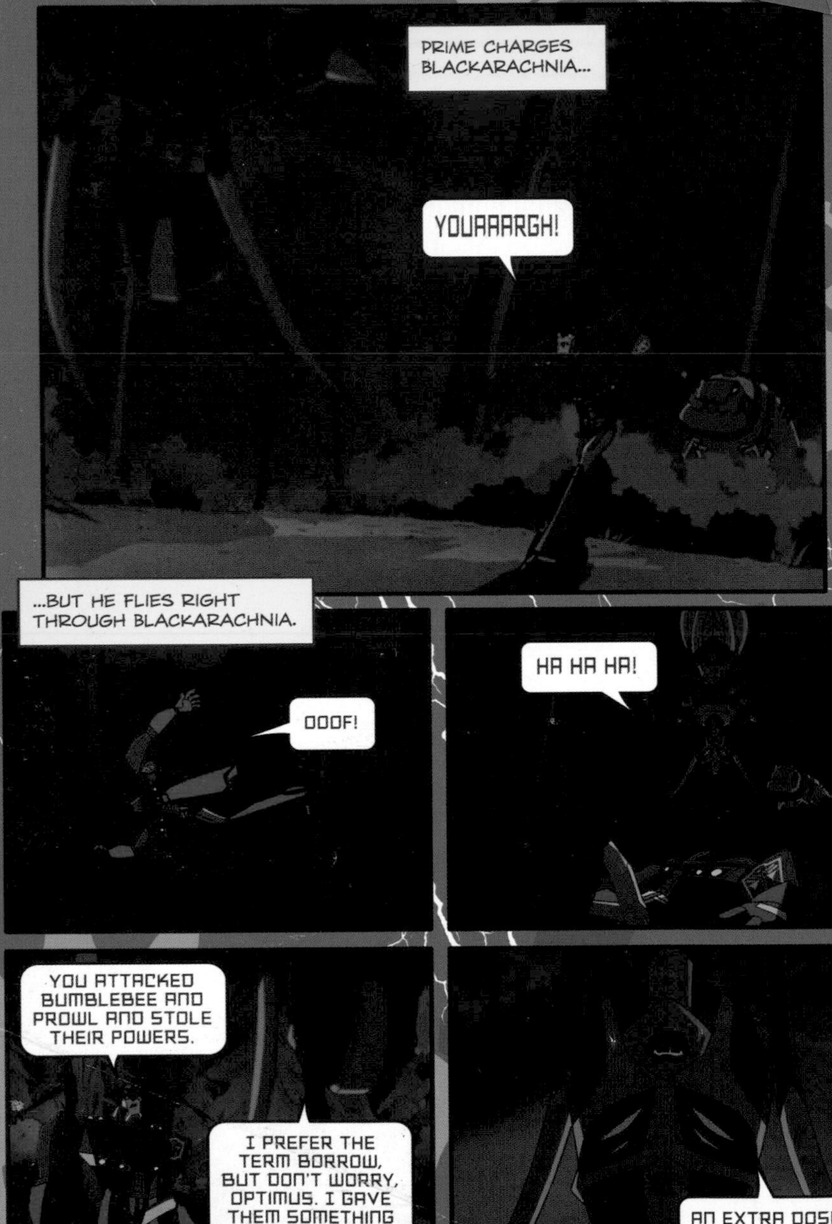
PRIME CHARGES BLACKARACHNIA...
YOUAAARGH!
...BUT HE FLIES RIGHT THROUGH BLACKARACHNIA.
OOOF!
HA HA HA!
YOU ATTACKED BUMBLEBEE AND PROWL AND STOLE THEIR POWERS.
I PREFER THE TERM BORROW, BUT DON'T WORRY, OPTIMUS. I GAVE THEM SOMETHING IN RETURN.
AN EXTRA DOSE OF VENOM.

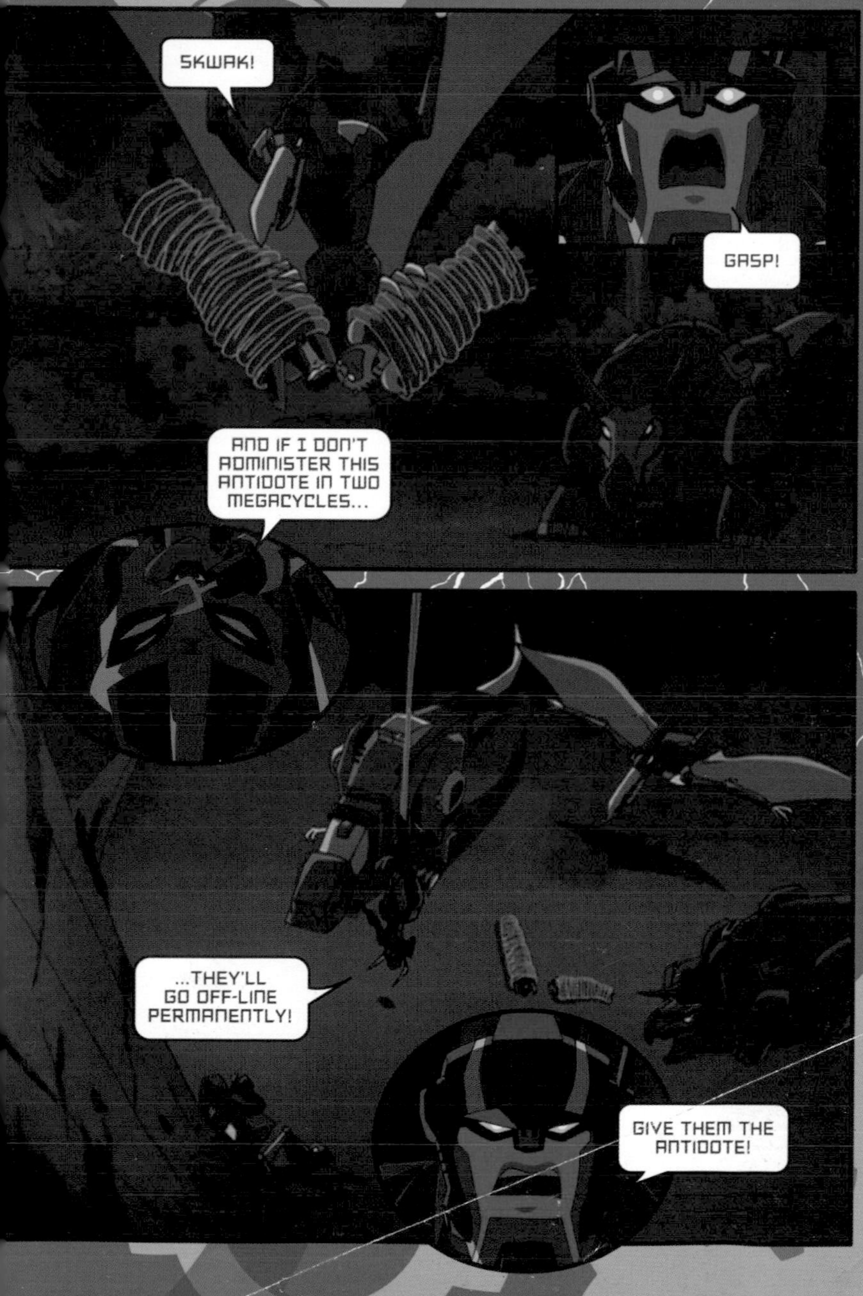
SKWAK!
GASP!
AND IF I DON'T ADMINISTER THIS ANTIDOTE IN TWO MEGACYCLES...
...THEY'LL GO OFF-LINE PERMANENTLY!
GIVE THEM THE ANTIDOTE!

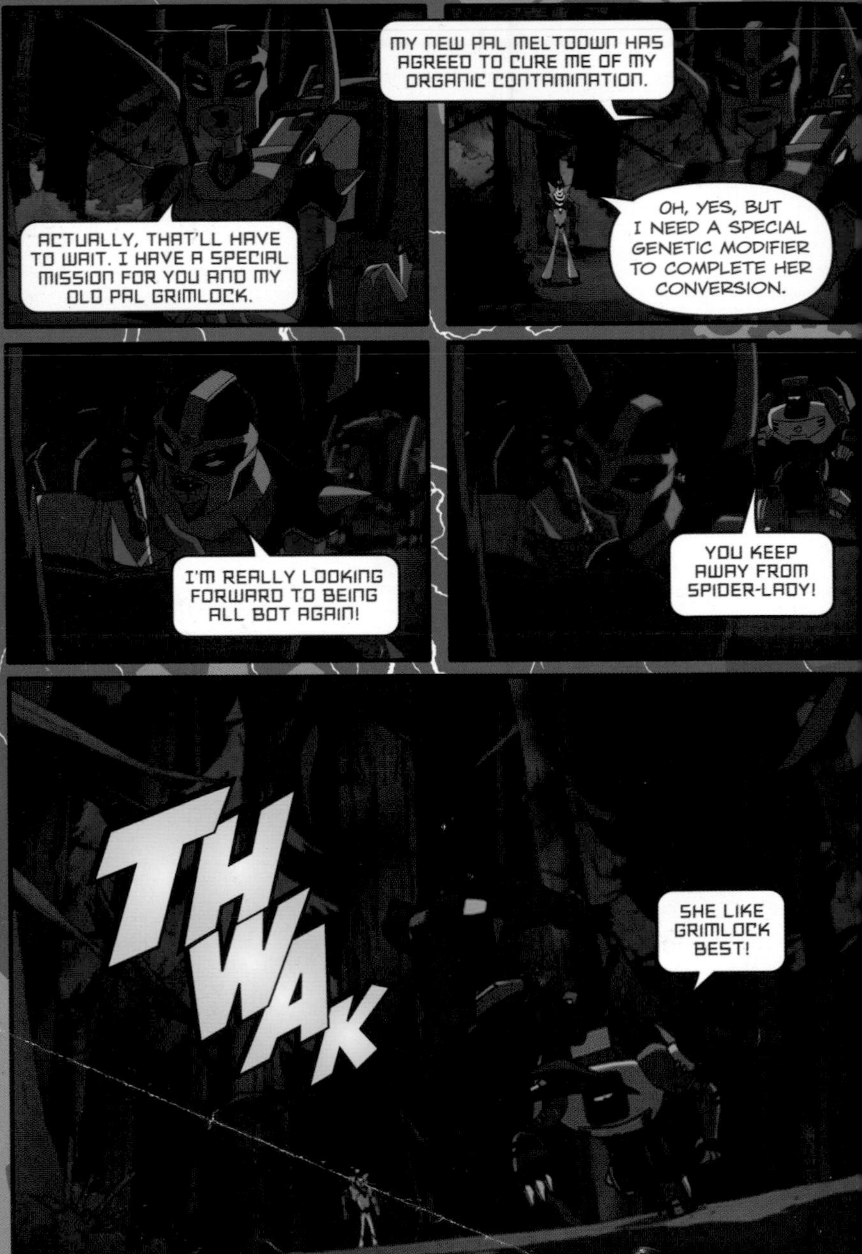
ACTUALLY, THAT'LL HAVE TO WAIT. I HAVE A SPECIAL MISSION FOR YOU AND MY OLD PAL GRIMLOCK.
MY NEW PAL MELTDOWN HAS AGREED TO CURE ME OF MY ORGANIC CONTAMINATION.
OH, YES, BUT I NEED A SPECIAL GENETIC MODIFIER TO COMPLETE HER CONVERSION.
I'M REALLY LOOKING FORWARD TO BEING ALL BOT AGAIN!
YOU KEEP AWAY FROM SPIDER-LADY!
THWAK
SHE LIKE GRIMLOCK BEST!

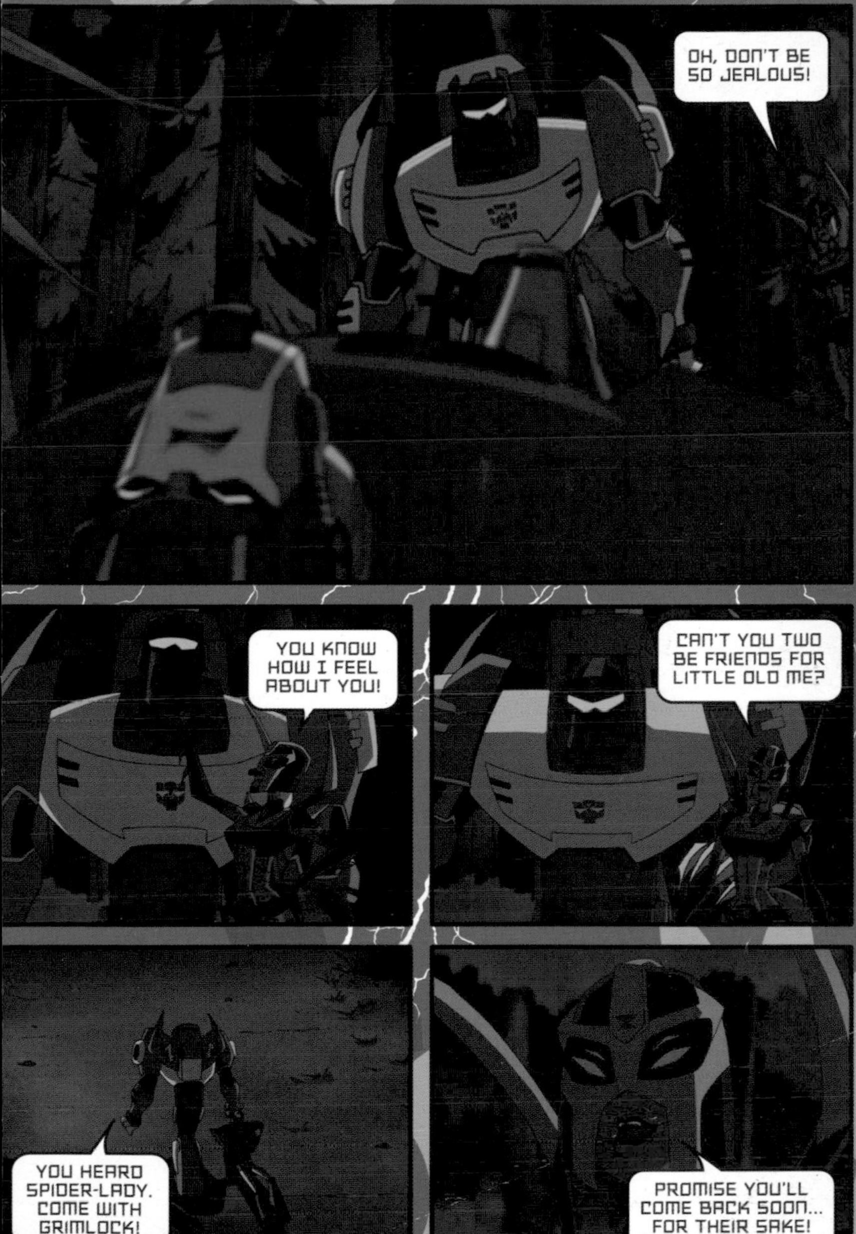
OH, DON'T BE SO JEALOUS!
YOU KNOW HOW I FEEL ABOUT YOU!
CAN'T YOU TWO BE FRIENDS FOR LITTLE OLD ME?
YOU HEARD SPIDER-LADY. COME WITH GRIMLOCK!
PROMISE YOU'LL COME BACK SOON... FOR THEIR SAKE!

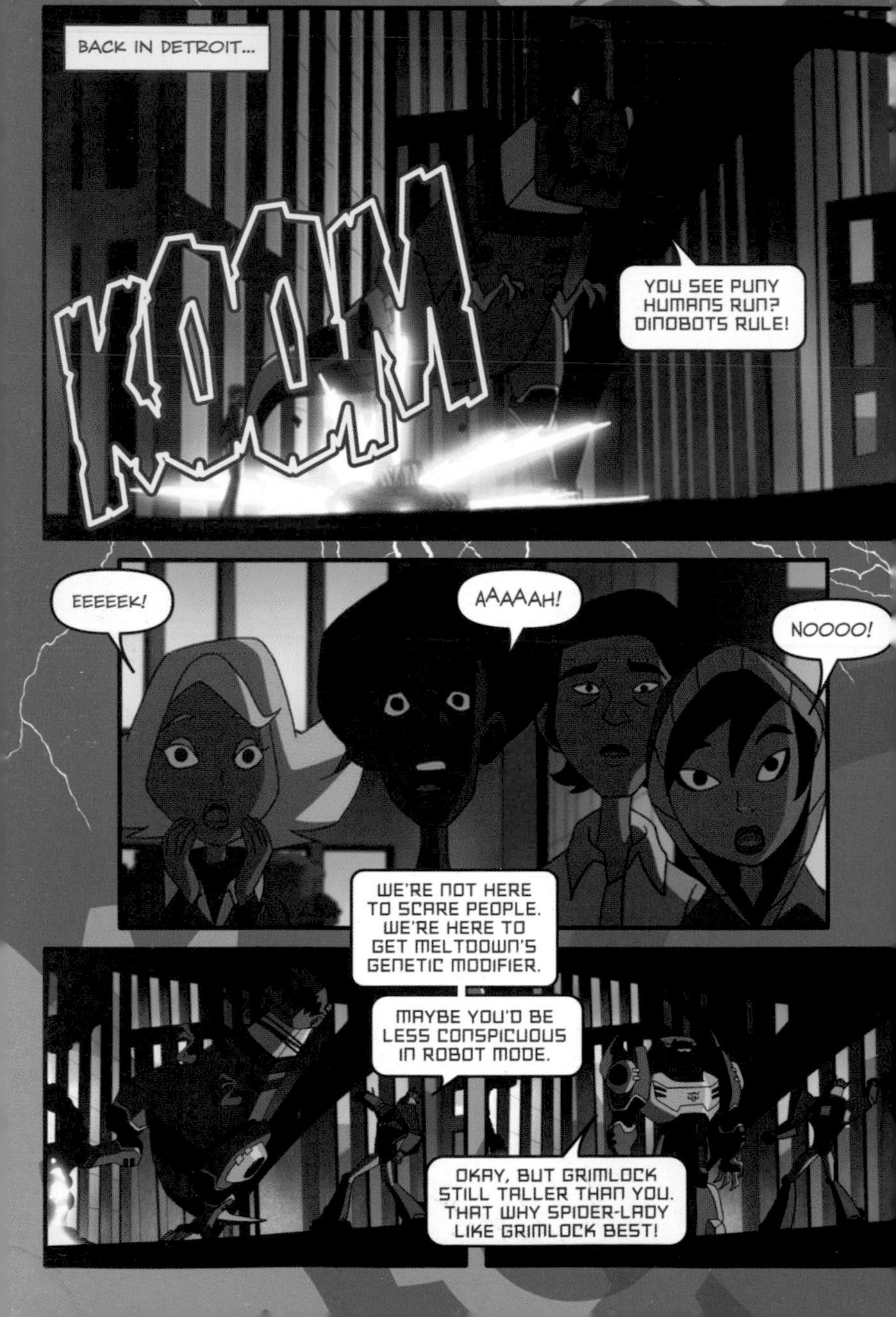
BACK IN DETROIT...
KOOOM
YOU SEE PUNY HUMANS RUN? DINOBOTS RULE!
EEEEEK!
AAAAAH!
NOOOO!
WE'RE NOT HERE TO SCARE PEOPLE. WE'RE HERE TO GET MELTDOWN'S GENETIC MODIFIER.
MAYBE YOU'D BE LESS CONSPICUOUS IN ROBOT MODE.
OKAY, BUT GRIMLOCK STILL TALLER THAN YOU. THAT WHY SPIDER-LADY LIKE GRIMLOCK BEST!

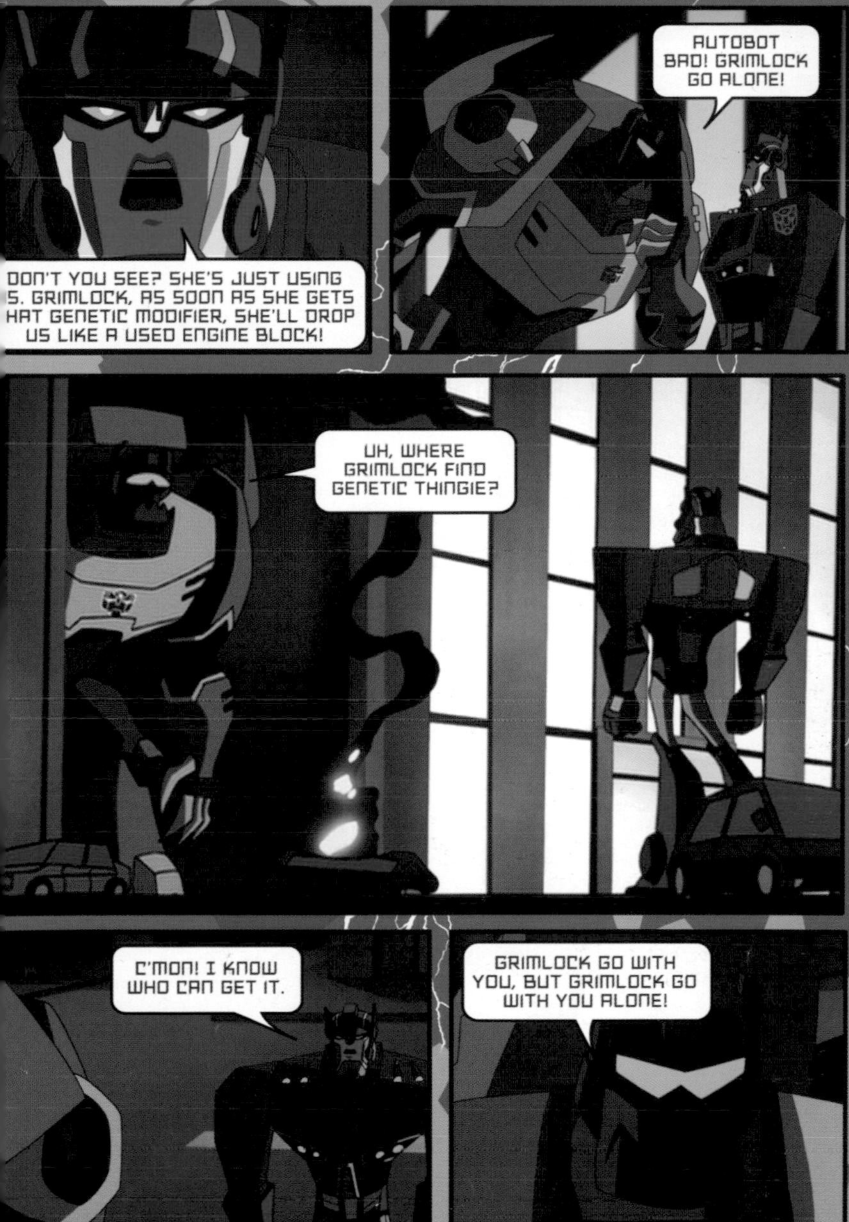
DON'T YOU SEE? SHE'S JUST USING
S. GRIMLOCK, AS SOON AS SHE GETS
HAT GENETIC MODIFIER, SHE'LL DROP
US LIKE A USED ENGINE BLOCK!
AUTOBOT BAD! GRIMLOCK GO ALONE!
UH, WHERE GRIMLOCK FIND GENETIC THINGIE?
C'MON! I KNOW WHO CAN GET IT.
GRIMLOCK GO WITH YOU, BUT GRIMLOCK GO WITH YOU ALONE!

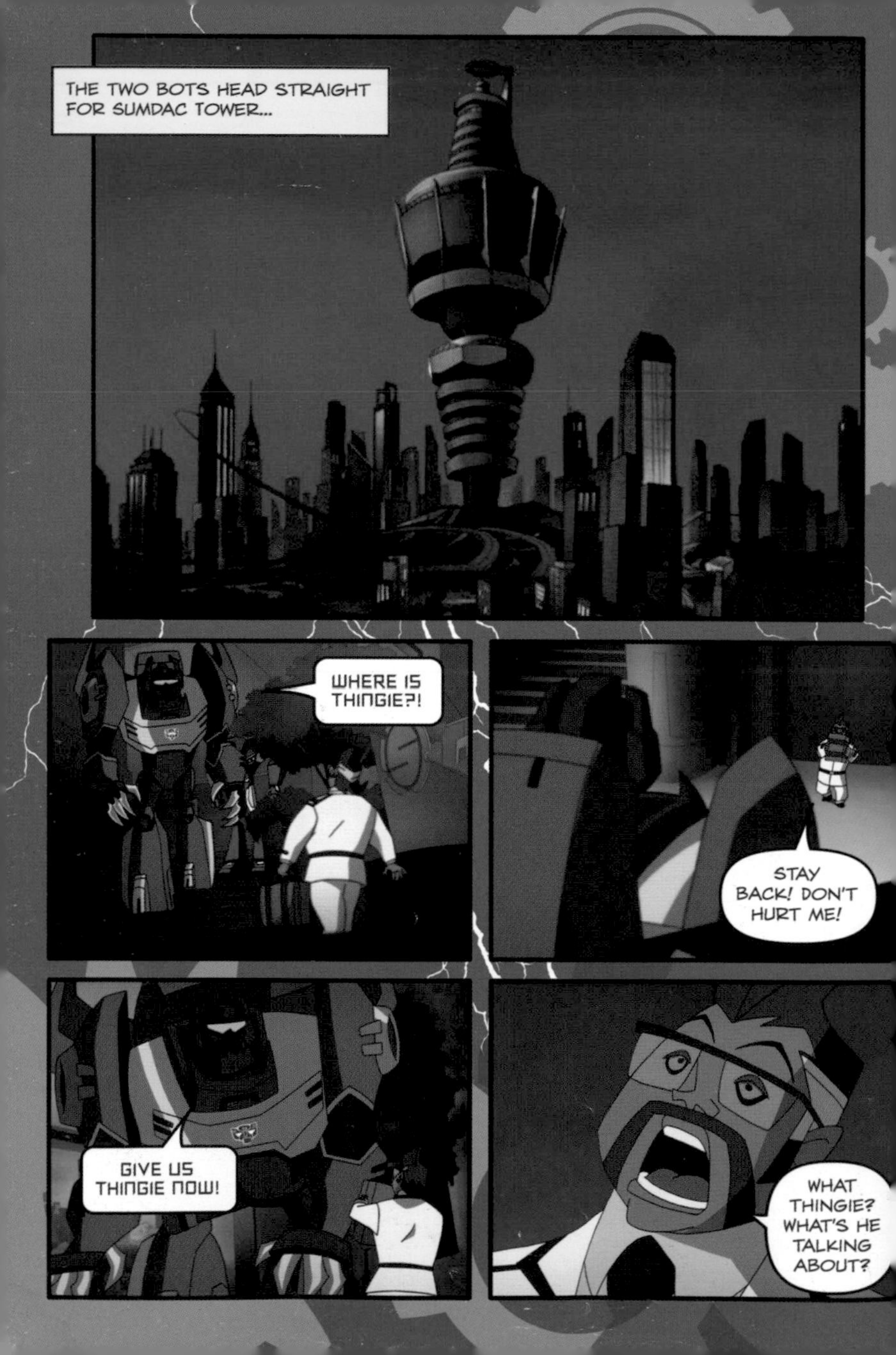
THE TWO BOTS HEAD STRAIGHT FOR SUMDAC TOWER...
WHERE IS THINGIE?!
STAY BACK! DON'T HURT ME!
GIVE US THINGIE NOW!
WHAT THINGIE? WHAT'S HE TALKING ABOUT?

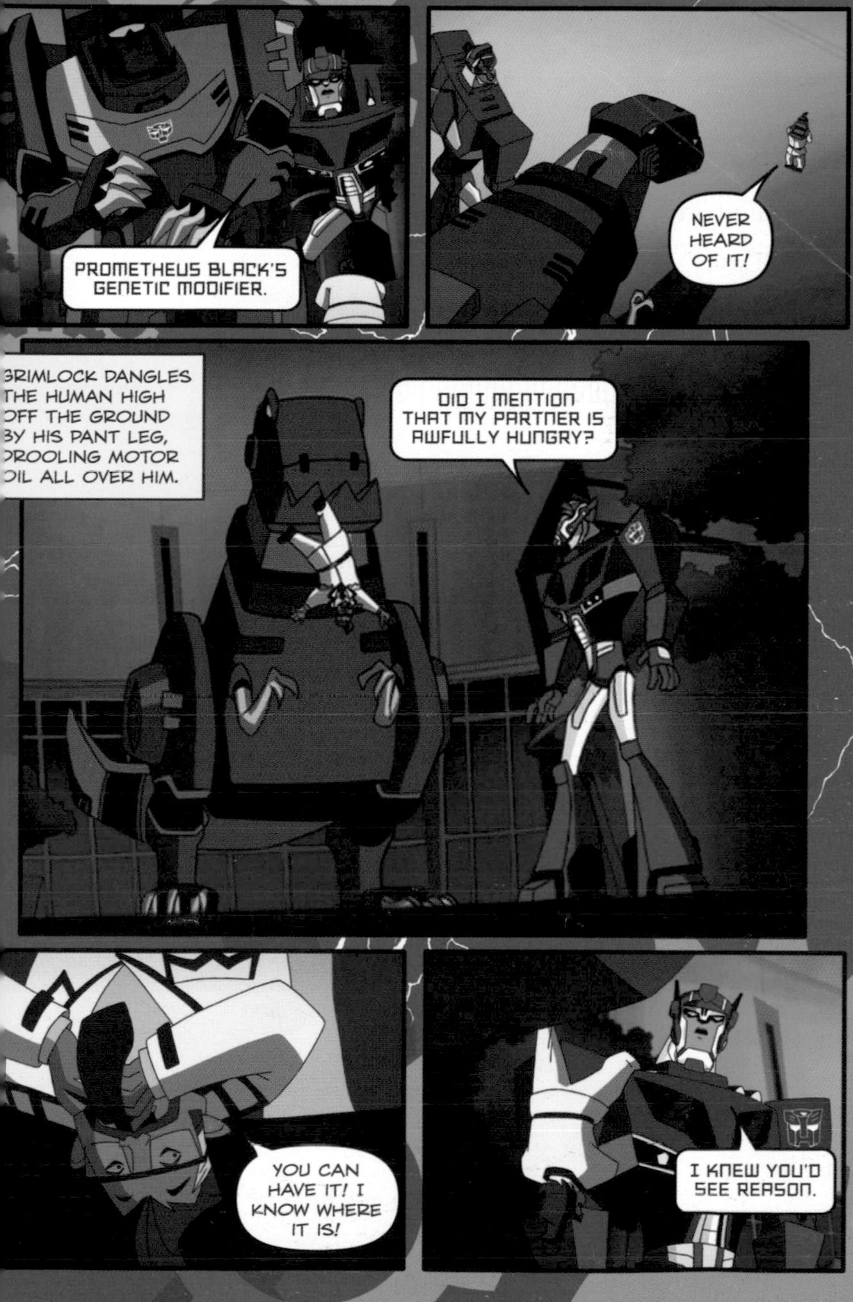

PROMETHEUS BLACK'S GENETIC MODIFIER.
NEVER HEARD OF IT!
GRIMLOCK DANGLES THE HUMAN HIGH OFF THE GROUND BY HIS PANT LEG, DROOLING MOTOR OIL ALL OVER HIM.
DID I MENTION THAT MY PARTNER IS AWFULLY HUNGRY?
YOU CAN HAVE IT! I KNOW WHERE IT IS!
I KNEW YOU'D SEE REASON.

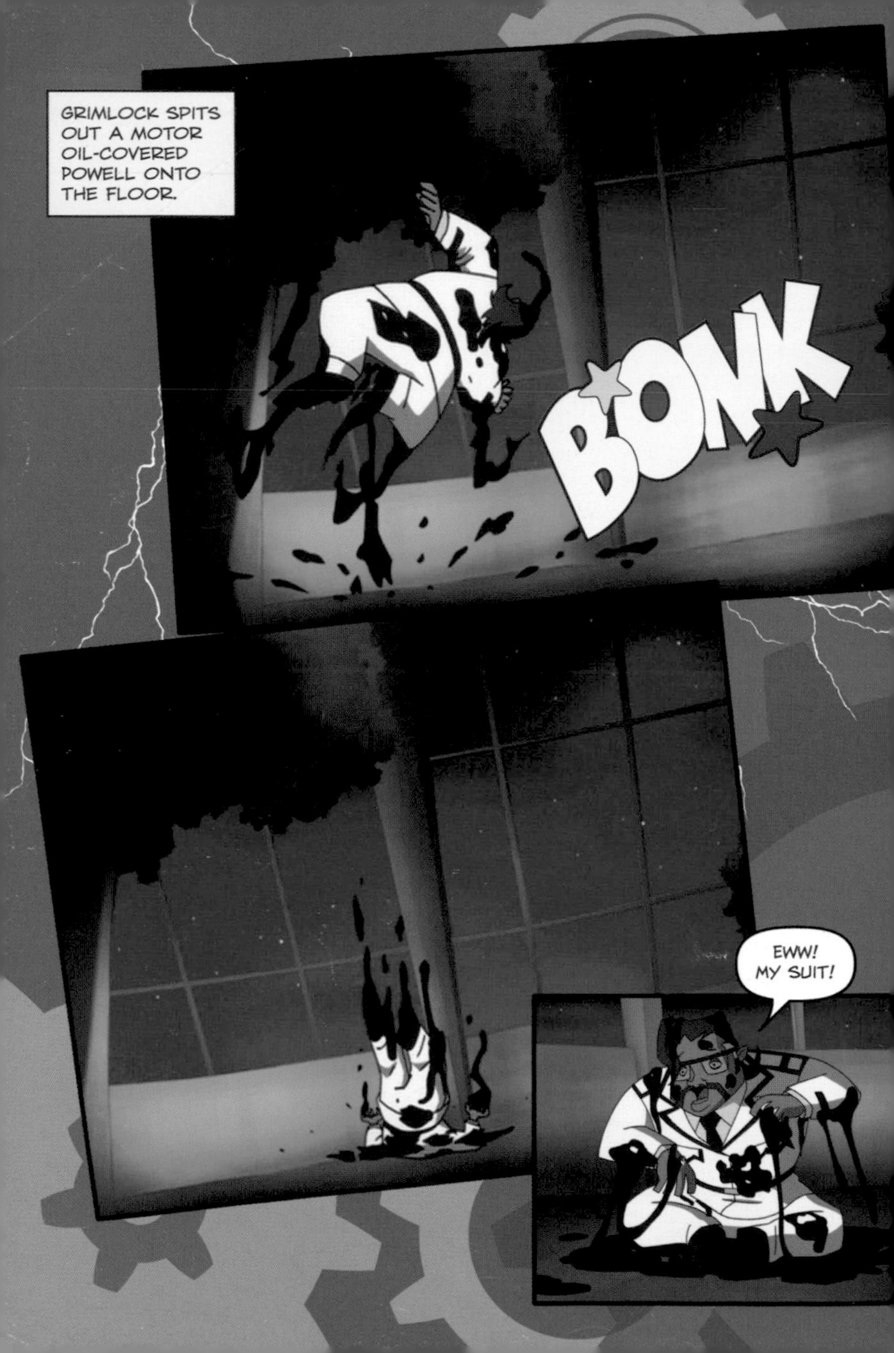
GRIMLOCK SPITS OUT A MOTOR OIL-COVERED POWELL ONTO THE FLOOR.
BONK
EWW! MY SUIT!

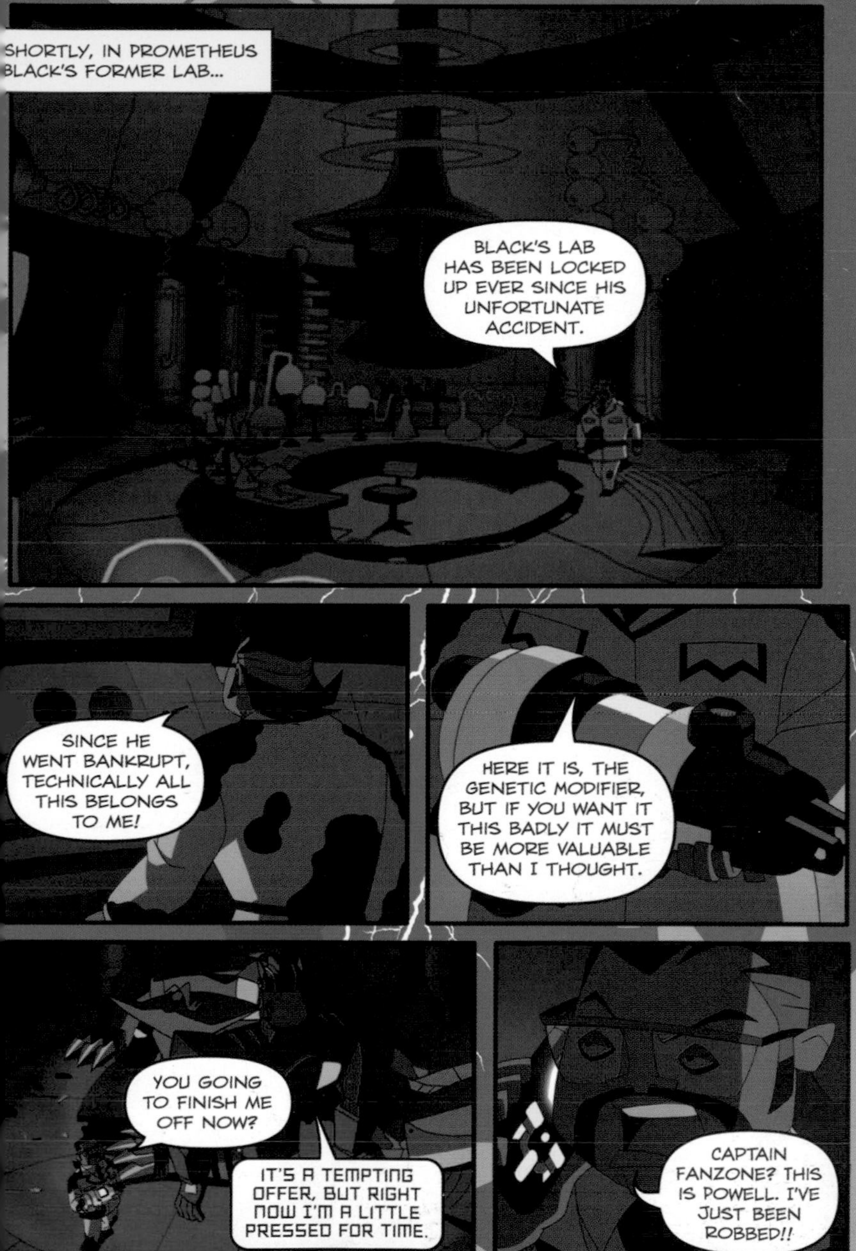
SHORTLY, IN PROMETHEUS BLACK'S FORMER LAB...
BLACK'S LAB HAS BEEN LOCKED UP EVER SINCE HIS UNFORTUNATE ACCIDENT.
SINCE HE WENT BANKRUPT, TECHNICALLY ALL THIS BELONGS TO ME!
HERE IT IS, THE GENETIC MODIFIER, BUT IF YOU WANT IT THIS BADLY IT MUST BE MORE VALUABLE THAN I THOUGHT.
YOU GOING TO FINISH ME OFF NOW?
IT'S A TEMPTING OFFER, BUT RIGHT NOW I'M A LITTLE PRESSED FOR TIME.
CAPTAIN FANZONE? THIS IS POWELL. I'VE JUST BEEN ROBBED!!

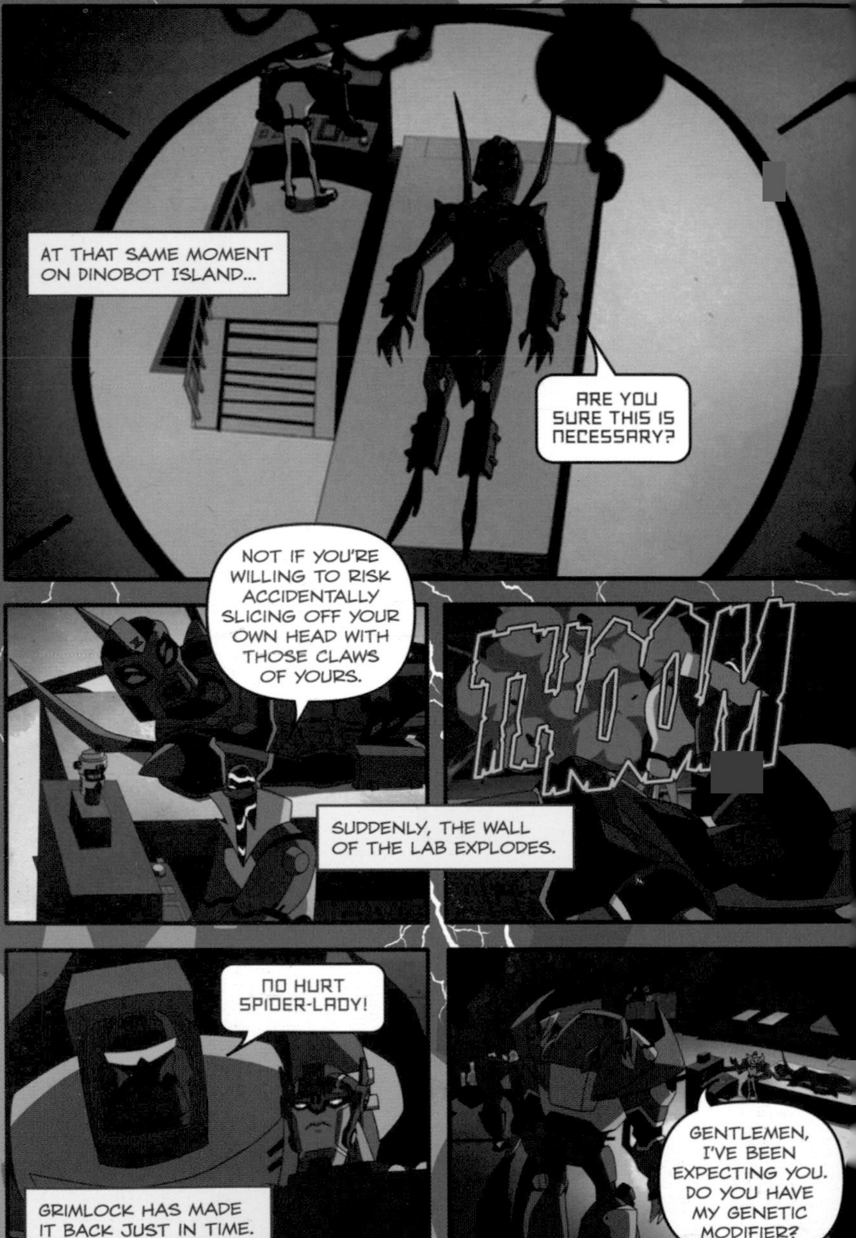
AT THAT SAME MOMENT ON DINOBOT ISLAND...
ARE YOU SURE THIS IS NECESSARY?
NOT IF YOU'RE WILLING TO RISK ACCIDENTALLY SLICING OFF YOUR OWN HEAD WITH THOSE CLAWS OF YOURS.
THOOM
SUDDENLY, THE WALL OF THE LAB EXPLODES.
NO HURT SPIDER-LADY!
GRIMLOCK HAS MADE IT BACK JUST IN TIME.
GENTLEMEN, I'VE BEEN EXPECTING YOU. DO YOU HAVE MY GENETIC MODIFIER?

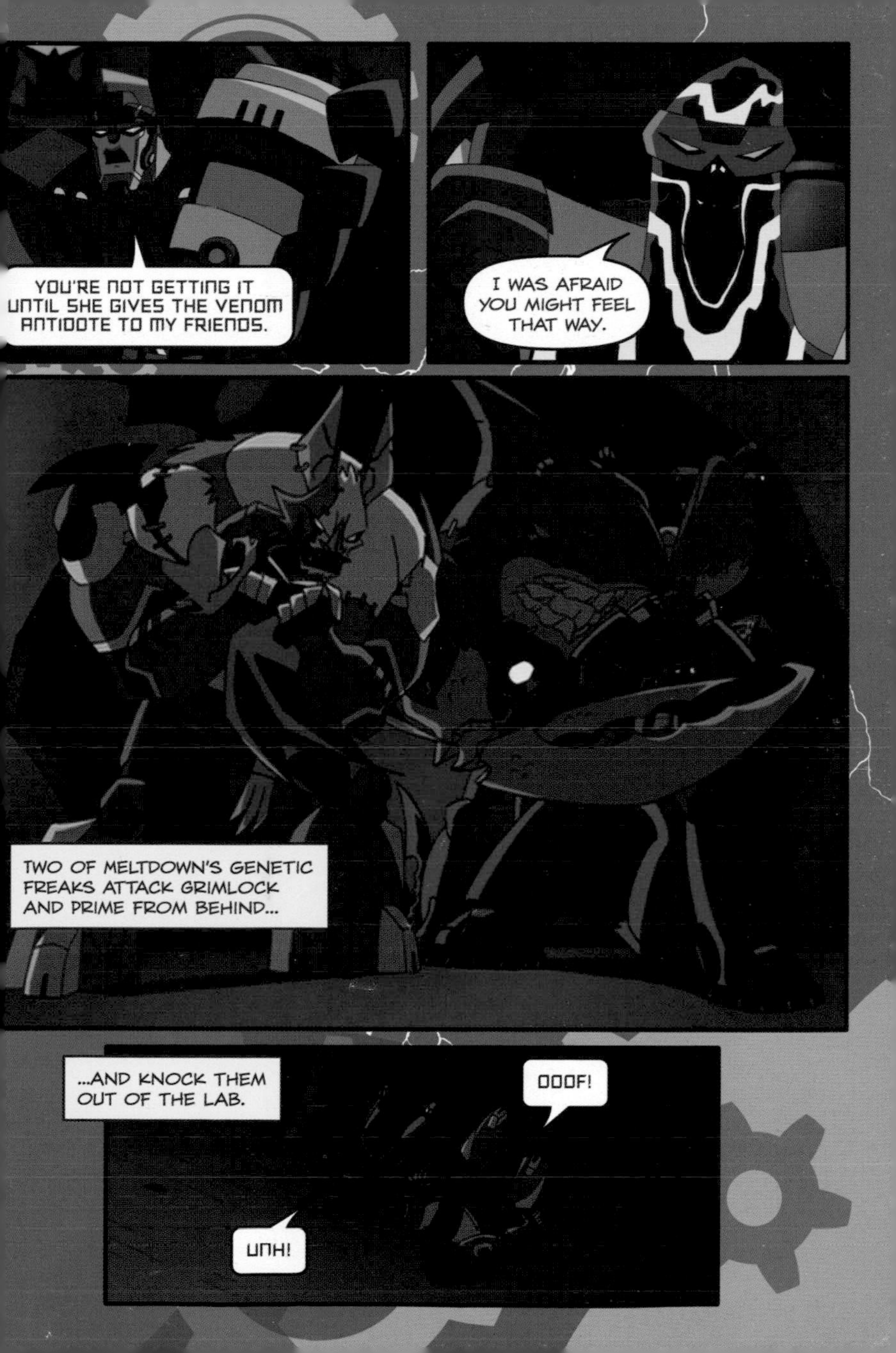
YOU'RE NOT GETTING IT UNTIL SHE GIVES THE VENOM ANTIDOTE TO MY FRIENDS.
I WAS AFRAID YOU MIGHT FEEL THAT WAY.
TWO OF MELTDOWN'S GENETIC FREAKS ATTACK GRIMLOCK AND PRIME FROM BEHIND...
...AND KNOCK THEM OUT OF THE LAB.
OOOF!
UNH!

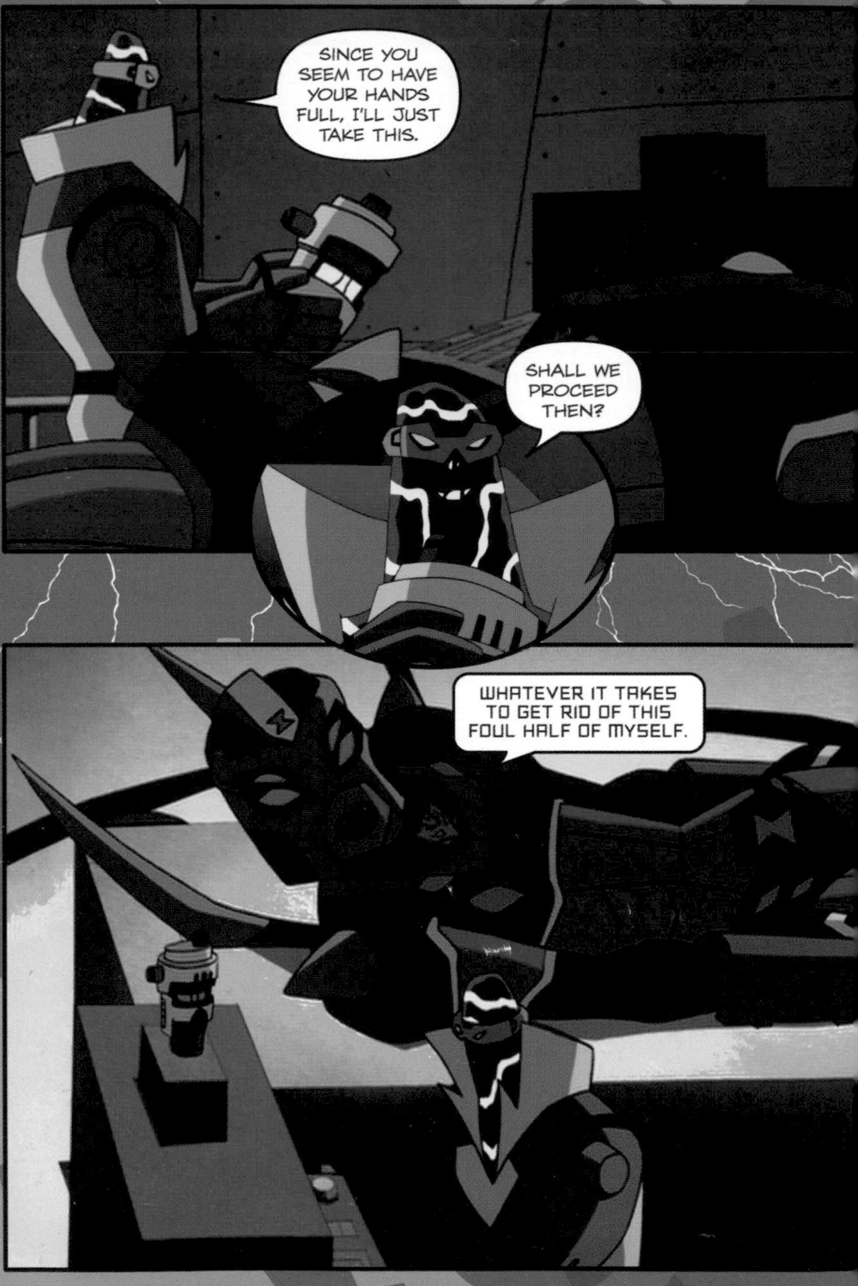
SINCE YOU SEEM TO HAVE YOUR HANDS FULL, I'LL JUST TAKE THIS.
SHALL WE PROCEED THEN?
WHATEVER IT TAKES TO GET RID OF THIS FOUL HALF OF MYSELF.

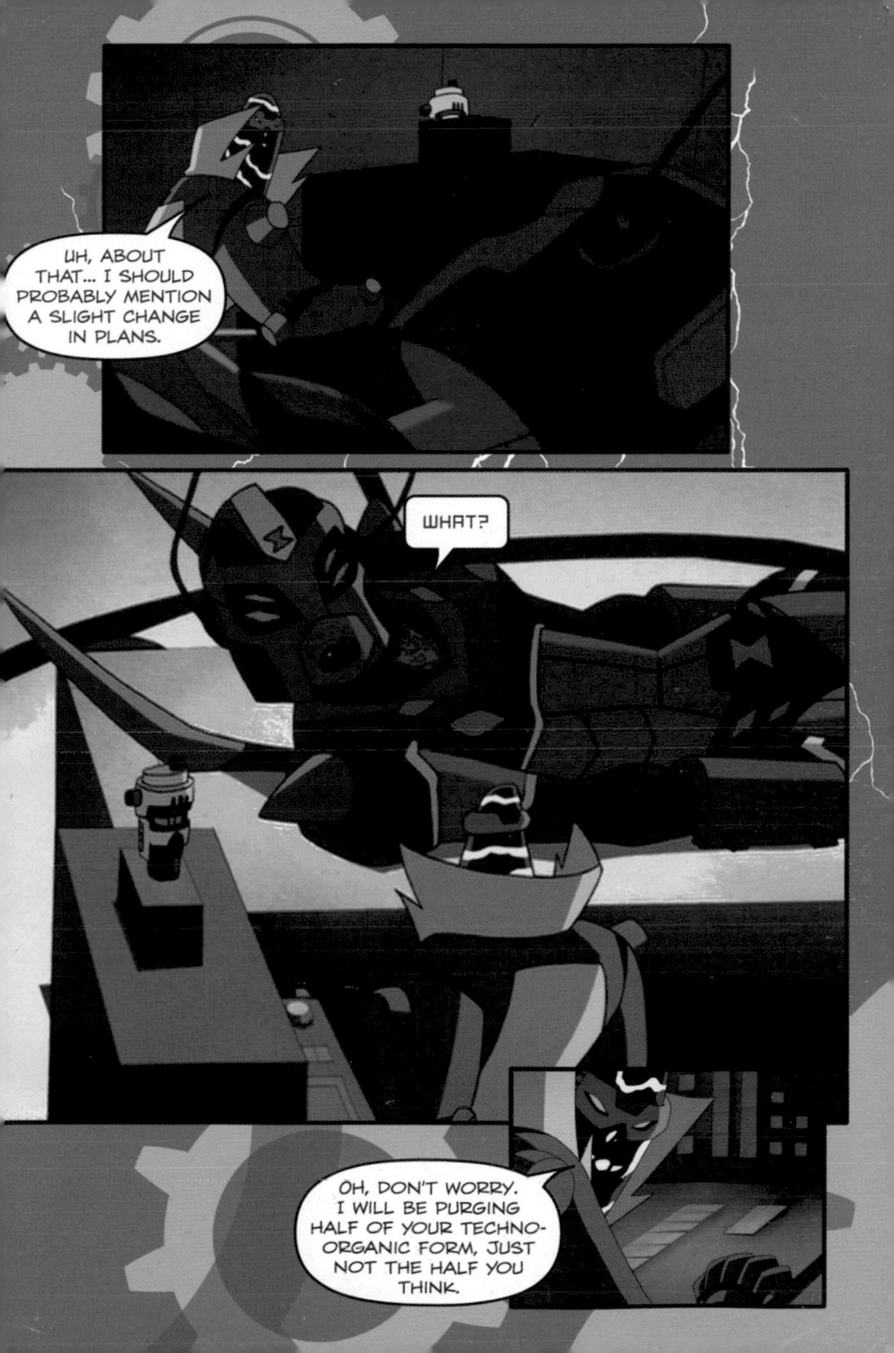
UH, ABOUT THAT... I SHOULD PROBABLY MENTION A SLIGHT CHANGE IN PLANS.
WHAT?
OH, DON'T WORRY. I WILL BE PURGING HALF OF YOUR TECHNO-ORGANIC FORM, JUST NOT THE HALF YOU THINK.

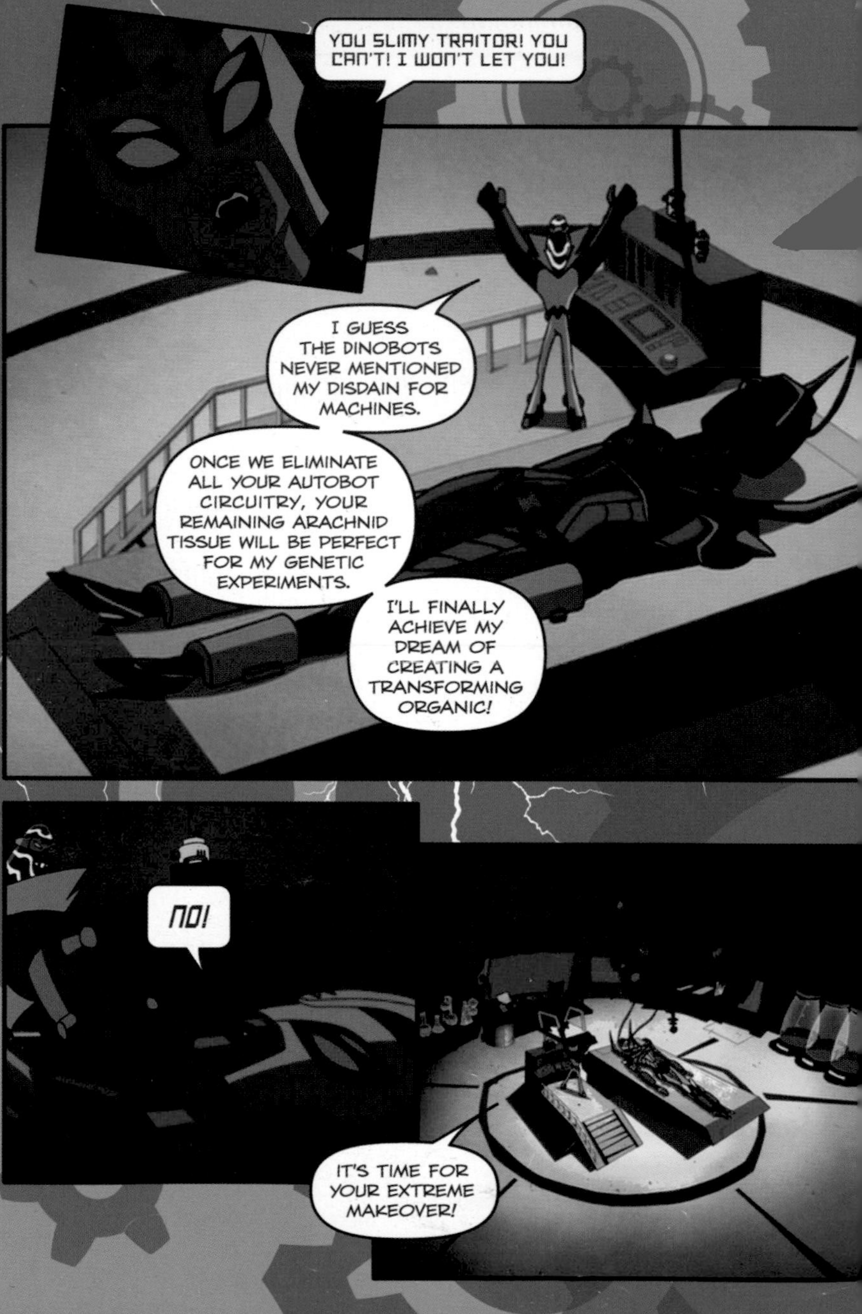
YOU SLIMY TRAITOR! YOU CAN'T! I WON'T LET YOU!
I GUESS THE DINOBOTS NEVER MENTIONED MY DISDAIN FOR MACHINES.
ONCE WE ELIMINATE ALL YOUR AUTOBOT CIRCUITRY, YOUR REMAINING ARACHNID TISSUE WILL BE PERFECT FOR MY GENETIC EXPERIMENTS.
I'LL FINALLY ACHIEVE MY DREAM OF CREATING A TRANSFORMING ORGANIC!
NO!
IT'S TIME FOR YOUR EXTREME MAKEOVER!

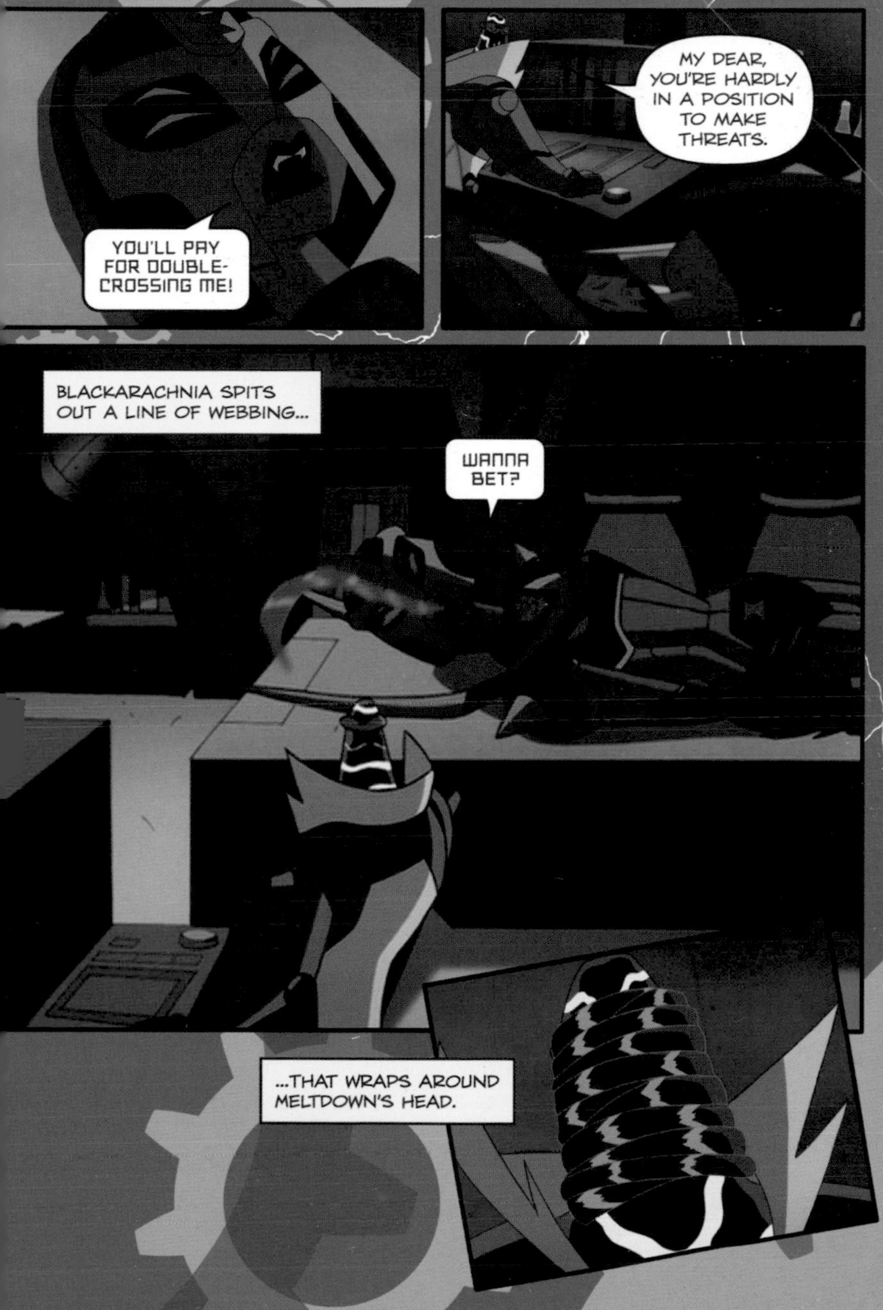
YOU'LL PAY FOR DOUBLE-CROSSING ME!
MY DEAR, YOU'RE HARDLY IN A POSITION TO MAKE THREATS.
BLACKARACHNIA SPITS OUT A LINE OF WEBBING...
WANNA BET?
...THAT WRAPS AROUND MELTDOWN'S HEAD.

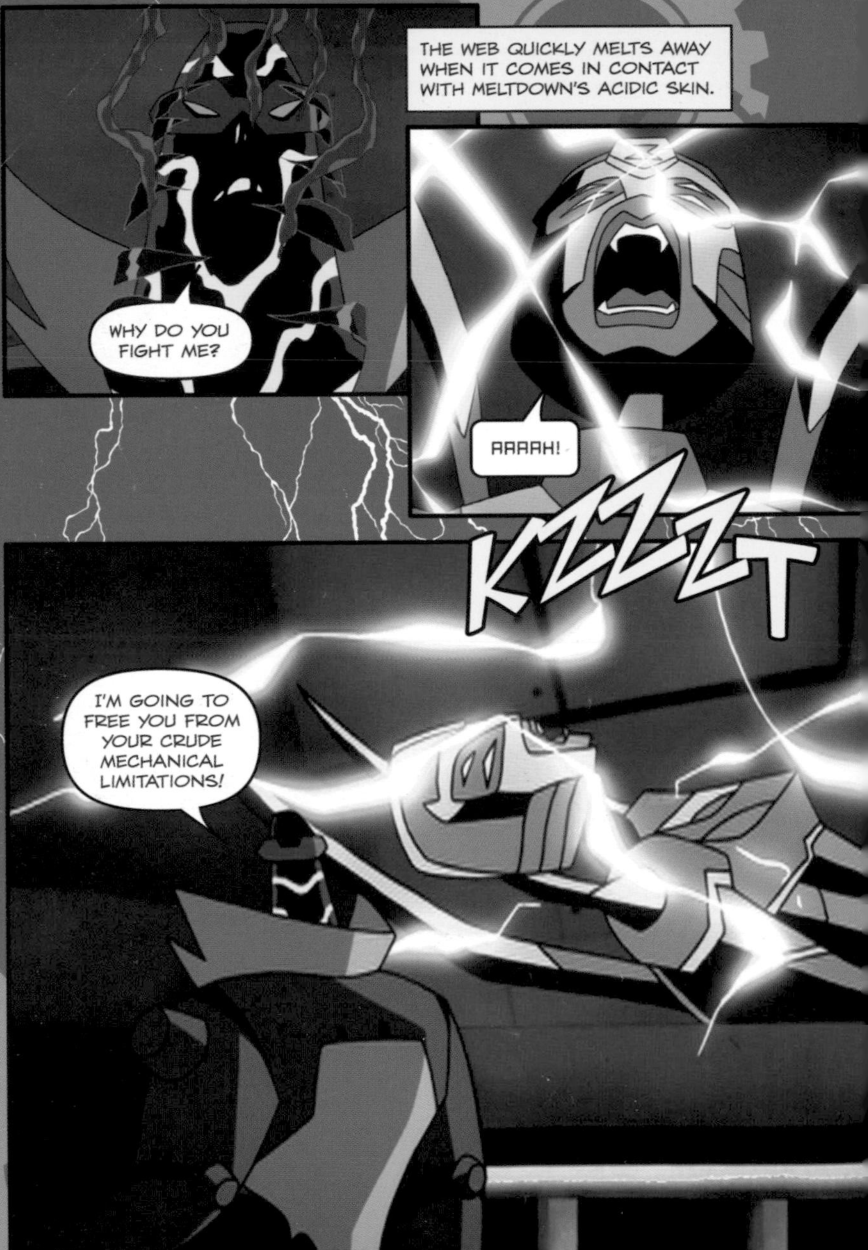
THE WEB QUICKLY MELTS AWAY WHEN IT COMES IN CONTACT WITH MELTDOWN'S ACIDIC SKIN.
WHY DO YOU FIGHT ME?
AAAAH!
KZZZT
I'M GOING TO FREE YOU FROM YOUR CRUDE MECHANICAL LIMITATIONS!

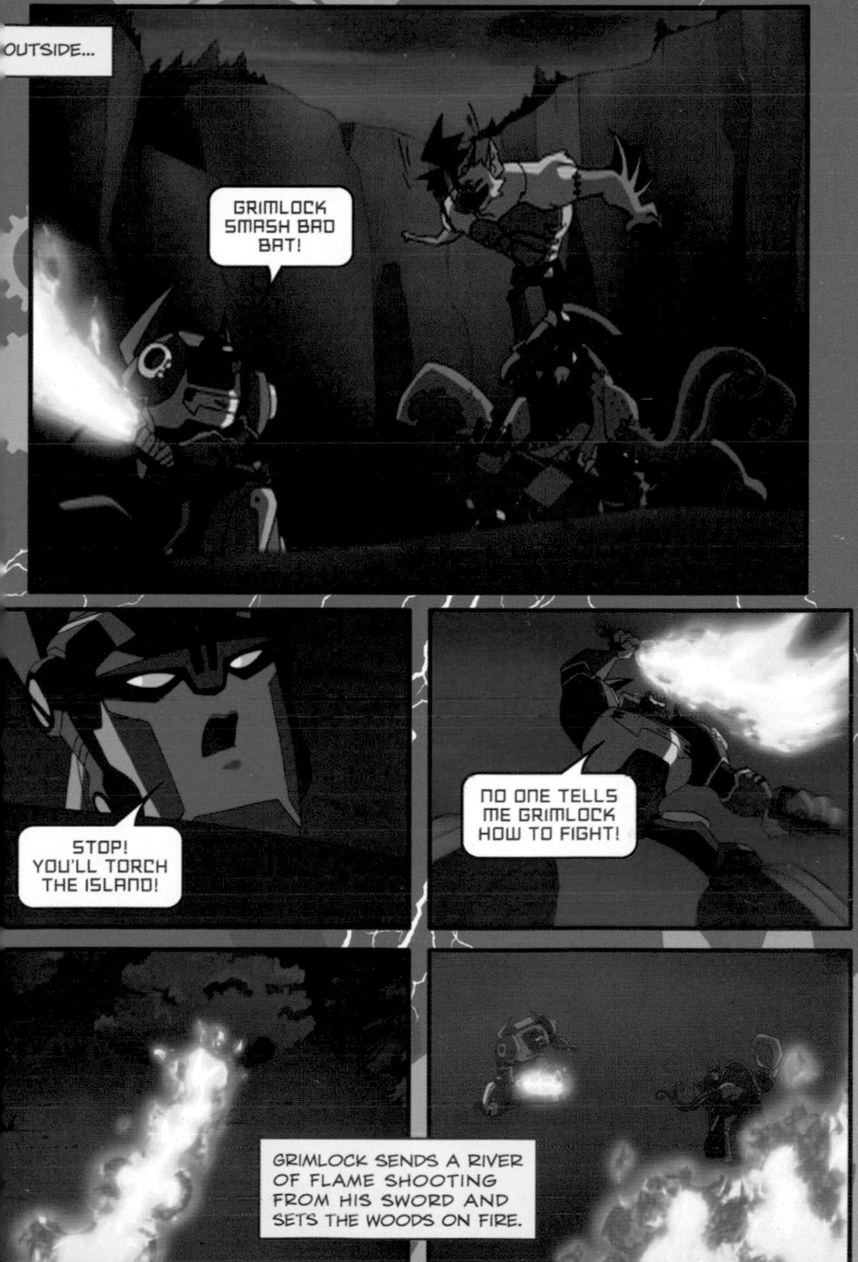
OUTSIDE...
GRIMLOCK SMASH BAD BAT!
STOP! YOU'LL TORCH THE ISLAND!
NO ONE TELLS ME GRIMLOCK HOW TO FIGHT!
GRIMLOCK SENDS A RIVER OF FLAME SHOOTING FROM HIS SWORD AND SETS THE WOODS ON FIRE.

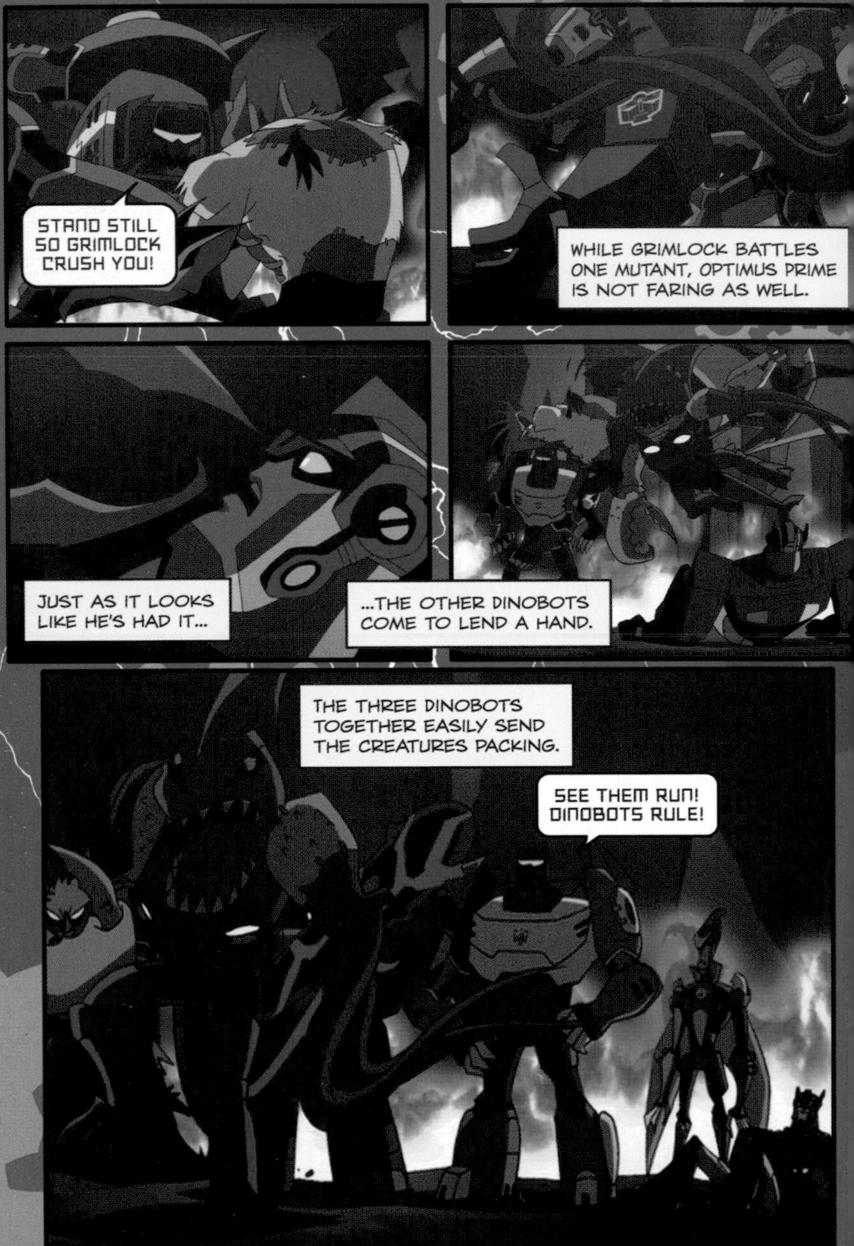
STAND STILL SO GRIMLOCK CRUSH YOU!
WHILE GRIMLOCK BATTLES ONE MUTANT, OPTIMUS PRIME IS NOT FARING AS WELL.
JUST AS IT LOOKS LIKE HE'S HAD IT...
...THE OTHER DINOBOTS COME TO LEND A HAND.
THE THREE DINOBOTS TOGETHER EASILY SEND THE CREATURES PACKING.
SEE THEM RUN! DINOBOTS RULE!

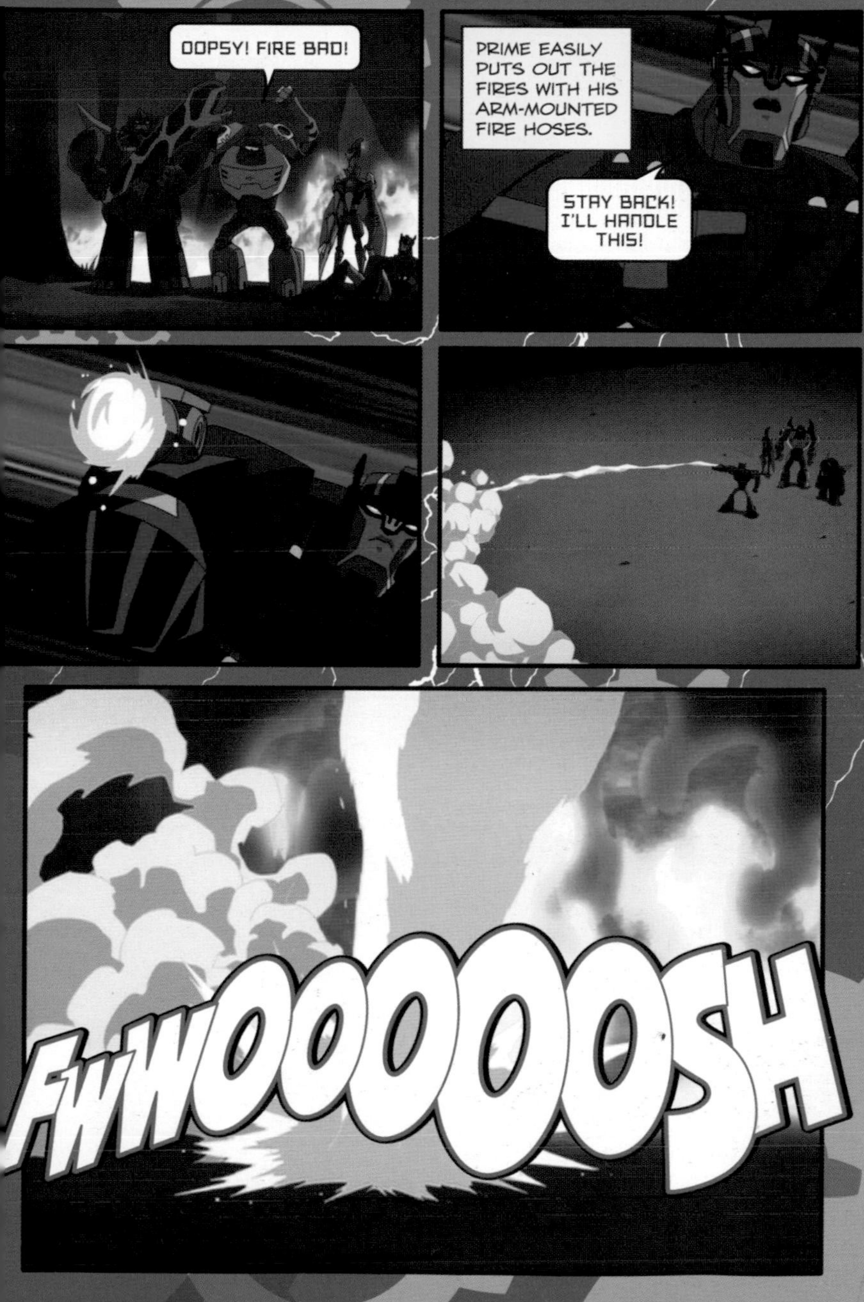
OOPSY! FIRE BAD!
PRIME EASILY PUTS OUT THE FIRES WITH HIS ARM-MOUNTED FIRE HOSES.
STAY BACK! I'LL HANDLE THIS!
FWWOOOOOOSH

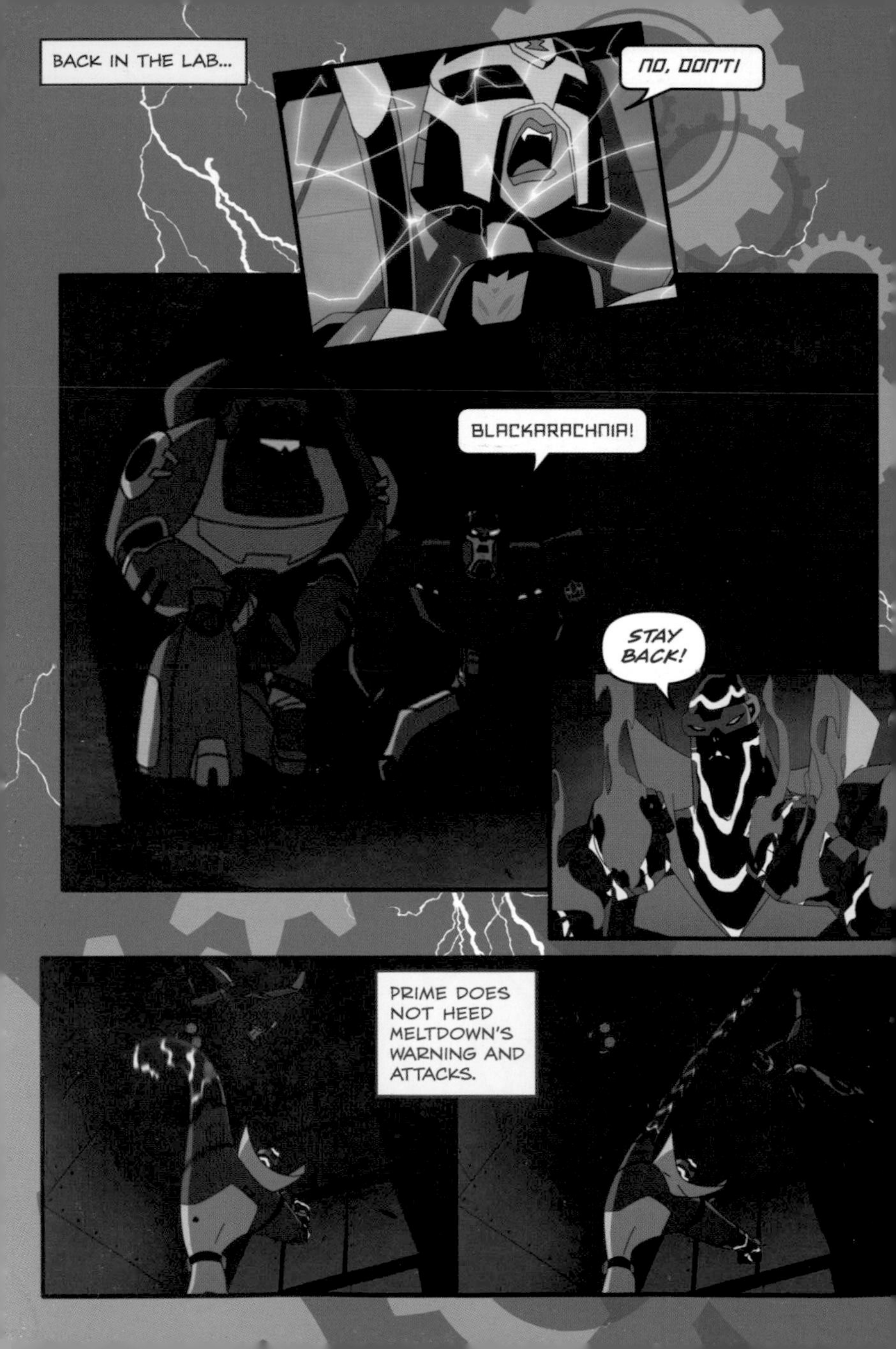
BACK IN THE LAB...
NO, DON'T!
BLACKARACHNIA!
STAY BACK!
PRIME DOES NOT HEED MELTDOWN'S WARNING AND ATTACKS.

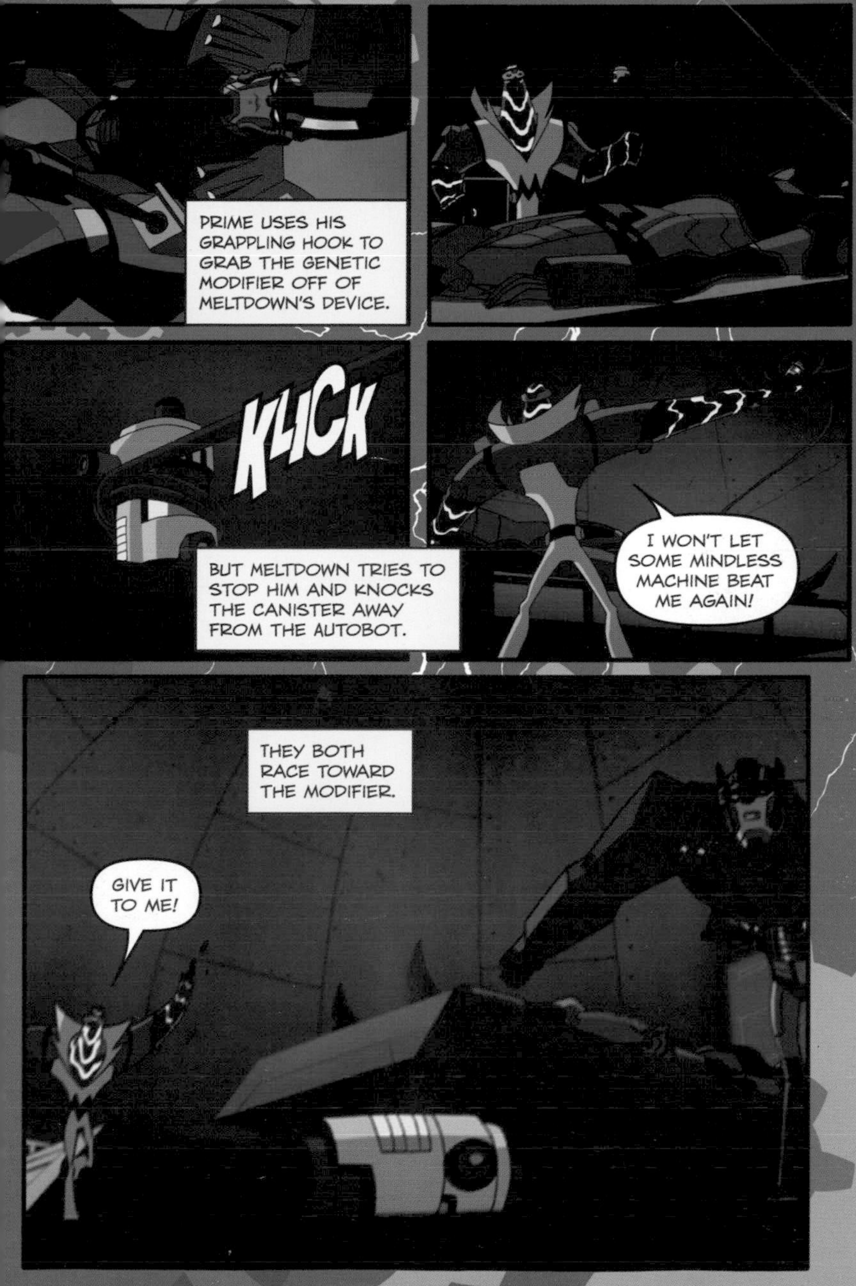

PRIME USES HIS GRAPPLING HOOK TO GRAB THE GENETIC MODIFIER OFF OF MELTDOWN'S DEVICE.
KLICK
BUT MELTDOWN TRIES TO STOP HIM AND KNOCKS THE CANISTER AWAY FROM THE AUTOBOT.
I WON'T LET SOME MINDLESS MACHINE BEAT ME AGAIN!
THEY BOTH RACE TOWARD THE MODIFIER.
GIVE IT TO ME!

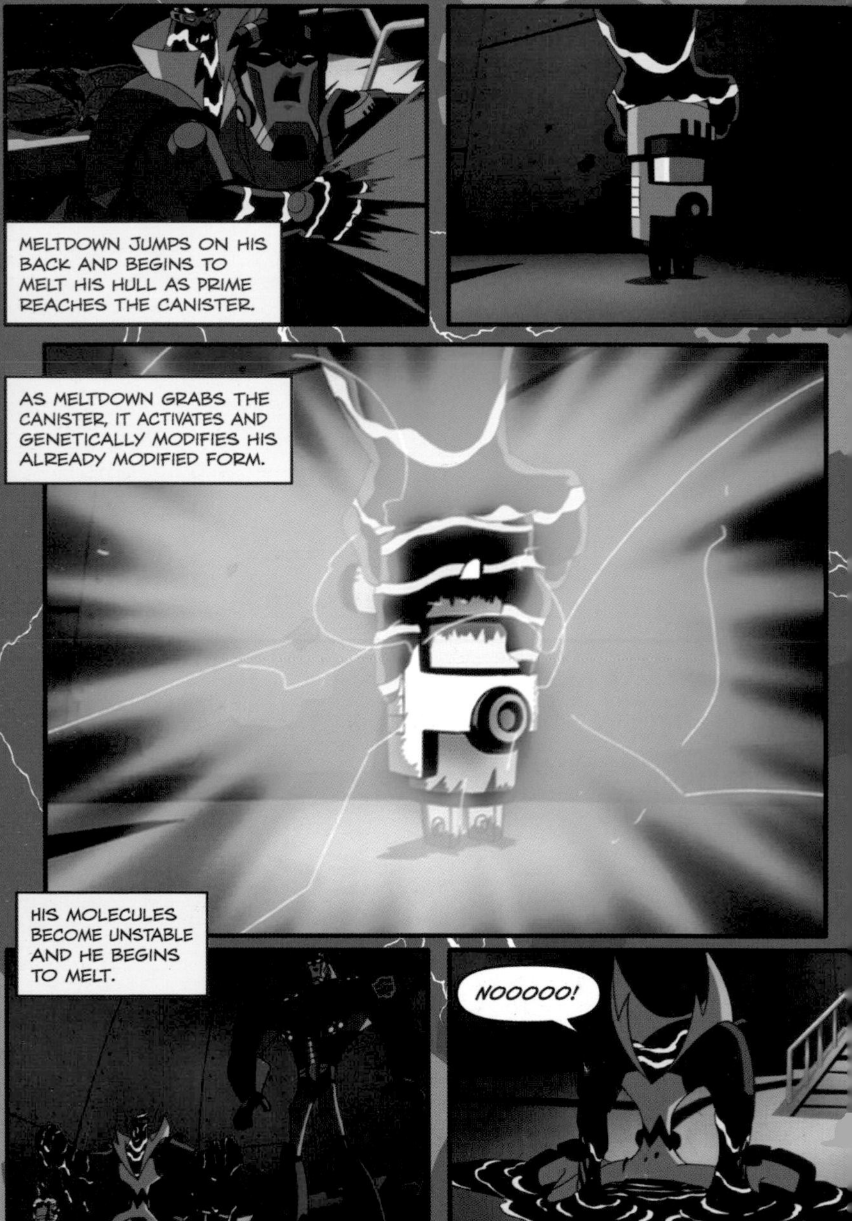
MELTDOWN JUMPS ON HIS BACK AND BEGINS TO MELT HIS HULL AS PRIME REACHES THE CANISTER.
AS MELTDOWN GRABS THE CANISTER, IT ACTIVATES AND GENETICALLY MODIFIES HIS ALREADY MODIFIED FORM.
HIS MOLECULES BECOME UNSTABLE AND HE BEGINS TO MELT.
NOOOOO!

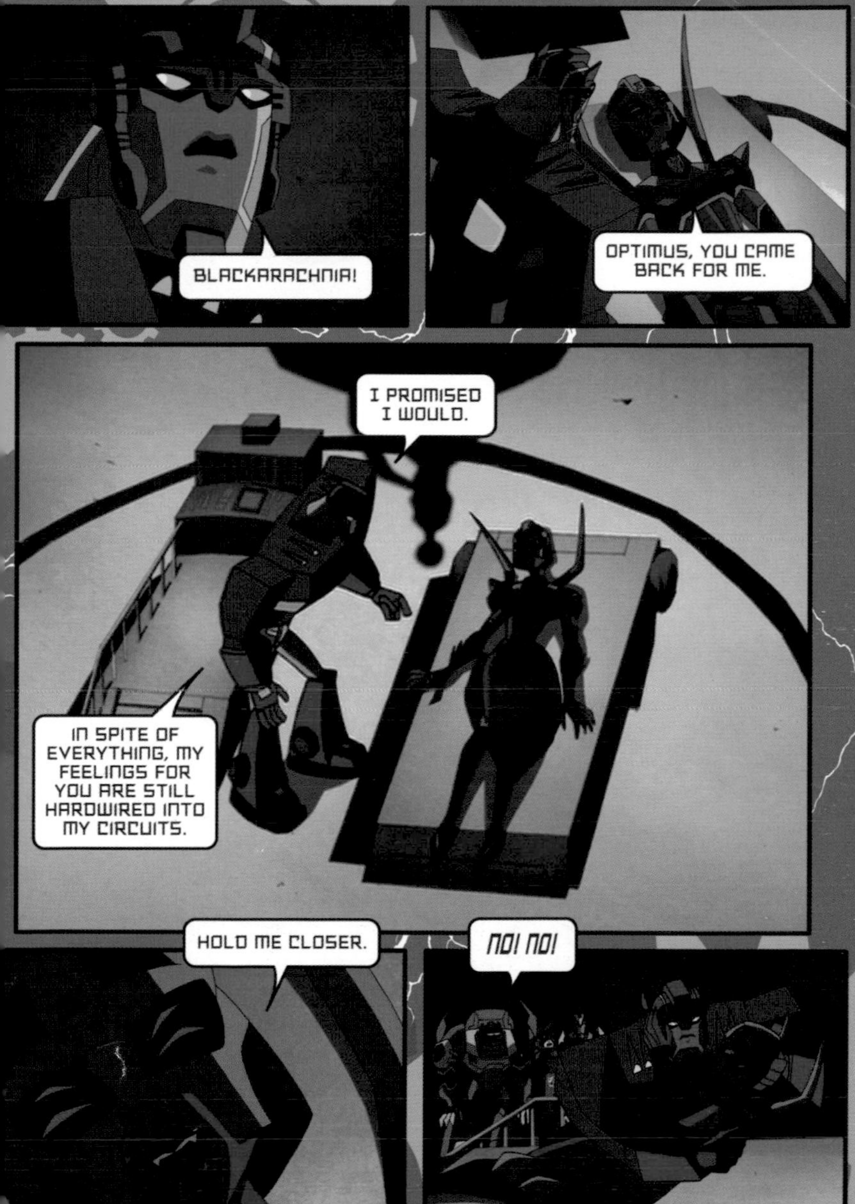
BLACKARACHNIA!
OPTIMUS, YOU CAME BACK FOR ME.
I PROMISED I WOULD.
IN SPITE OF EVERYTHING, MY FEELINGS FOR YOU ARE STILL HARDWIRED INTO MY CIRCUITS.
HOLD ME CLOSER.
NO! NO!

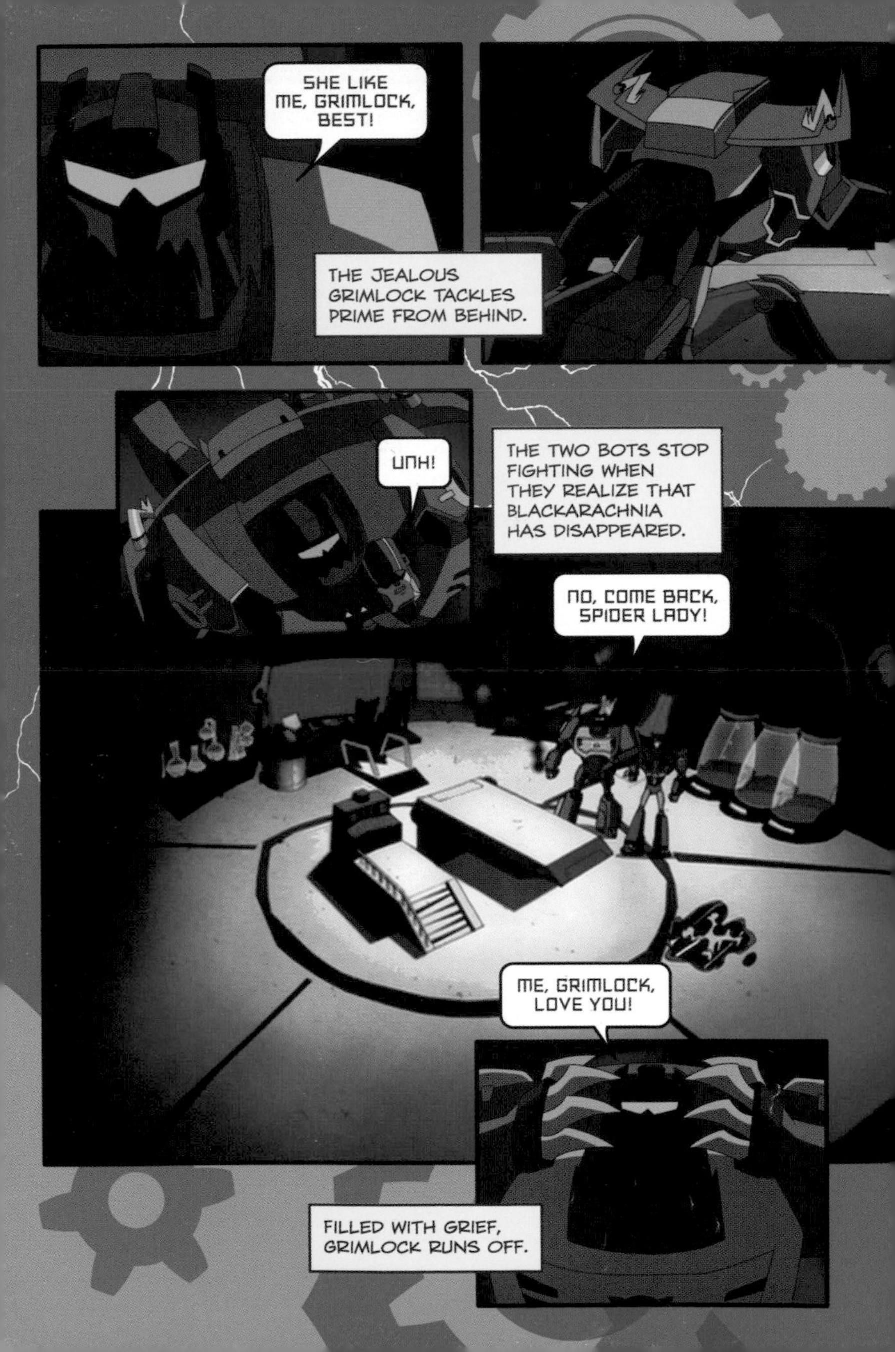
SHE LIKE ME, GRIMLOCK, BEST!
THE JEALOUS GRIMLOCK TACKLES PRIME FROM BEHIND.
UNH!
THE TWO BOTS STOP FIGHTING WHEN THEY REALIZE THAT BLACKARACHNIA HAS DISAPPEARED.
NO, COME BACK, SPIDER LADY!
ME, GRIMLOCK, LOVE YOU!
FILLED WITH GRIEF, GRIMLOCK RUNS OFF.

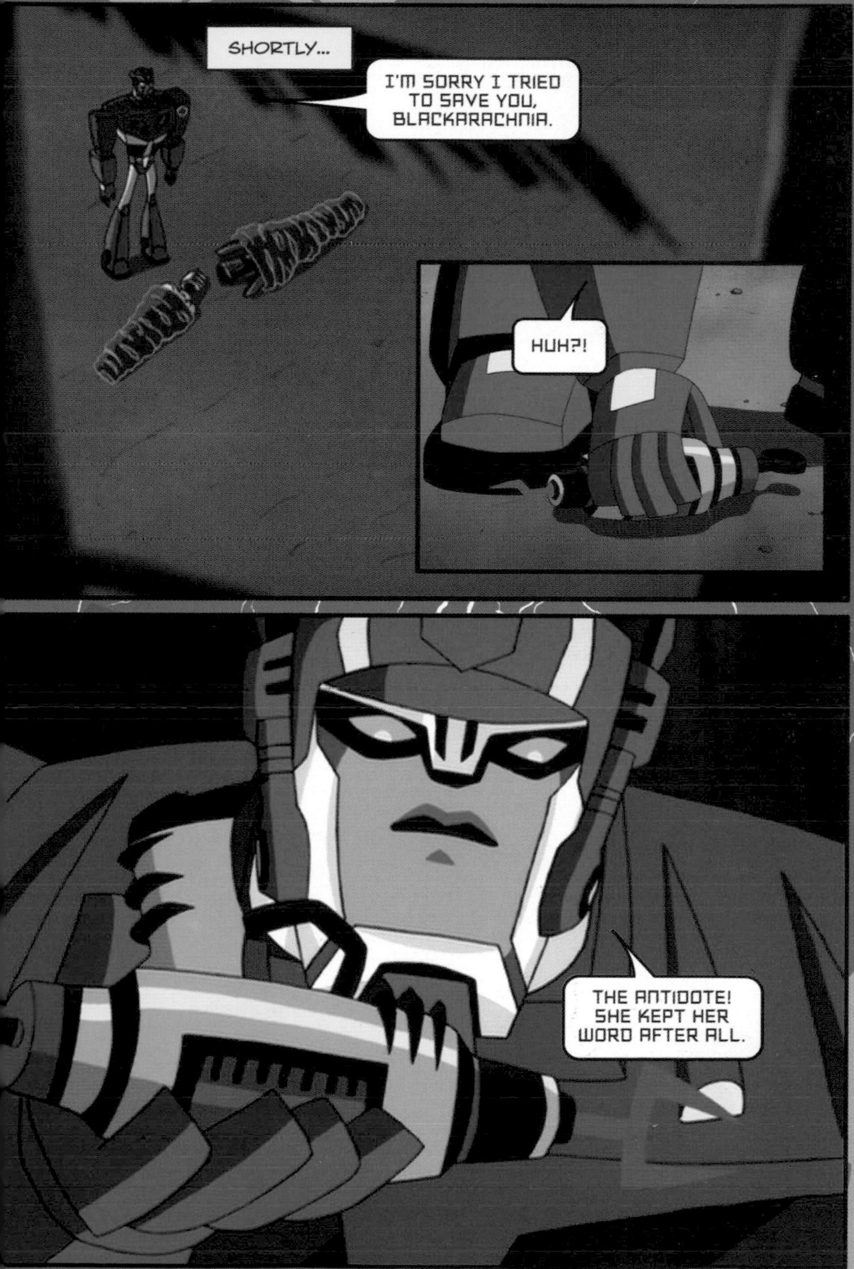
SHORTLY...
I'M SORRY I TRIED TO SAVE YOU, BLACKARACHNIA.
HUH?!
THE ANTIDOTE! SHE KEPT HER WORD AFTER ALL.

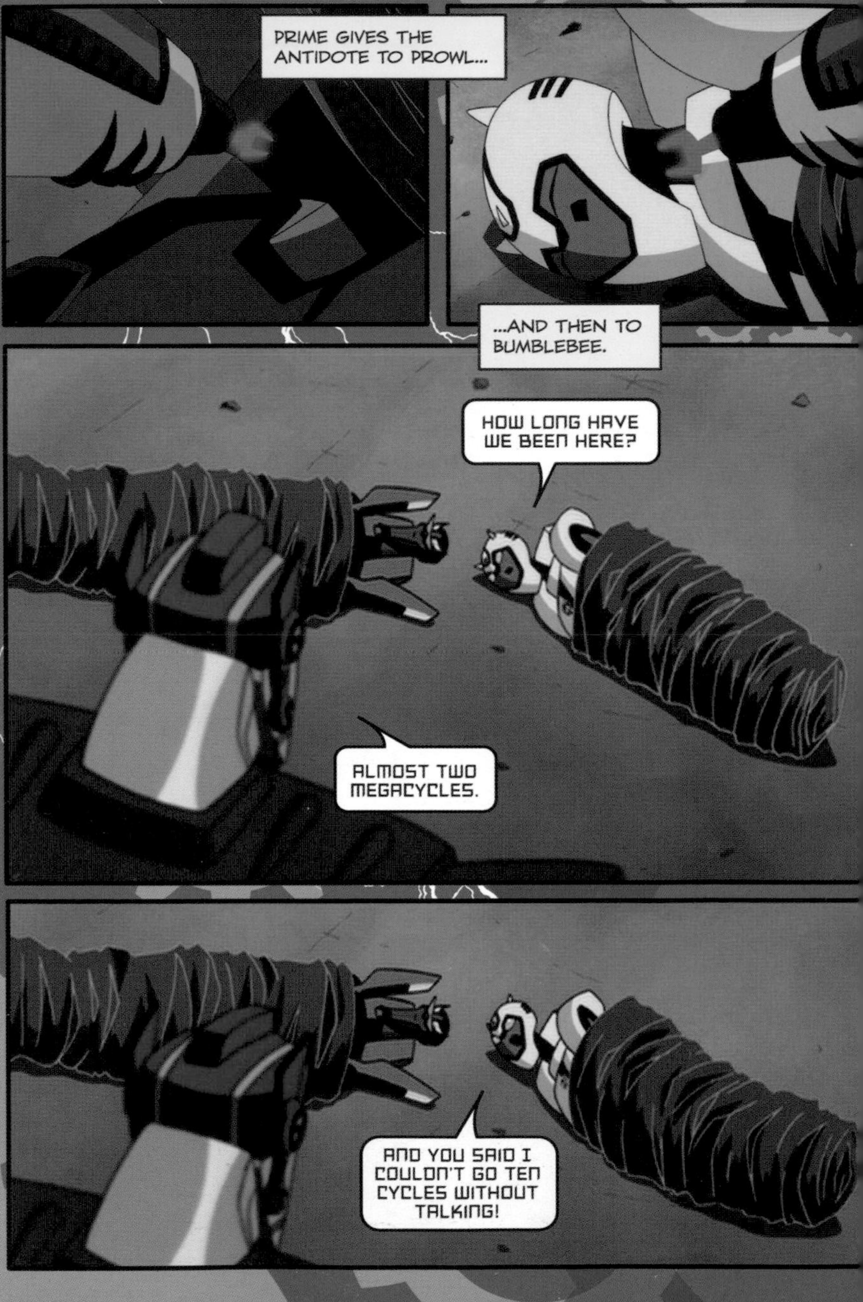
PRIME GIVES THE ANTIDOTE TO PROWL...
...AND THEN TO BUMBLEBEE.
HOW LONG HAVE WE BEEN HERE?
ALMOST TWO MEGACYCLES.
AND YOU SAID I COULDN'T GO TEN CYCLES WITHOUT TALKING!

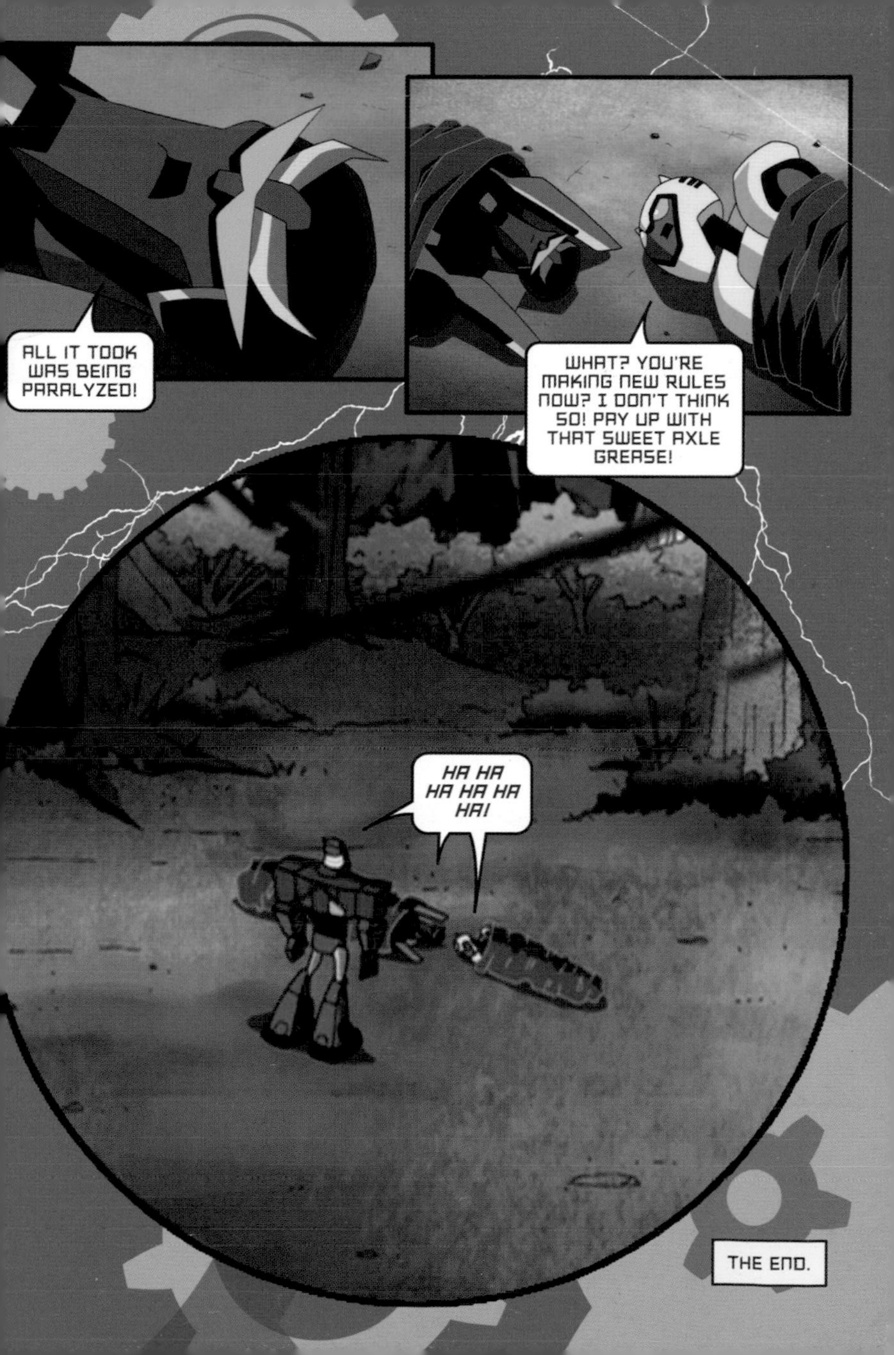
ALL IT TOOK WAS BEING PARALYZED!
WHAT? YOU'RE MAKING NEW RULES NOW? I DON'T THINK SO! PAY UP WITH THAT SWEET AXLE GREASE!
HA HA HA HA HA HA!
THE END.

Sari, No One's Home

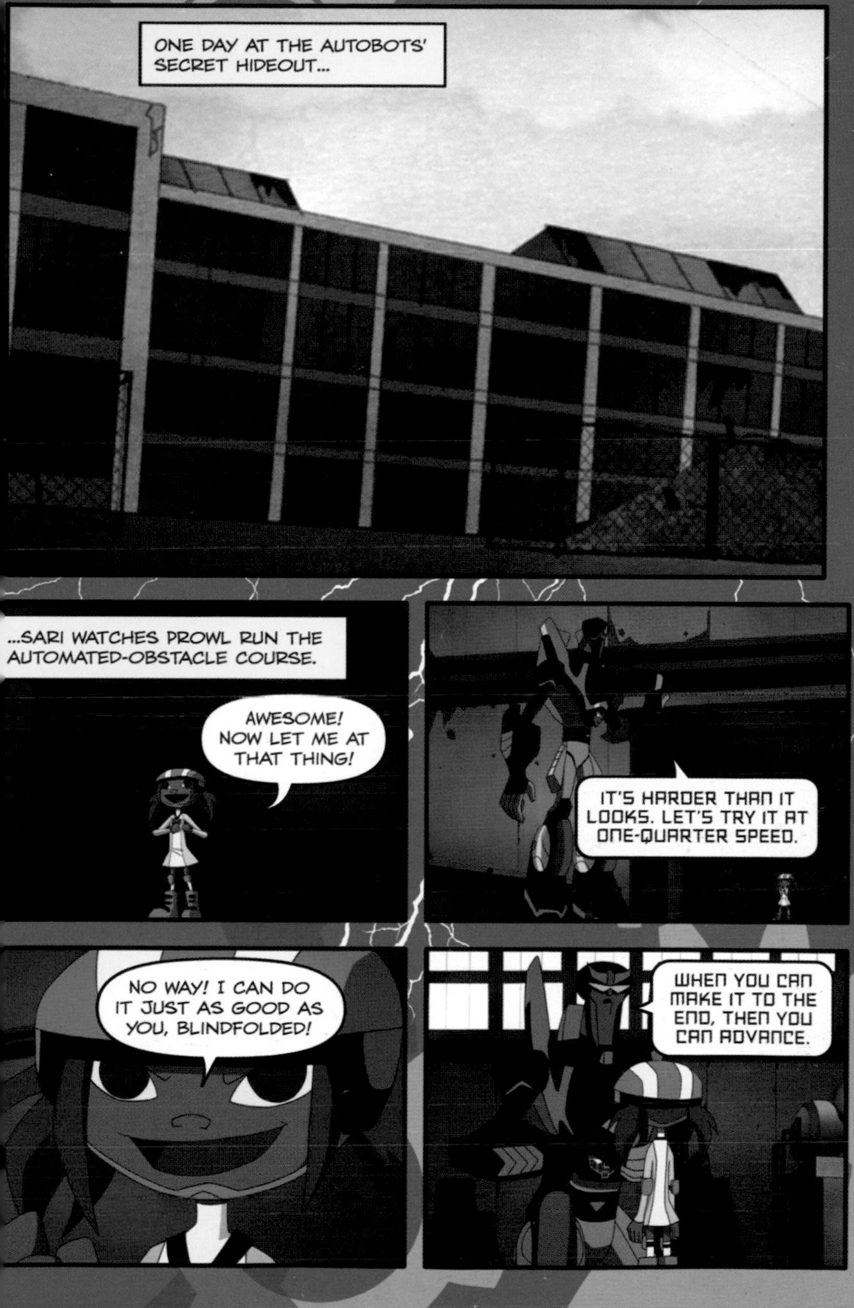
ONE DAY AT THE AUTOBOTS' SECRET HIDEOUT...
...SARI WATCHES PROWL RUN THE AUTOMATED-OBSTACLE COURSE.
AWESOME! NOW LET ME AT THAT THING!
IT'S HARDER THAN IT LOOKS. LET'S TRY IT AT ONE-QUARTER SPEED.
NO WAY! I CAN DO IT JUST AS GOOD AS YOU, BLINDFOLDED!
WHEN YOU CAN MAKE IT TO THE END, THEN YOU CAN ADVANCE.

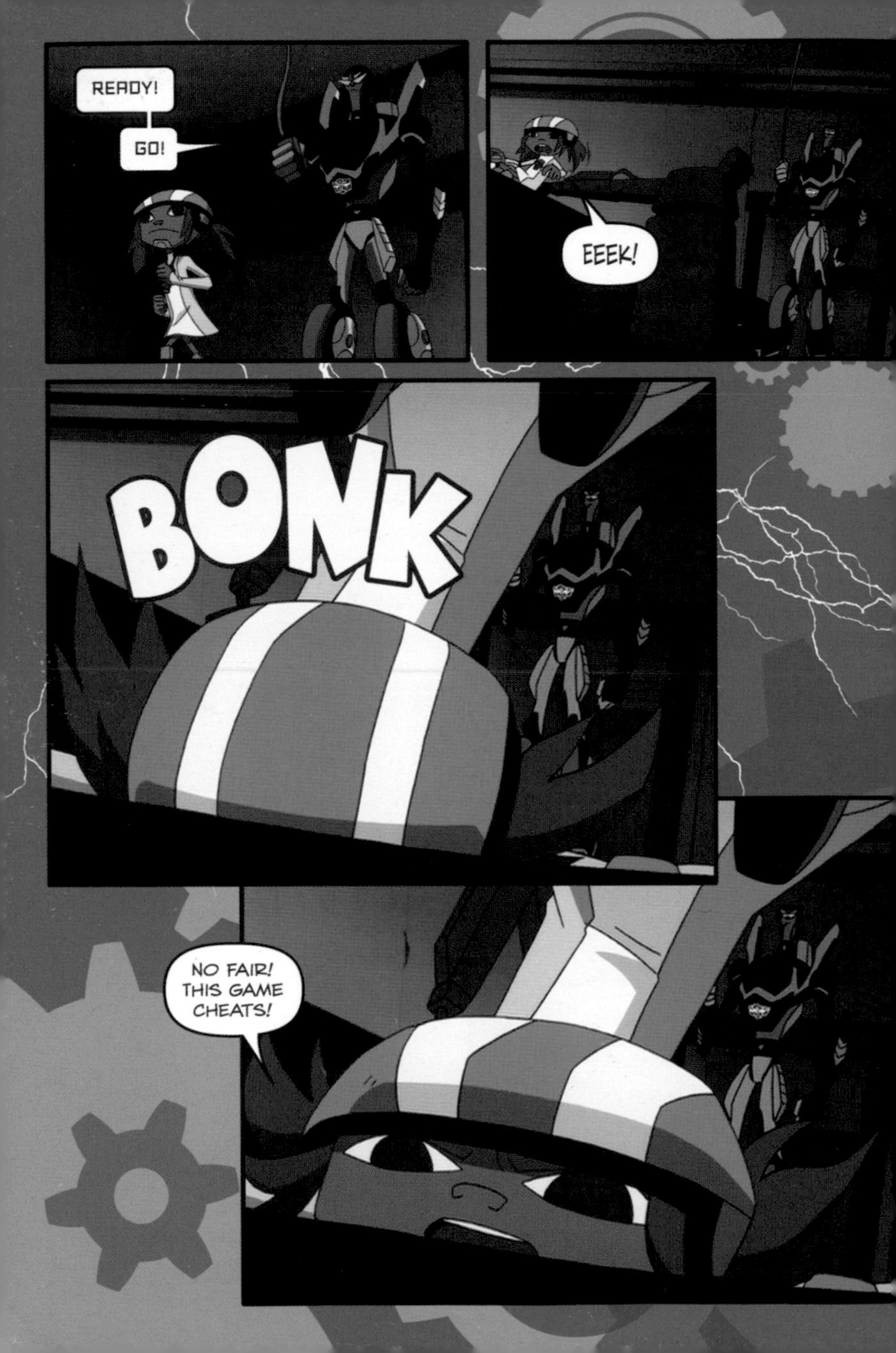
READY!
GO!
EEEK!
BONK
NO FAIR! THIS GAME CHEATS!

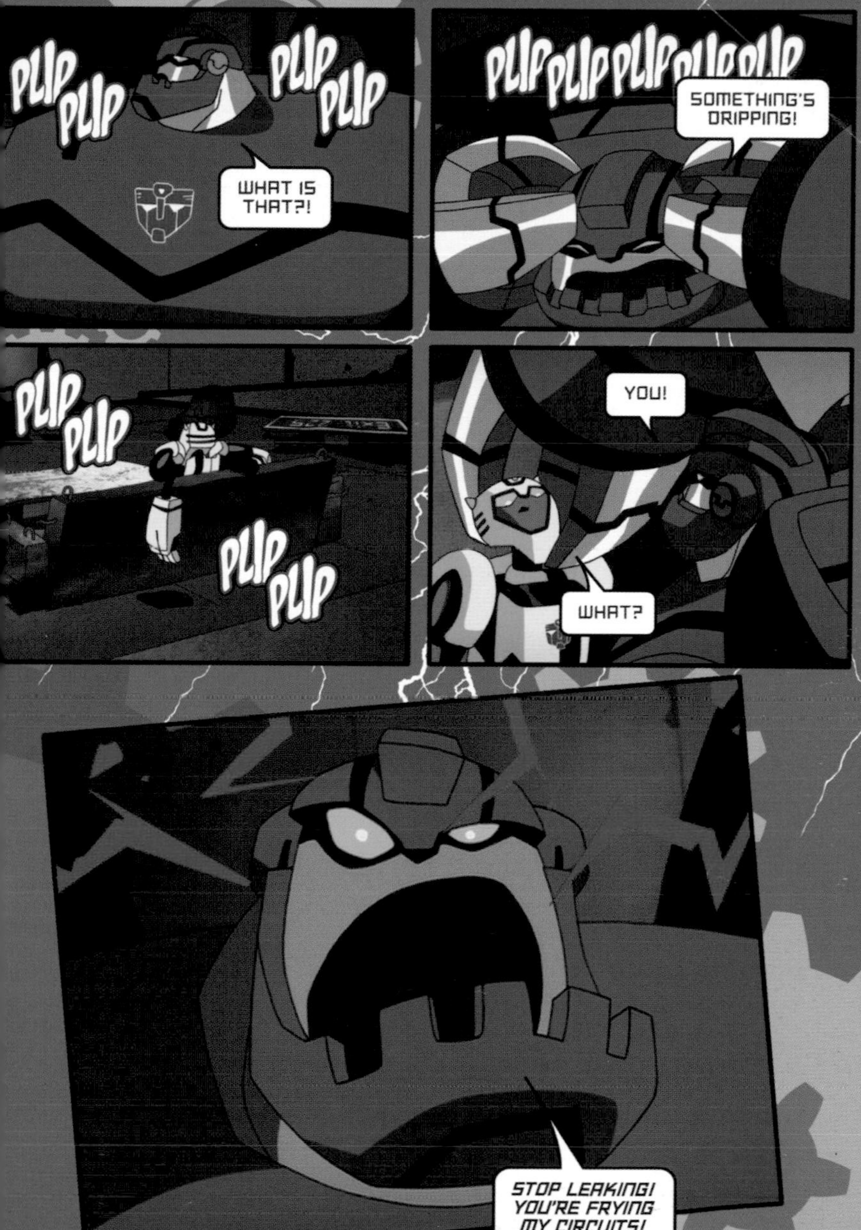

PLIP PLIP
PLIP PLIP
WHAT IS THAT?!
PLIP PLIP PLIP
SOMETHING'S DRIPPING!
PLIP PLIP
PLIP PLIP
YOU!
WHAT?
STOP LEAKING! YOU'RE FRYING MY CIRCUITS!

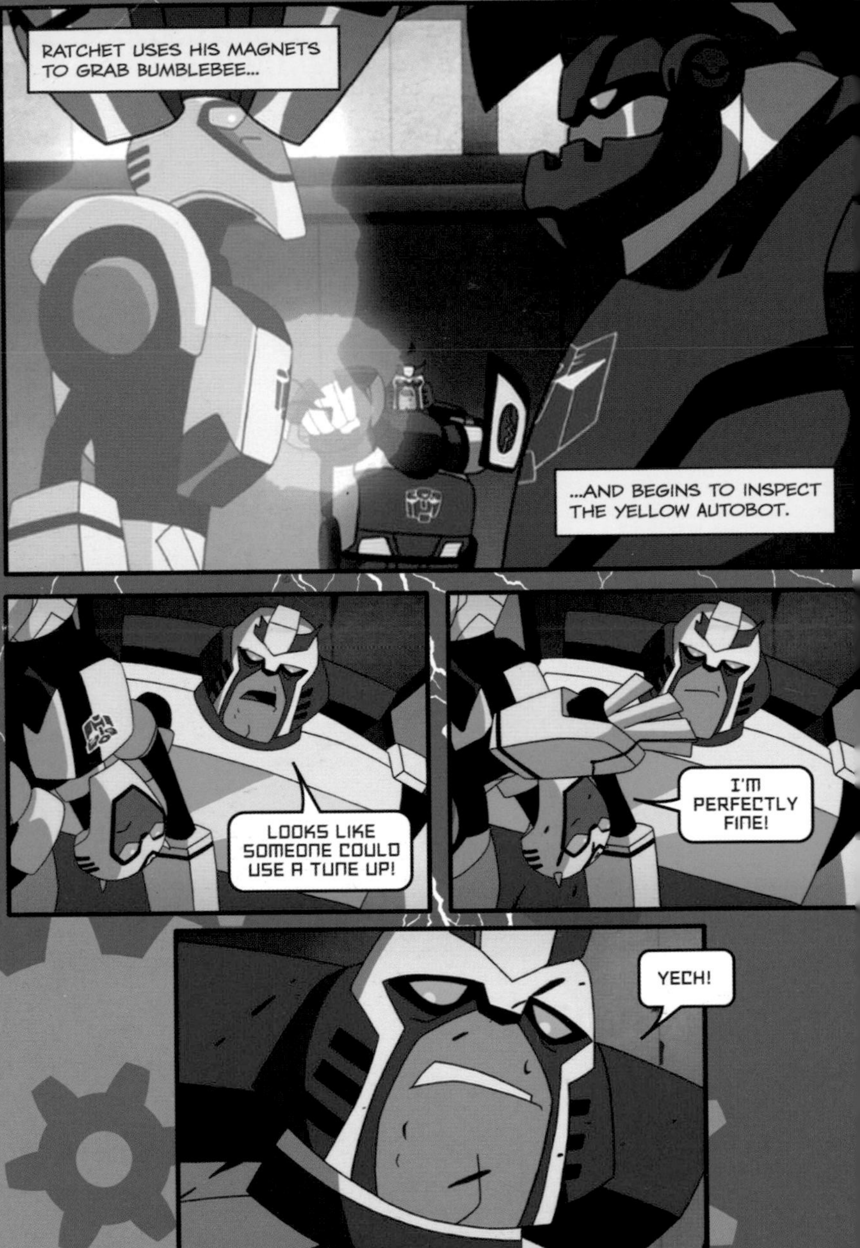
RATCHET USES HIS MAGNETS TO GRAB BUMBLEBEE...
...AND BEGINS TO INSPECT THE YELLOW AUTOBOT.
LOOKS LIKE SOMEONE COULD USE A TUNE UP!
I'M PERFECTLY FINE!
YECH!

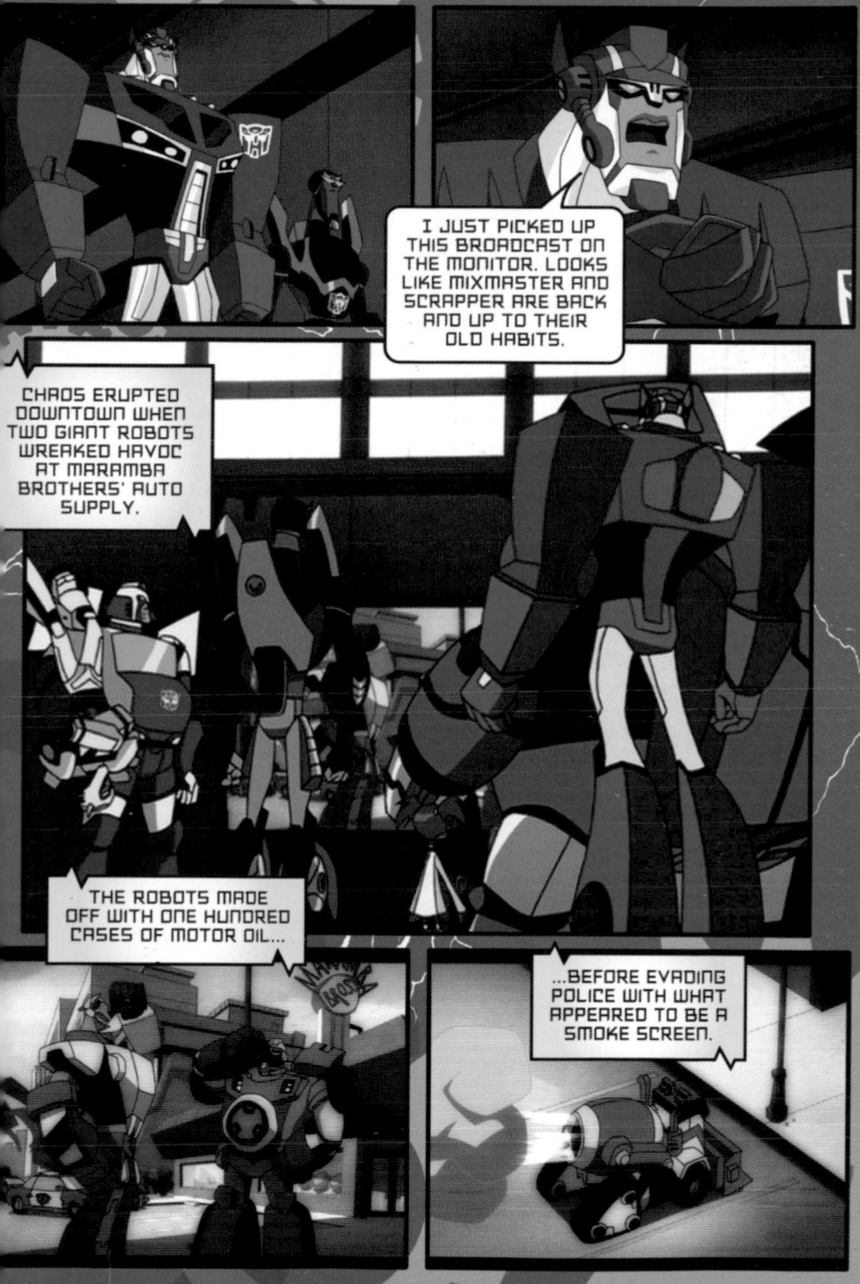
I JUST PICKED UP THIS BROADCAST ON THE MONITOR. LOOKS LIKE MIXMASTER AND SCRAPPER ARE BACK AND UP TO THEIR OLD HABITS.
CHAOS ERUPTED DOWNTOWN WHEN TWO GIANT ROBOTS WREAKED HAVOC AT MARAMBA BROTHERS' AUTO SUPPLY.
THE ROBOTS MADE OFF WITH ONE HUNDRED CASES OF MOTOR OIL...
...BEFORE EVADING POLICE WITH WHAT APPEARED TO BE A SMOKE SCREEN.

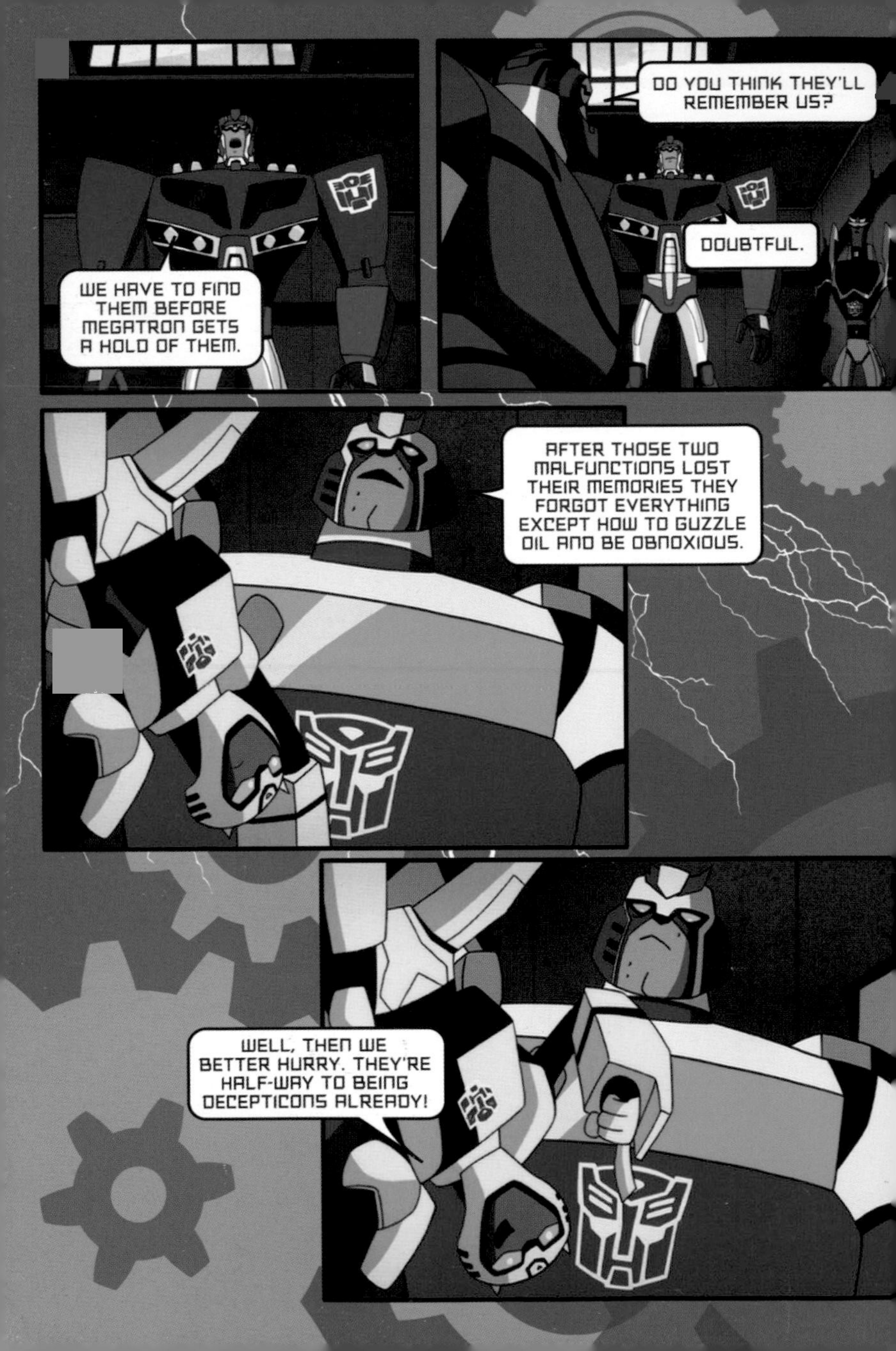
WE HAVE TO FIND THEM BEFORE MEGATRON GETS A HOLD OF THEM.
DO YOU THINK THEY'LL REMEMBER US?
DOUBTFUL.
AFTER THOSE TWO MALFUNCTIONS LOST THEIR MEMORIES THEY FORGOT EVERYTHING EXCEPT HOW TO GUZZLE OIL AND BE OBNOXIOUS.
WELL, THEN WE BETTER HURRY. THEY'RE HALF-WAY TO BEING DECEPTICONS ALREADY!

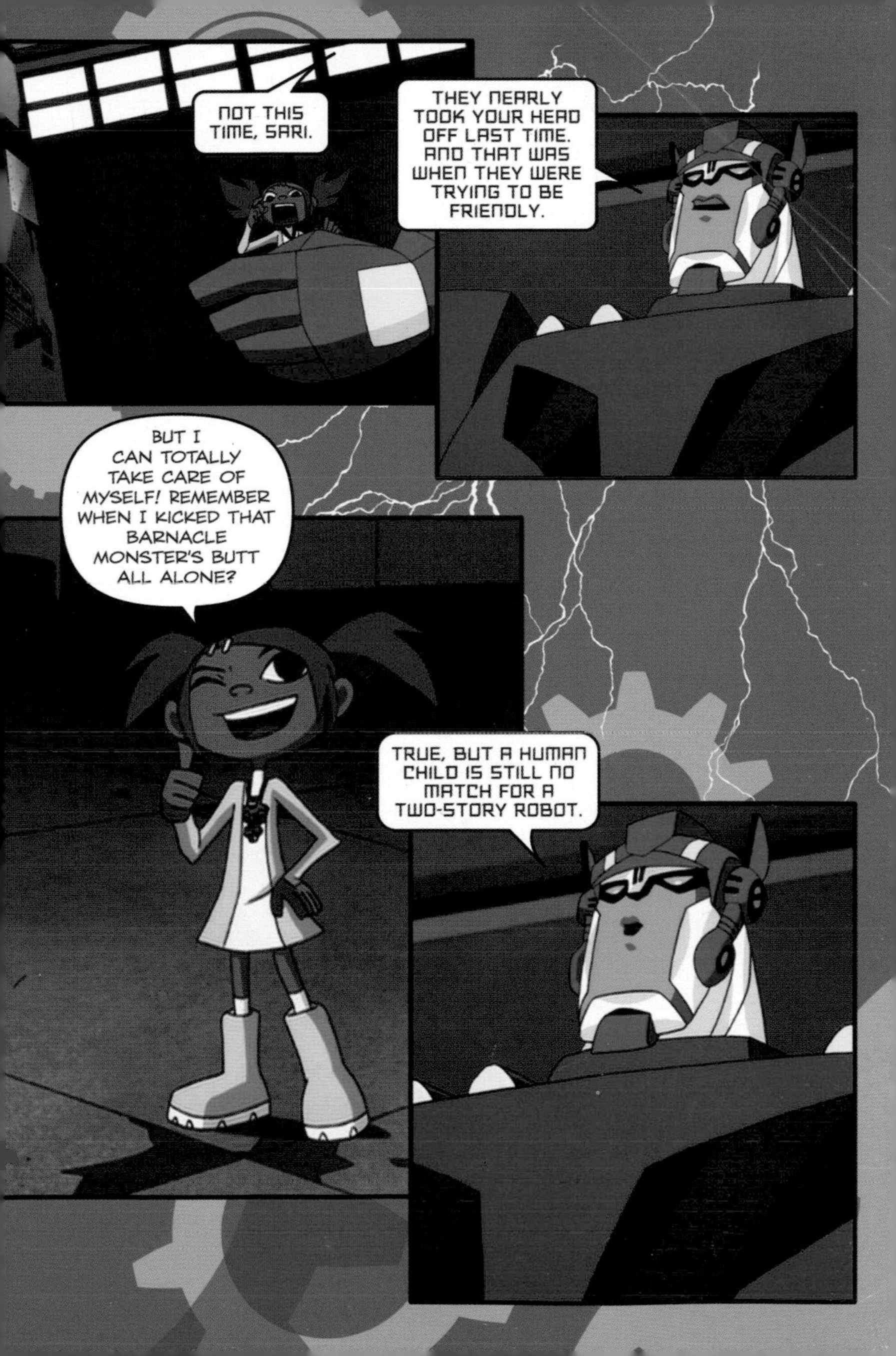
NOT THIS TIME, SARI.
THEY NEARLY TOOK YOUR HEAD OFF LAST TIME. AND THAT WAS WHEN THEY WERE TRYING TO BE FRIENDLY.
BUT I CAN TOTALLY TAKE CARE OF MYSELF! REMEMBER WHEN I KICKED THAT BARNACLE MONSTER'S BUTT ALL ALONE?
TRUE, BUT A HUMAN CHILD IS STILL NO MATCH FOR A TWO-STORY ROBOT.

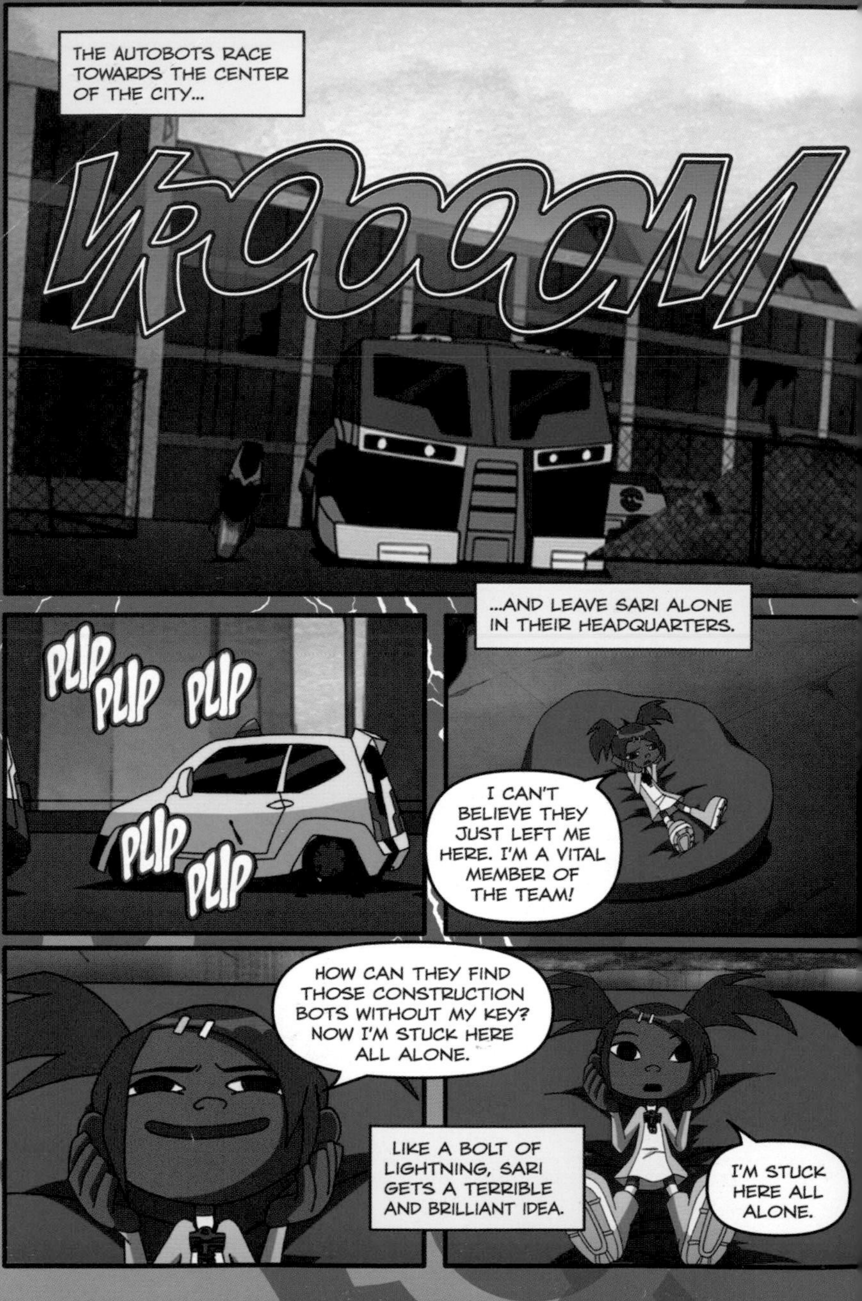
THE AUTOBOTS RACE TOWARDS THE CENTER OF THE CITY...
VROOOOM
...AND LEAVE SARI ALONE IN THEIR HEADQUARTERS.
PLIP PLIP PLIP
PLIP PLIP
I CAN'T BELIEVE THEY JUST LEFT ME HERE. I'M A VITAL MEMBER OF THE TEAM!
HOW CAN THEY FIND THOSE CONSTRUCTION BOTS WITHOUT MY KEY? NOW I'M STUCK HERE ALL ALONE.
LIKE A BOLT OF LIGHTNING, SARI GETS A TERRIBLE AND BRILLIANT IDEA.
I'M STUCK HERE ALL ALONE.

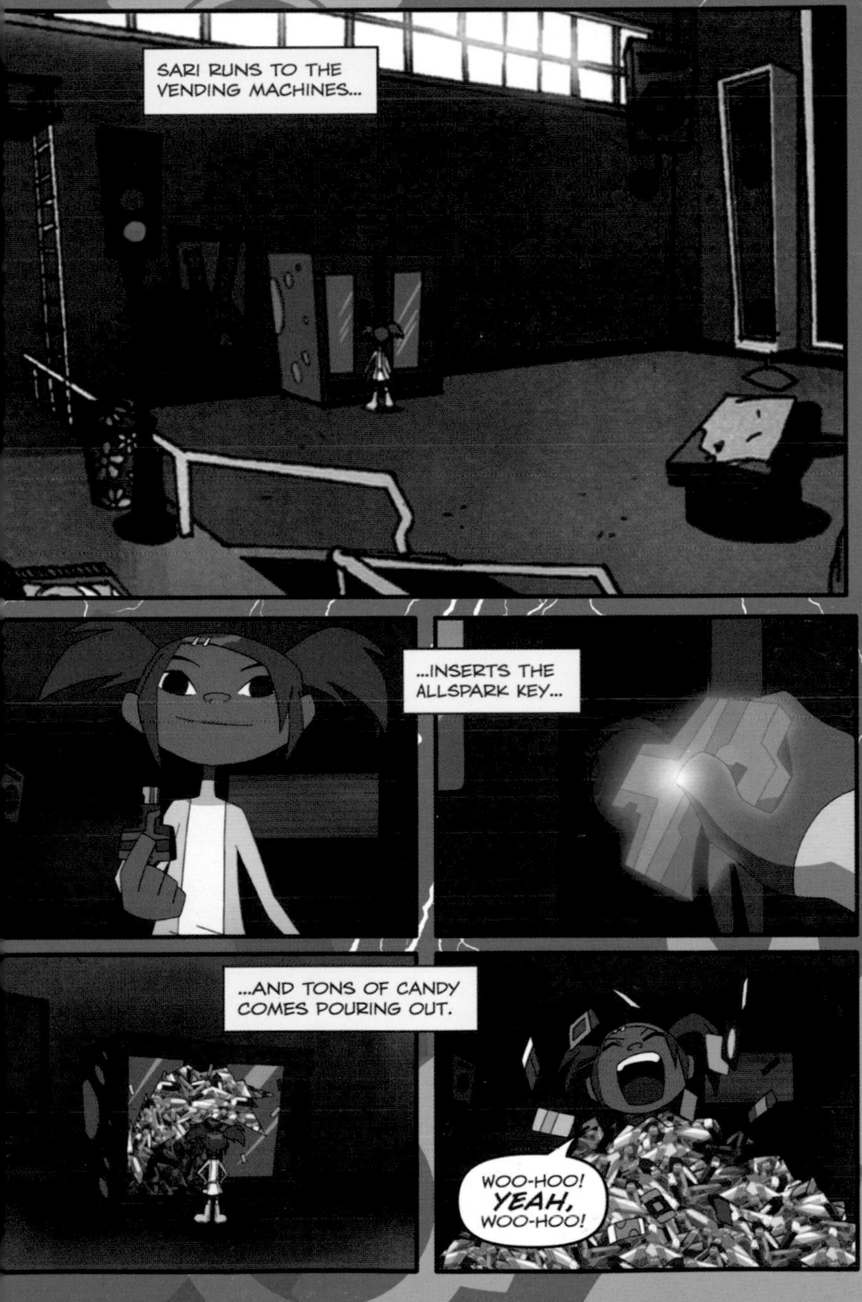
SARI RUNS TO THE VENDING MACHINES...
...INSERTS THE ALLSPARK KEY...
...AND TONS OF CANDY COMES POURING OUT.
WOO-HOO! YEAH, WOO-HOO!

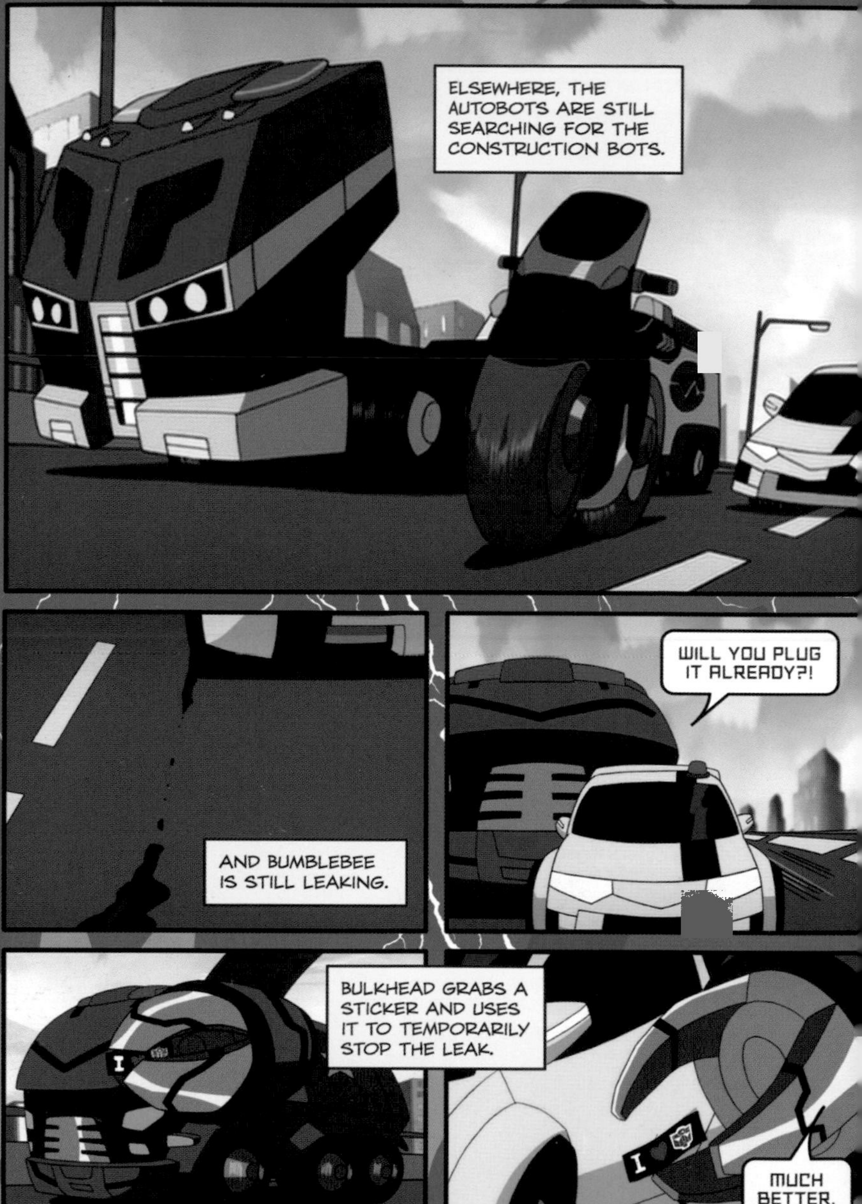
ELSEWHERE, THE AUTOBOTS ARE STILL SEARCHING FOR THE CONSTRUCTION BOTS.
AND BUMBLEBEE IS STILL LEAKING.
WILL YOU PLUG IT ALREADY?!
BULKHEAD GRABS A STICKER AND USES IT TO TEMPORARILY STOP THE LEAK.
MUCH BETTER.

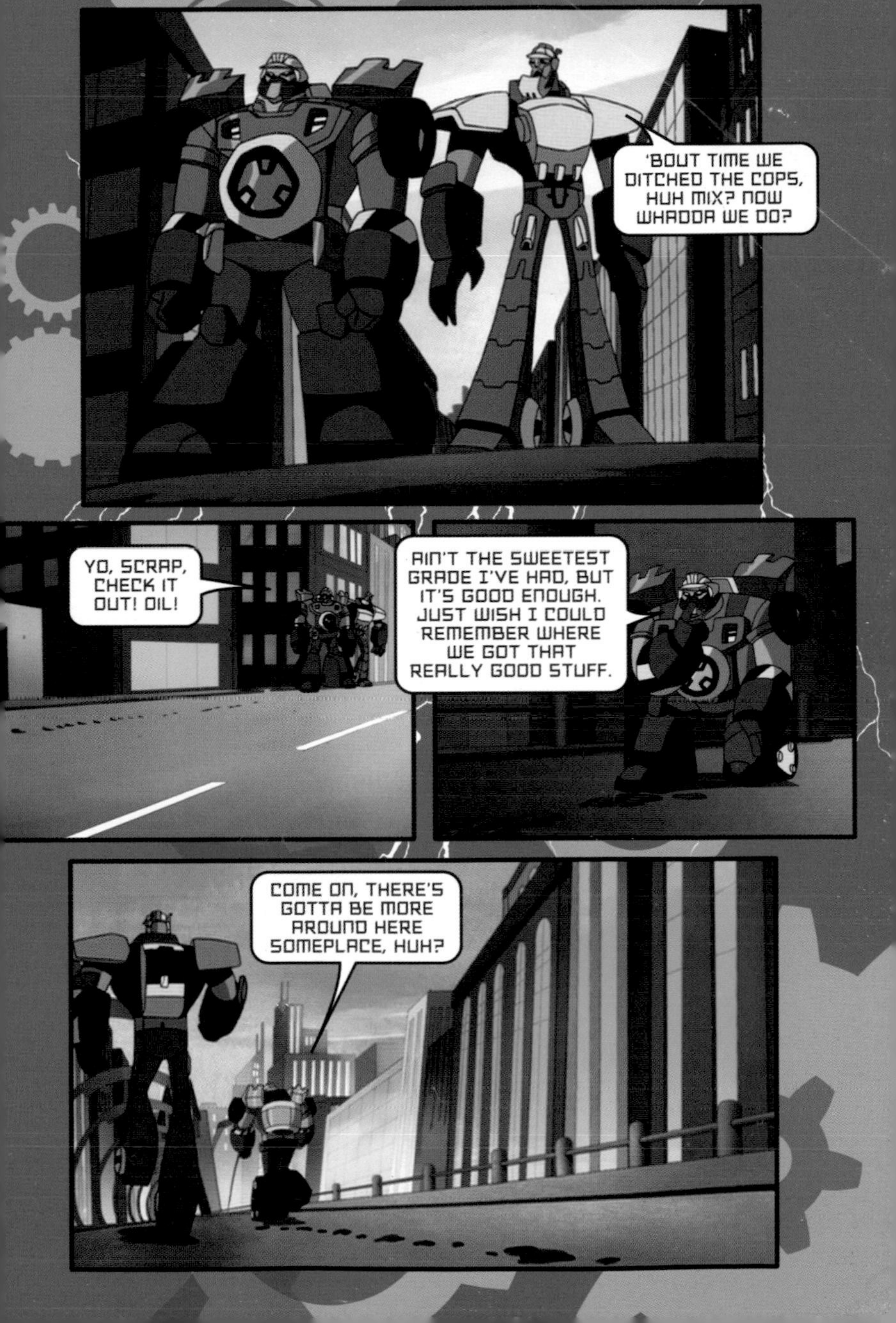
'BOUT TIME WE DITCHED THE COPS, HUH MIX? NOW WHADDA WE DO?
YO, SCRAP, CHECK IT OUT! OIL!
AIN'T THE SWEETEST GRADE I'VE HAD, BUT IT'S GOOD ENOUGH. JUST WISH I COULD REMEMBER WHERE WE GOT THAT REALLY GOOD STUFF.
COME ON, THERE'S GOTTA BE MORE AROUND HERE SOMEPLACE, HUH?

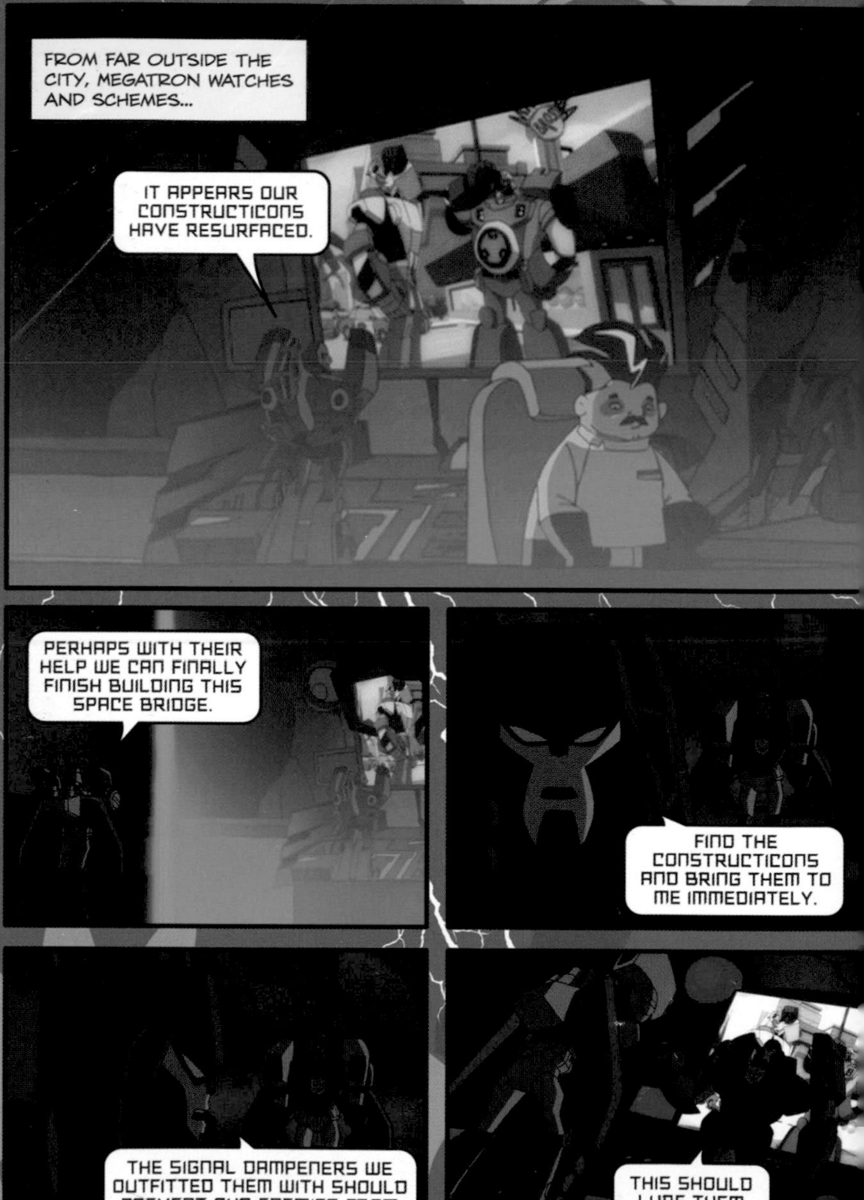
FROM FAR OUTSIDE THE CITY, MEGATRON WATCHES AND SCHEMES...
IT APPEARS OUR CONSTRUCTICONS HAVE RESURFACED.
PERHAPS WITH THEIR HELP WE CAN FINALLY FINISH BUILDING THIS SPACE BRIDGE.
FIND THE CONSTRUCTICONS AND BRING THEM TO ME IMMEDIATELY.
THE SIGNAL DAMPENERS WE OUTFITTED THEM WITH SHOULD PREVENT OUR ENEMIES FROM TRACKING THEM, BUT DO NOT ENGAGE THE AUTOBOTS.
THIS SHOULD LURE THEM OUT. NOW GO.

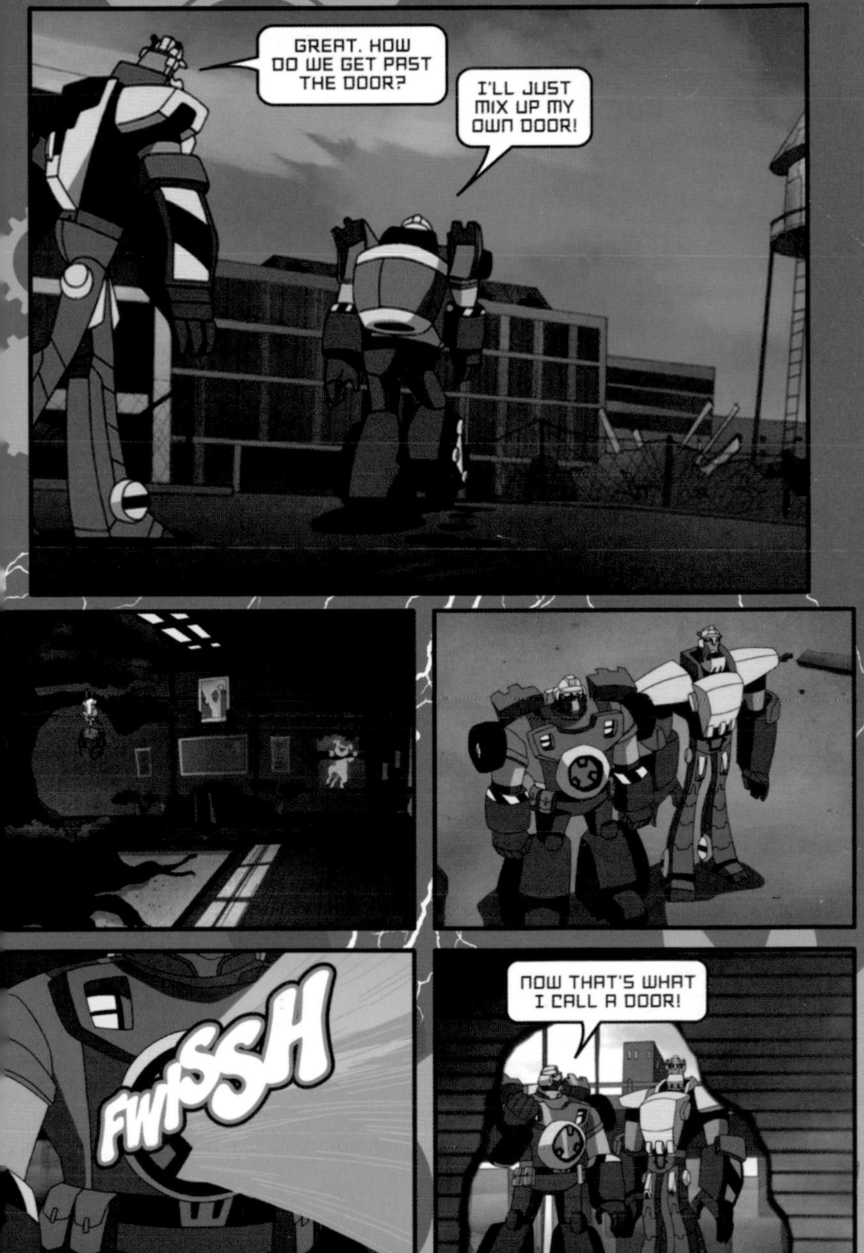
GREAT. HOW DO WE GET PAST THE DOOR?
I'LL JUST MIX UP MY OWN DOOR!
FWISSH
NOW THAT'S WHAT I CALL A DOOR!

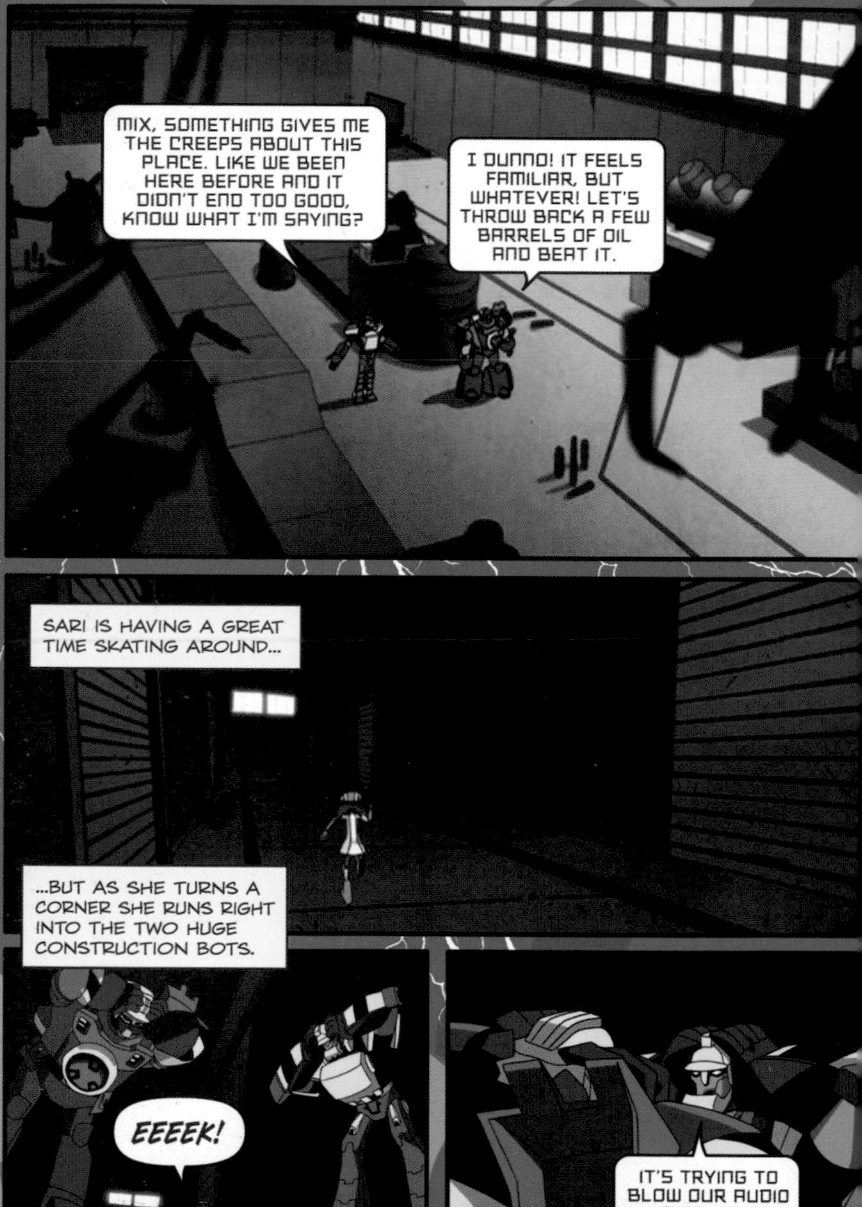
MIX, SOMETHING GIVES ME THE CREEPS ABOUT THIS PLACE. LIKE WE BEEN HERE BEFORE AND IT DIDN'T END TOO GOOD, KNOW WHAT I'M SAYING?
I DUNNO! IT FEELS FAMILIAR, BUT WHATEVER! LET'S THROW BACK A FEW BARRELS OF OIL AND BEAT IT.
SARI IS HAVING A GREAT TIME SKATING AROUND...
...BUT AS SHE TURNS A CORNER SHE RUNS RIGHT INTO THE TWO HUGE CONSTRUCTION BOTS.
EEEEK!
IT'S TRYING TO BLOW OUR AUDIO CIRCUITS!

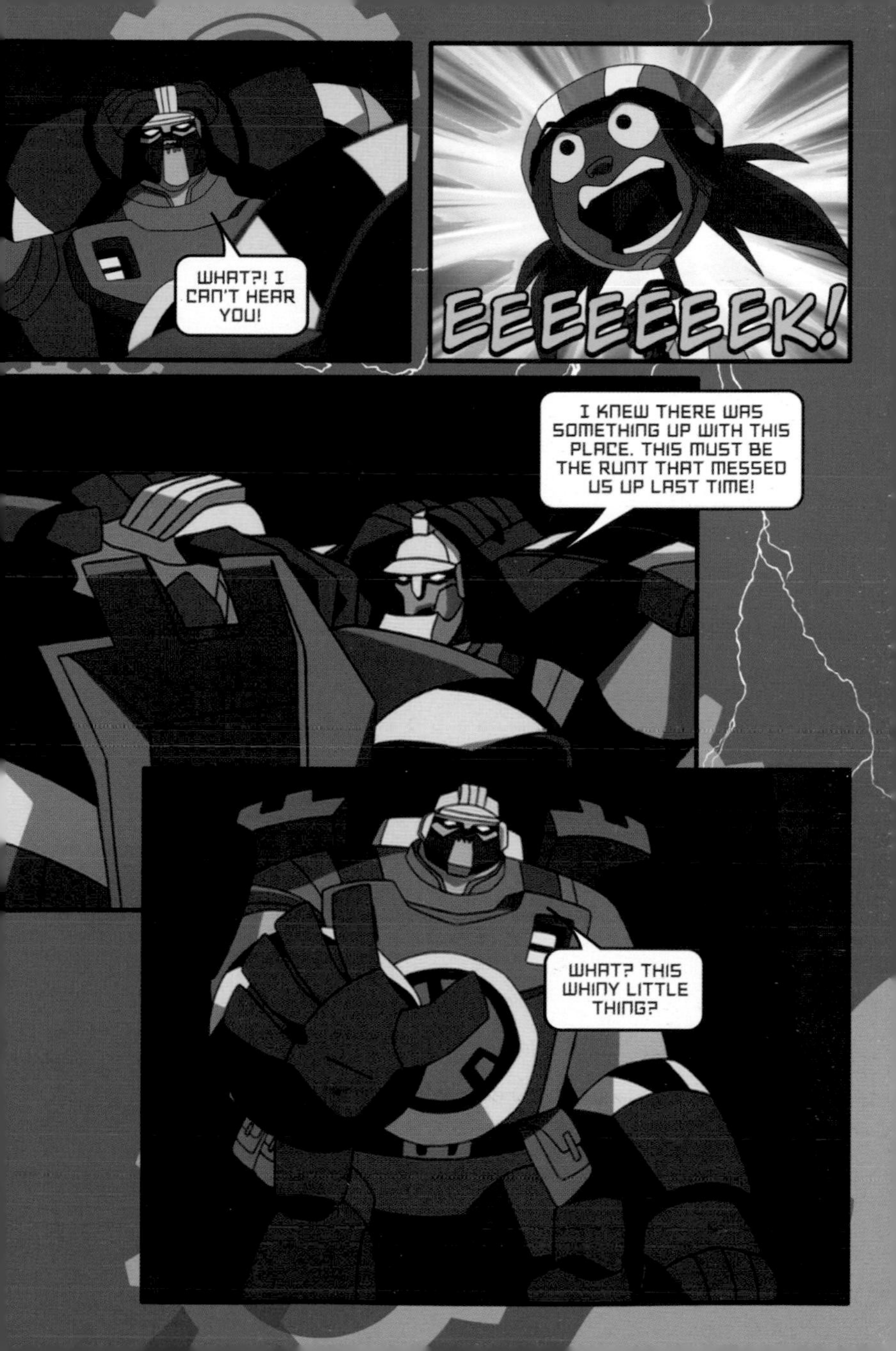
WHAT?! I CAN'T HEAR YOU!
EEEEEEEK!
I KNEW THERE WAS SOMETHING UP WITH THIS PLACE. THIS MUST BE THE RUNT THAT MESSED US UP LAST TIME!
WHAT? THIS WHINY LITTLE THING?

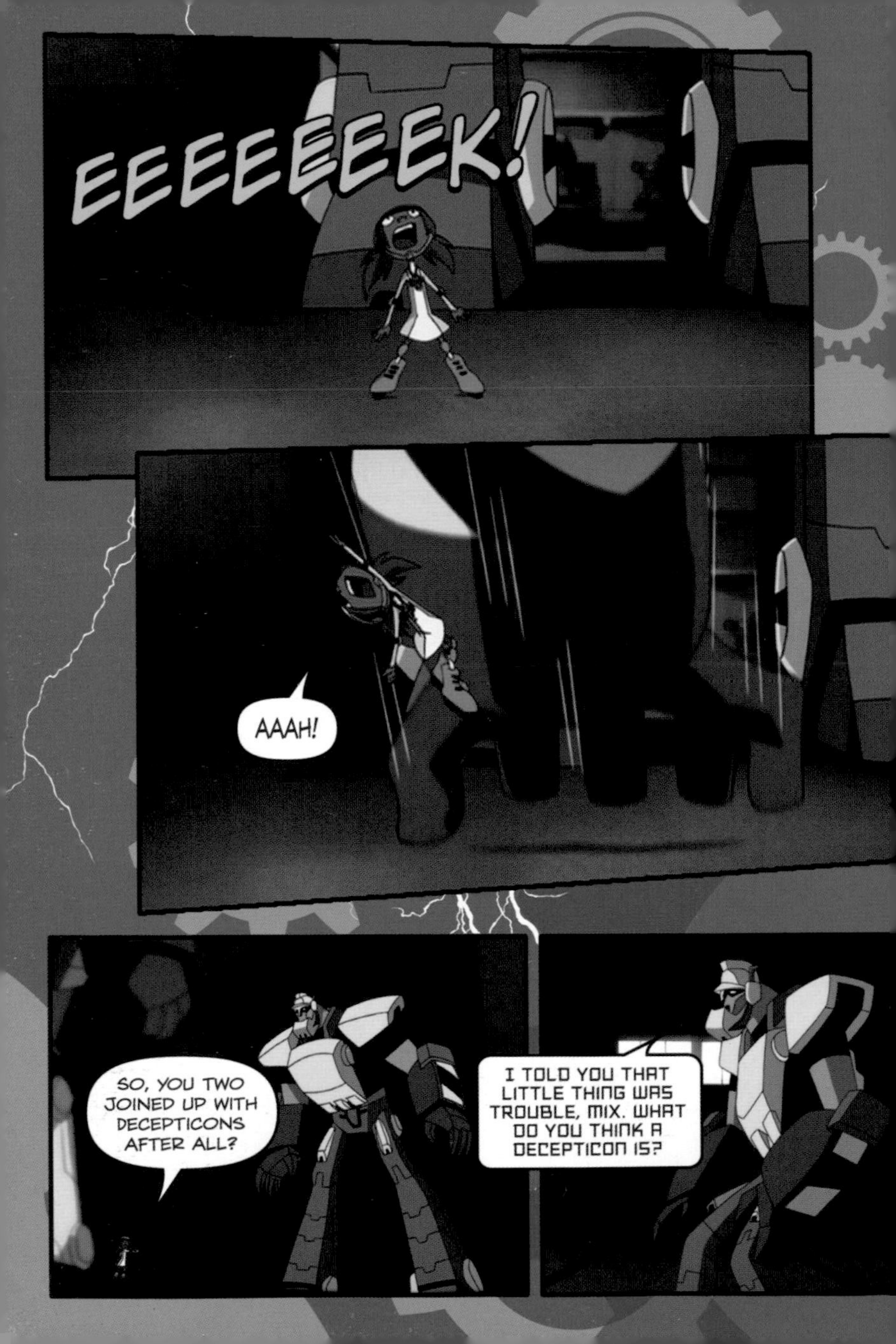
EEEEEEEK!
AAAH!
SO, YOU TWO JOINED UP WITH DECEPTICONS AFTER ALL?
I TOLD YOU THAT LITTLE THING WAS TROUBLE, MIX. WHAT DO YOU THINK A DECEPTICON IS?

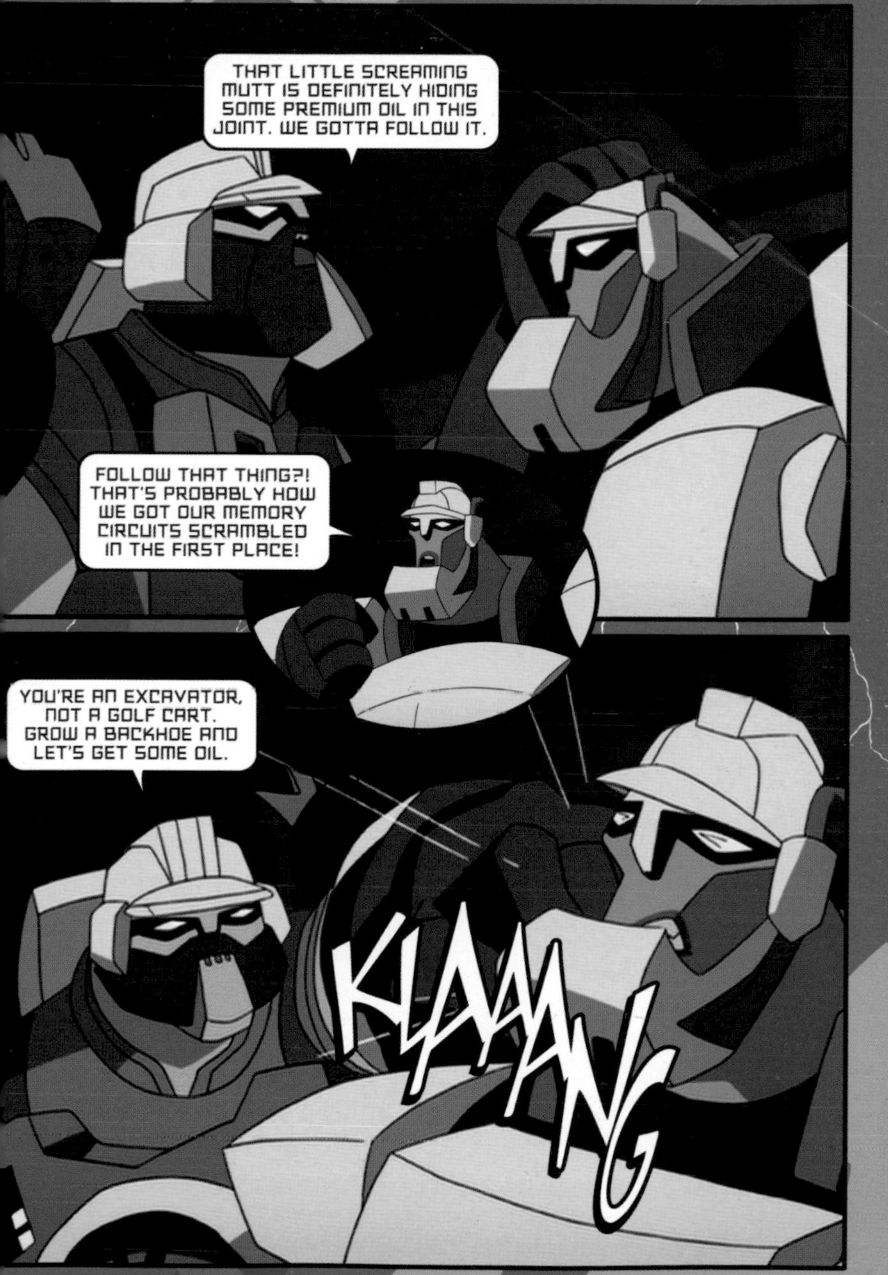

THAT LITTLE SCREAMING MUTT IS DEFINITELY HIDING SOME PREMIUM OIL IN THIS JOINT. WE GOTTA FOLLOW IT.
FOLLOW THAT THING?! THAT'S PROBABLY HOW WE GOT OUR MEMORY CIRCUITS SCRAMBLED IN THE FIRST PLACE!
YOU'RE AN EXCAVATOR, NOT A GOLF CART. GROW A BACKHOE AND LET'S GET SOME OIL.
KLAAAANG

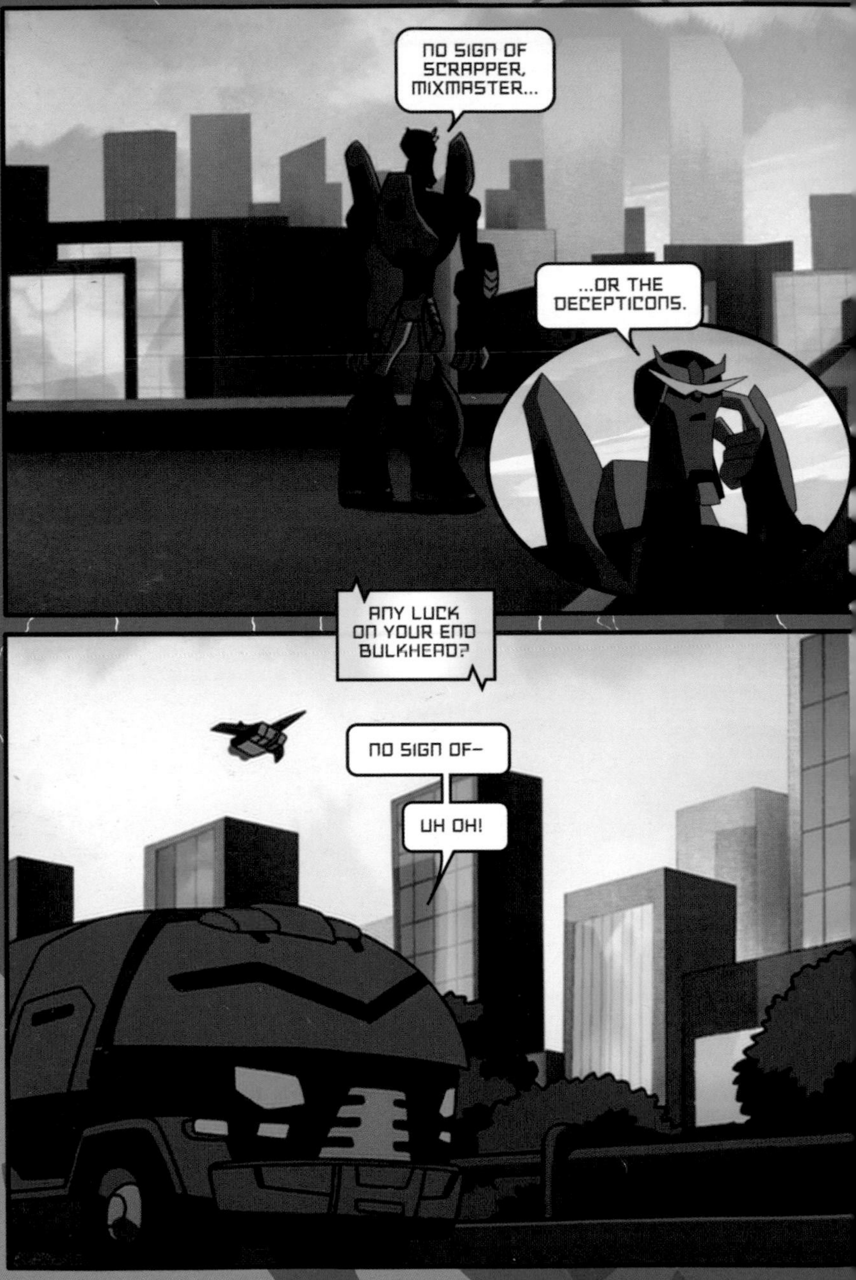
NO SIGN OF SCRAPPER, MIXMASTER...
...OR THE DECEPTICONS.
ANY LUCK ON YOUR END BULKHEAD?
NO SIGN OF–
UH OH!

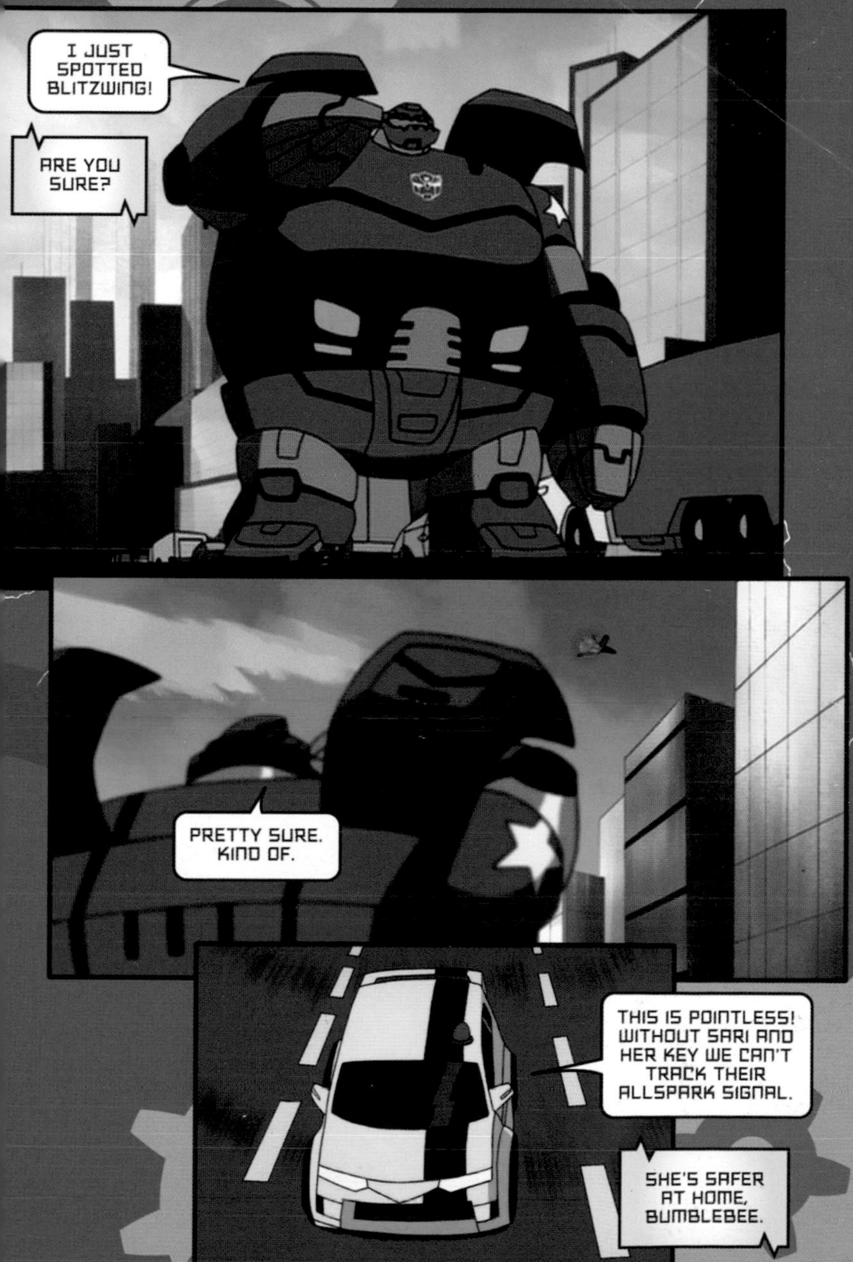
I JUST SPOTTED BLITZWING!
ARE YOU SURE?
PRETTY SURE. KIND OF.
THIS IS POINTLESS! WITHOUT SARI AND HER KEY WE CAN'T TRACK THEIR ALLSPARK SIGNAL.
SHE'S SAFER AT HOME, BUMBLEBEE.

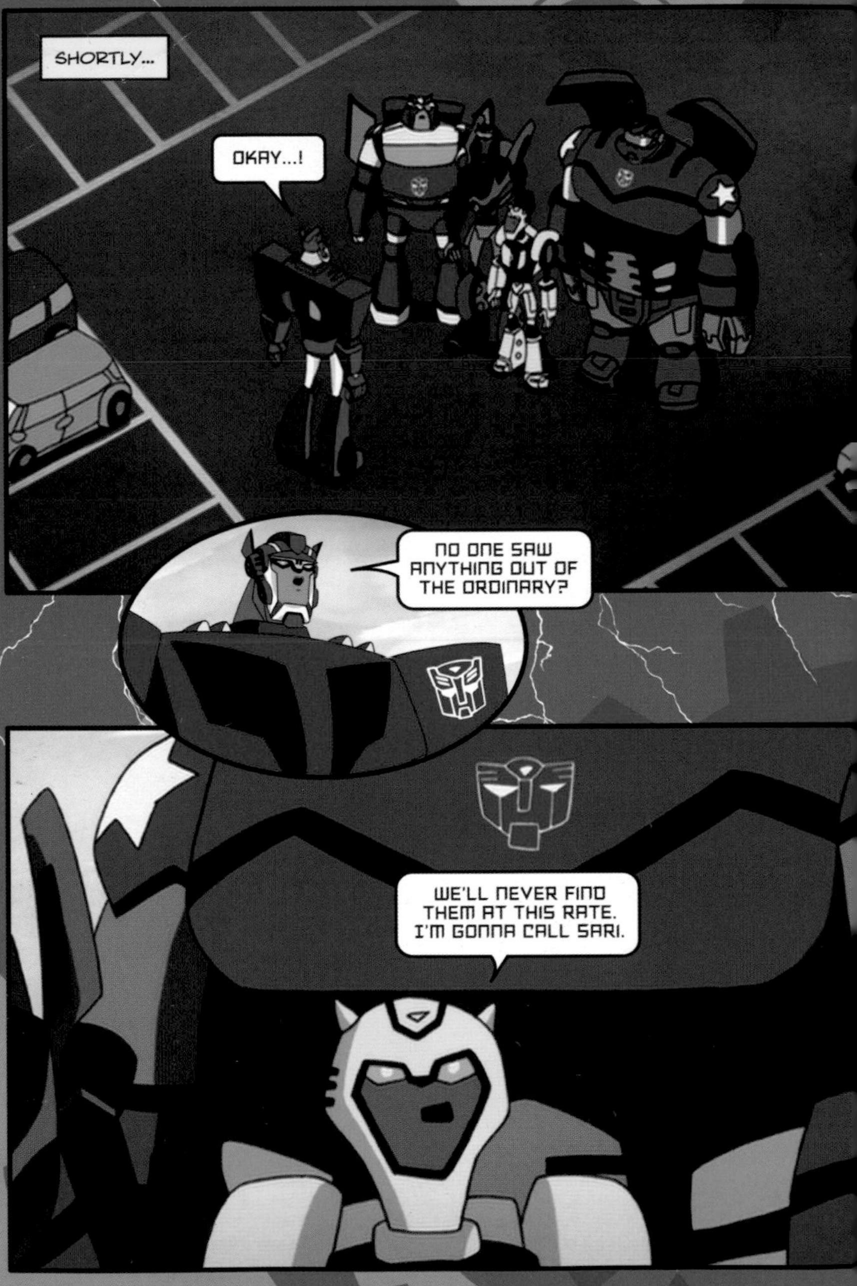
SHORTLY...
OKAY...!
NO ONE SAW ANYTHING OUT OF THE ORDINARY?
WE'LL NEVER FIND THEM AT THIS RATE. I'M GONNA CALL SARI.

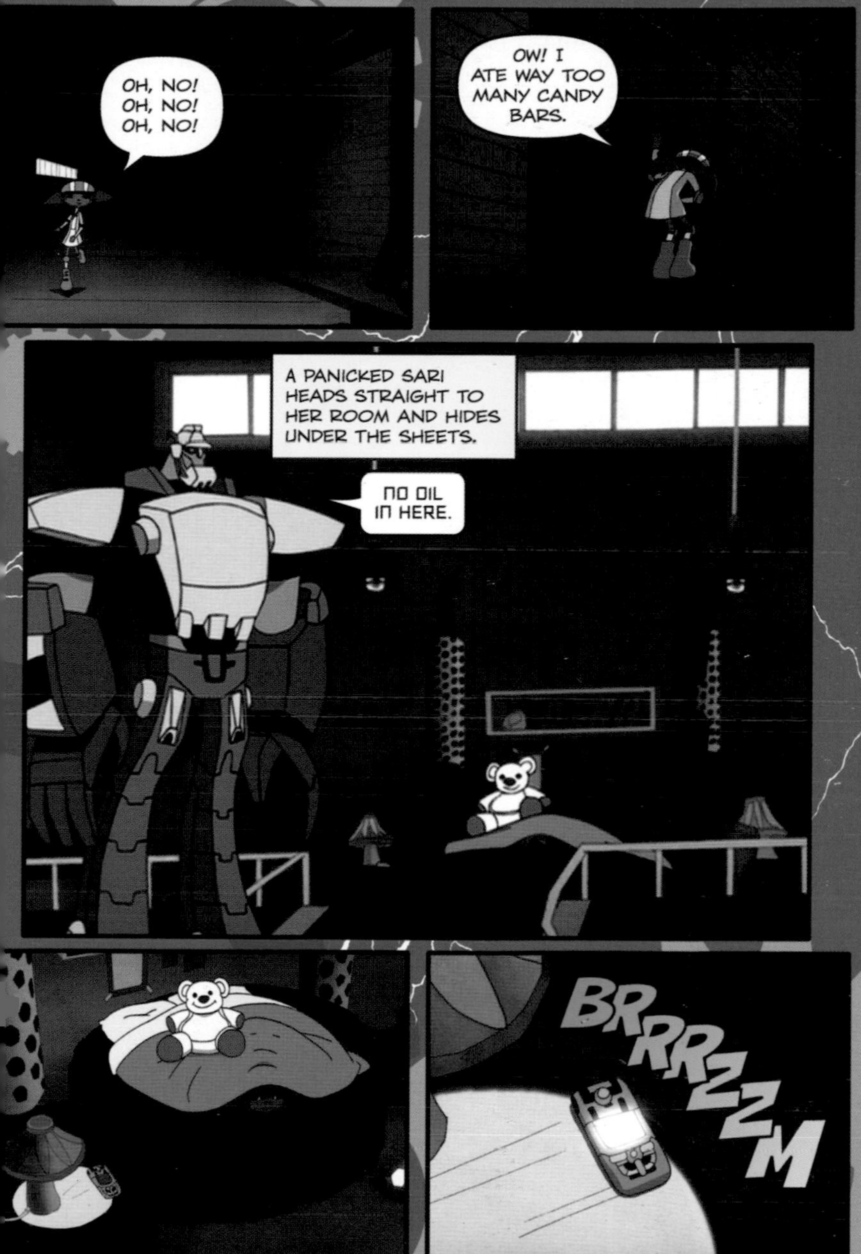
OH, NO!
OH, NO!
OH, NO!
OW! I ATE WAY TOO MANY CANDY BARS.
A PANICKED SARI HEADS STRAIGHT TO HER ROOM AND HIDES UNDER THE SHEETS.
NO OIL IN HERE.
BRRRZZM

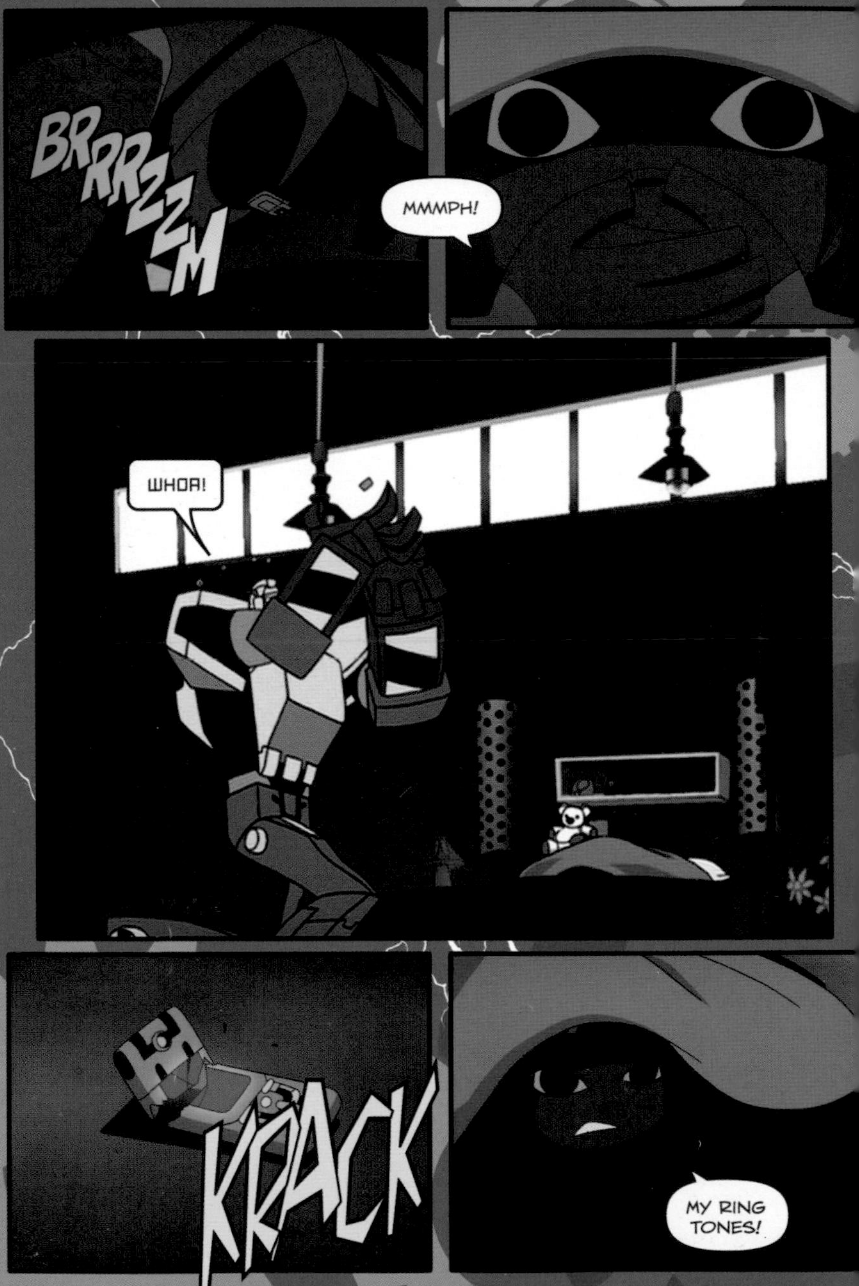
BRRRZZM
MMMPH!
WHOA!
KRACK
MY RING TONES!

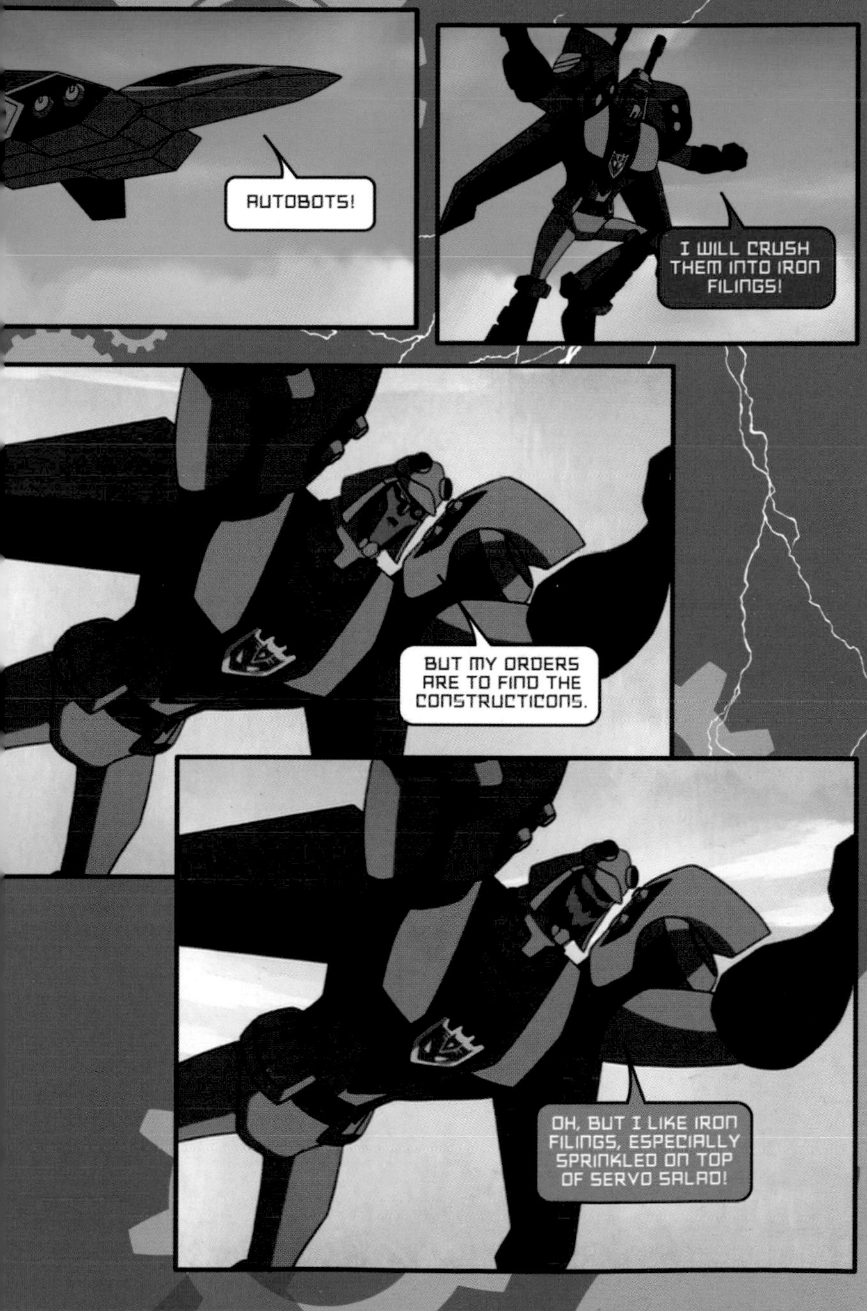
AUTOBOTS!
I WILL CRUSH THEM INTO IRON FILINGS!
BUT MY ORDERS ARE TO FIND THE CONSTRUCTICONS.
OH, BUT I LIKE IRON FILINGS, ESPECIALLY SPRINKLED ON TOP OF SERVO SALAD!

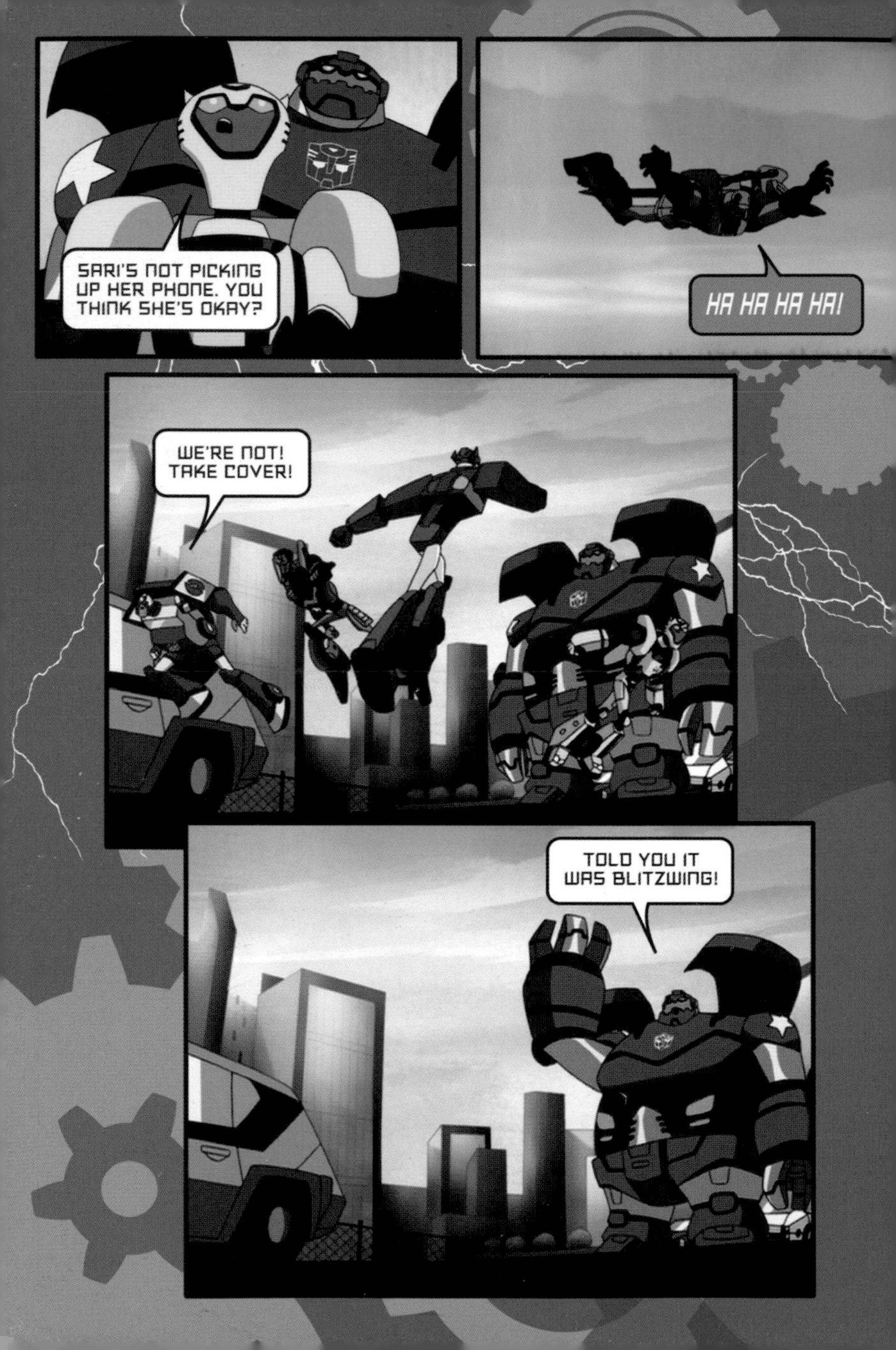
SARI'S NOT PICKING UP HER PHONE. YOU THINK SHE'S OKAY?
HA HA HA HA!
WE'RE NOT! TAKE COVER!
TOLD YOU IT WAS BLITZWING!

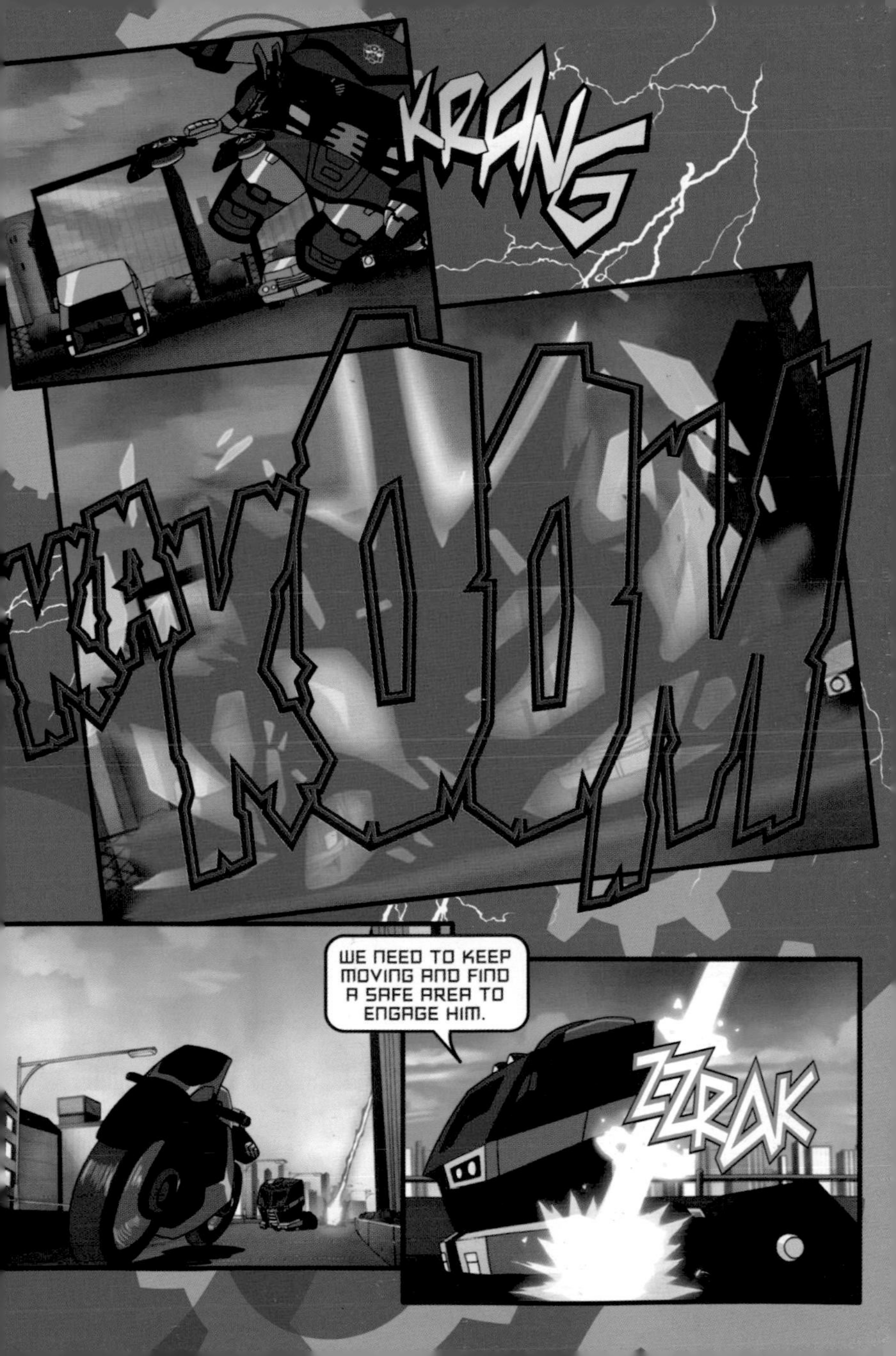
KRANG
KAWOOM
WE NEED TO KEEP MOVING AND FIND A SAFE AREA TO ENGAGE HIM.
ZZRAK

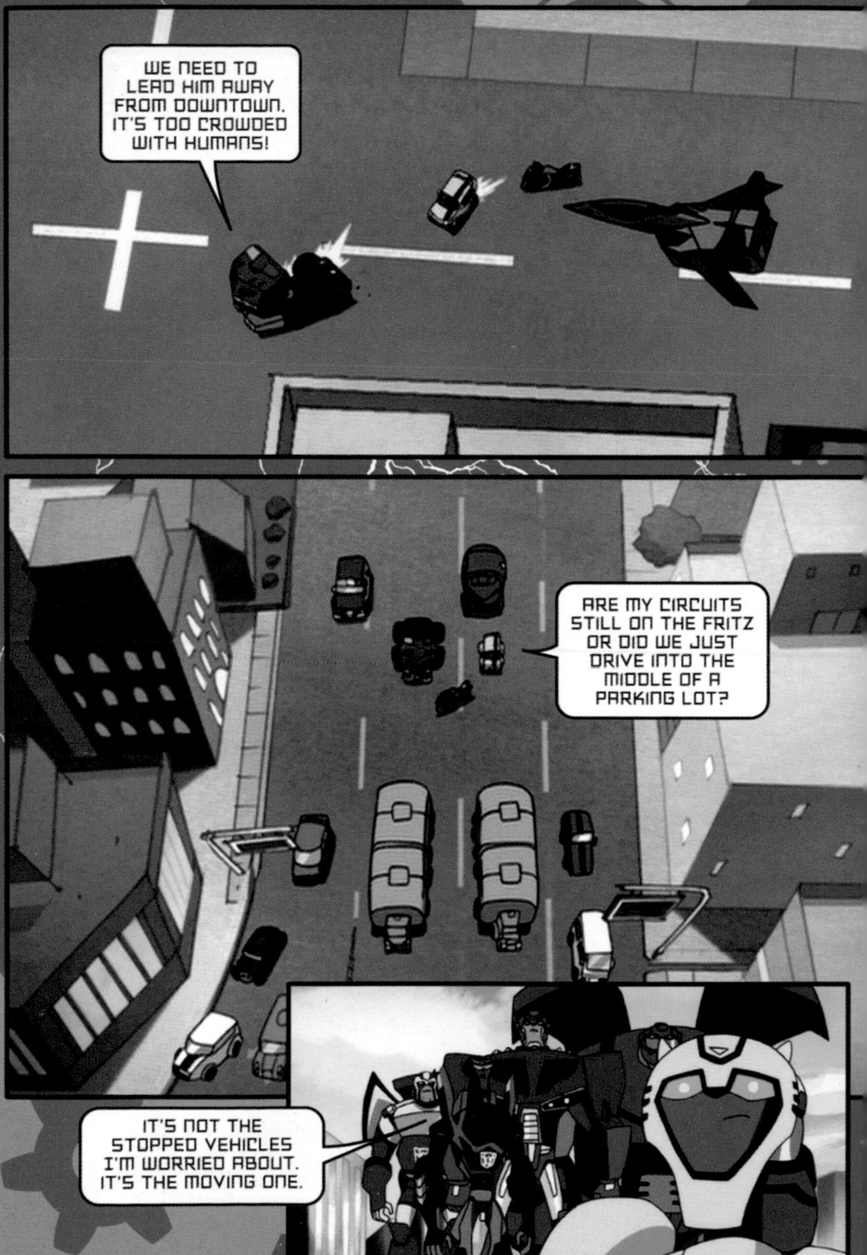
WE NEED TO LEAD HIM AWAY FROM DOWNTOWN. IT'S TOO CROWDED WITH HUMANS!
ARE MY CIRCUITS STILL ON THE FRITZ OR DID WE JUST DRIVE INTO THE MIDDLE OF A PARKING LOT?
IT'S NOT THE STOPPED VEHICLES I'M WORRIED ABOUT. IT'S THE MOVING ONE.

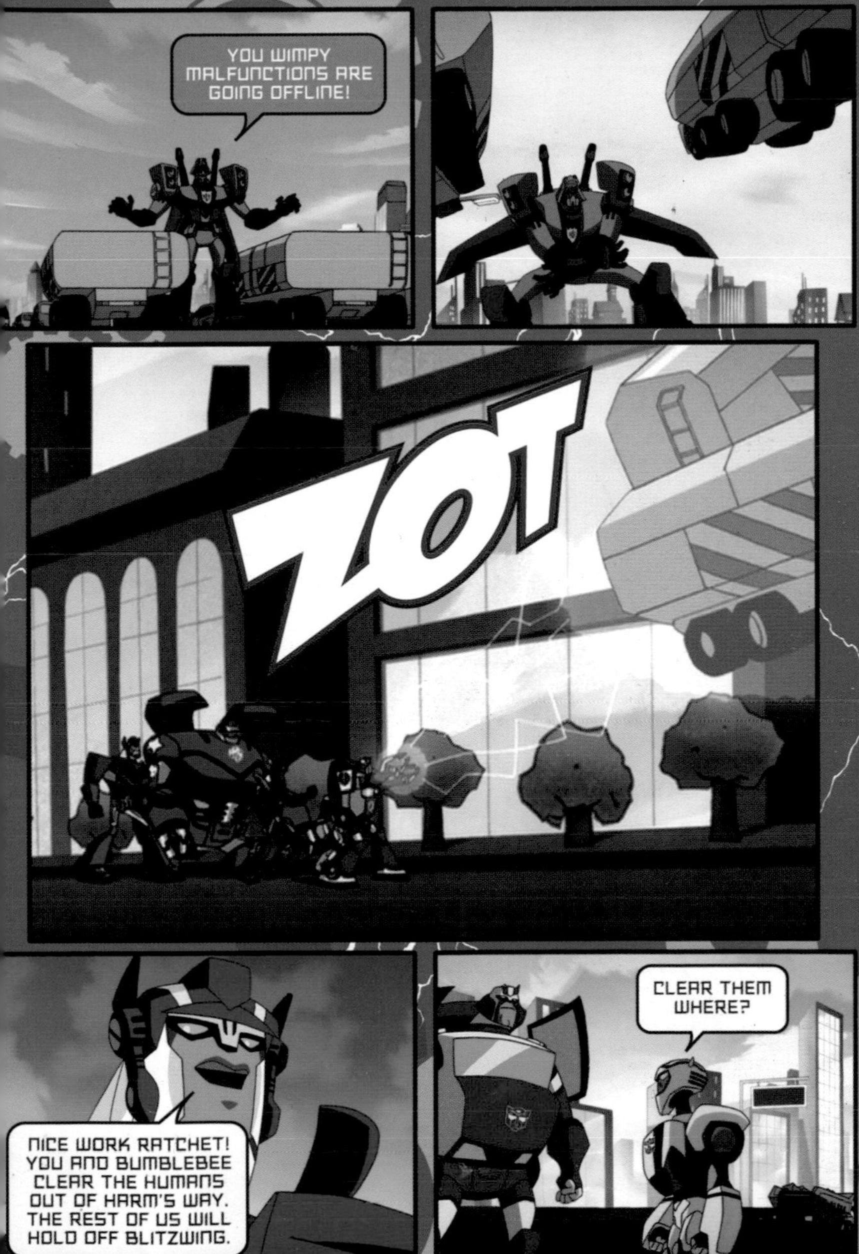
YOU WIMPY MALFUNCTIONS ARE GOING OFFLINE!
ZOT
NICE WORK RATCHET! YOU AND BUMBLEBEE CLEAR THE HUMANS OUT OF HARM'S WAY. THE REST OF US WILL HOLD OFF BLITZWING.
CLEAR THEM WHERE?

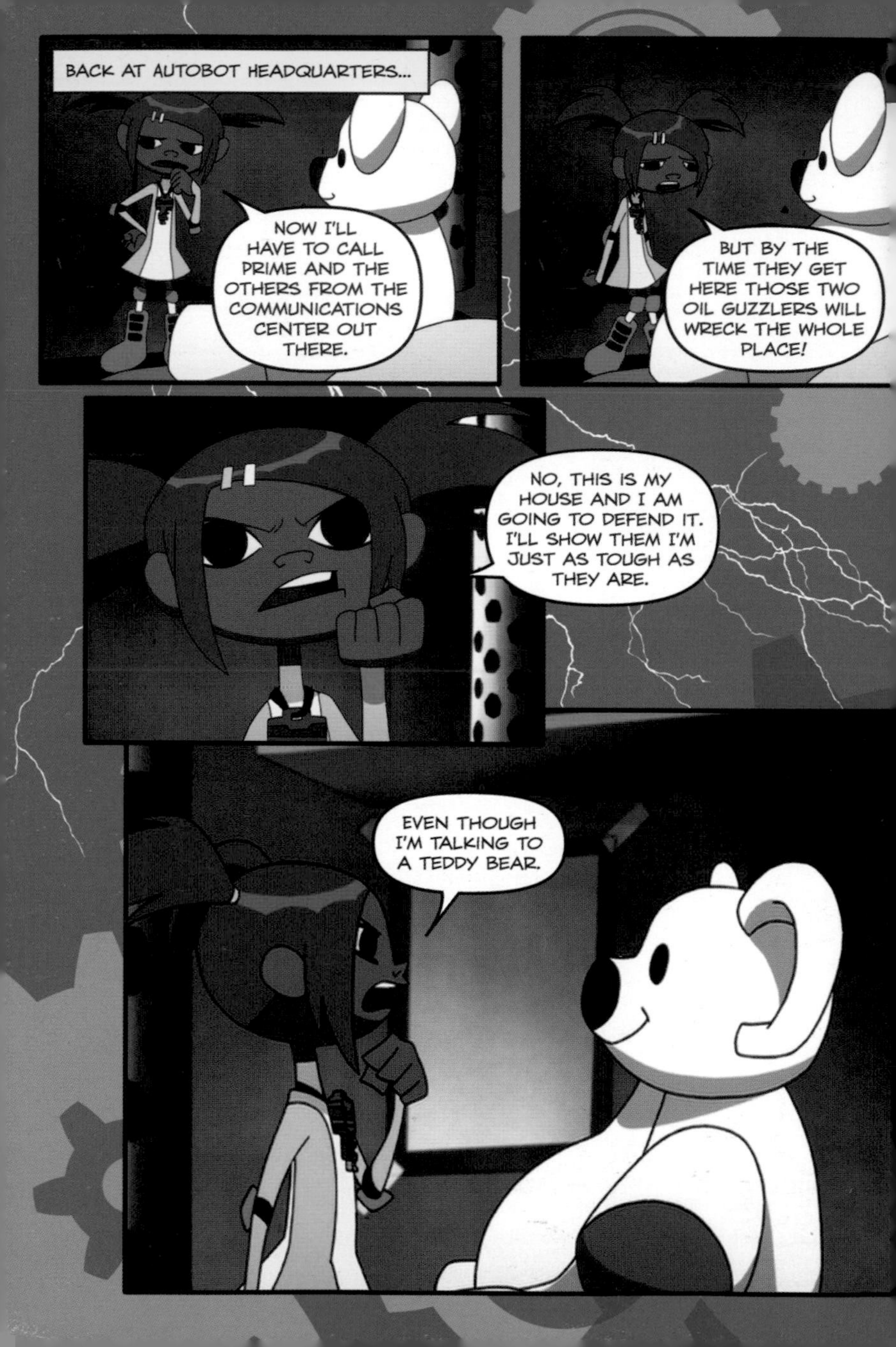
BACK AT AUTOBOT HEADQUARTERS...
NOW I'LL HAVE TO CALL PRIME AND THE OTHERS FROM THE COMMUNICATIONS CENTER OUT THERE.
BUT BY THE TIME THEY GET HERE THOSE TWO OIL GUZZLERS WILL WRECK THE WHOLE PLACE!
NO, THIS IS MY HOUSE AND I AM GOING TO DEFEND IT. I'LL SHOW THEM I'M JUST AS TOUGH AS THEY ARE.
EVEN THOUGH I'M TALKING TO A TEDDY BEAR.

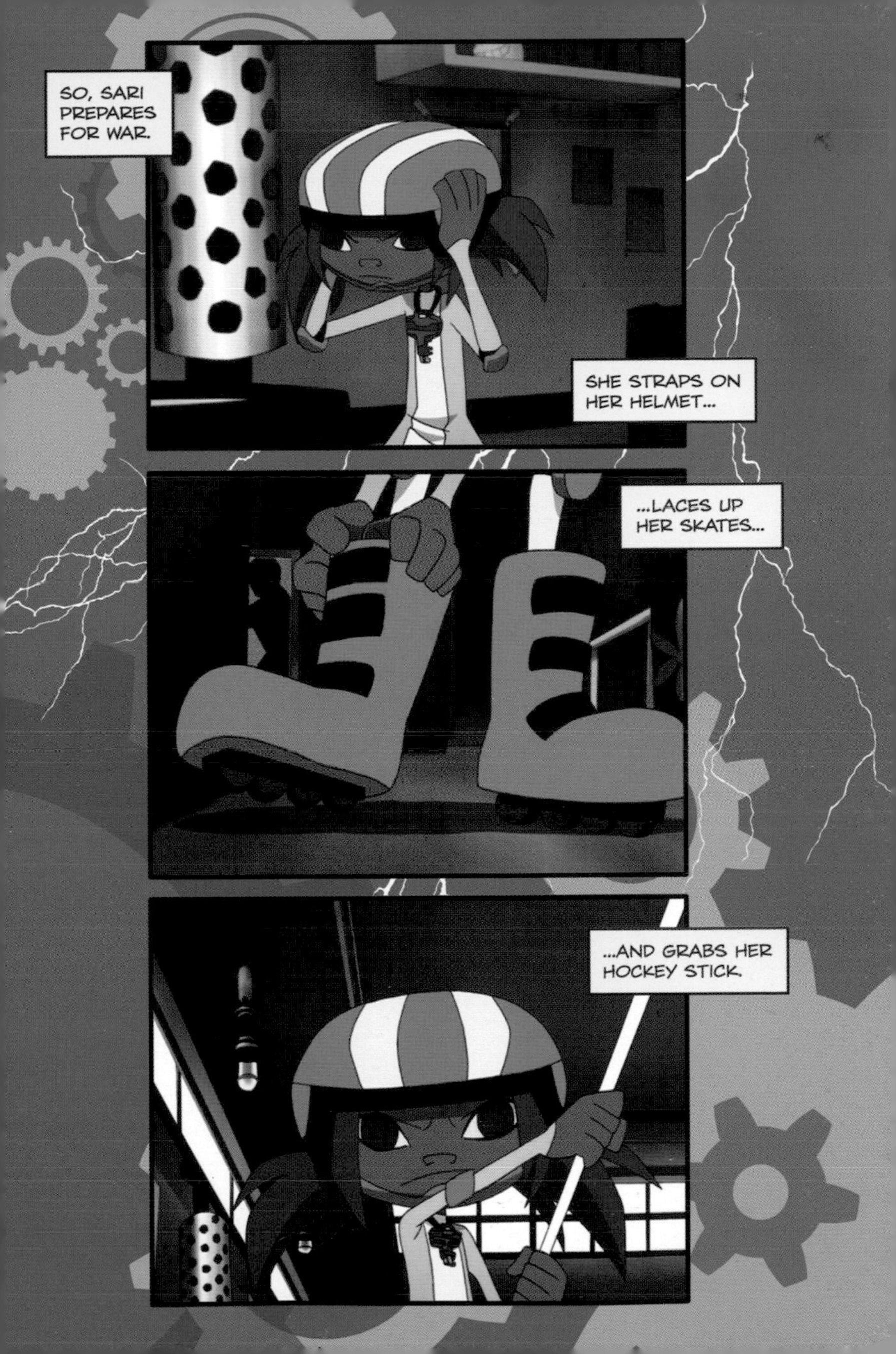
SO, SARI PREPARES FOR WAR.
SHE STRAPS ON HER HELMET...
...LACES UP HER SKATES...
...AND GRABS HER HOCKEY STICK.

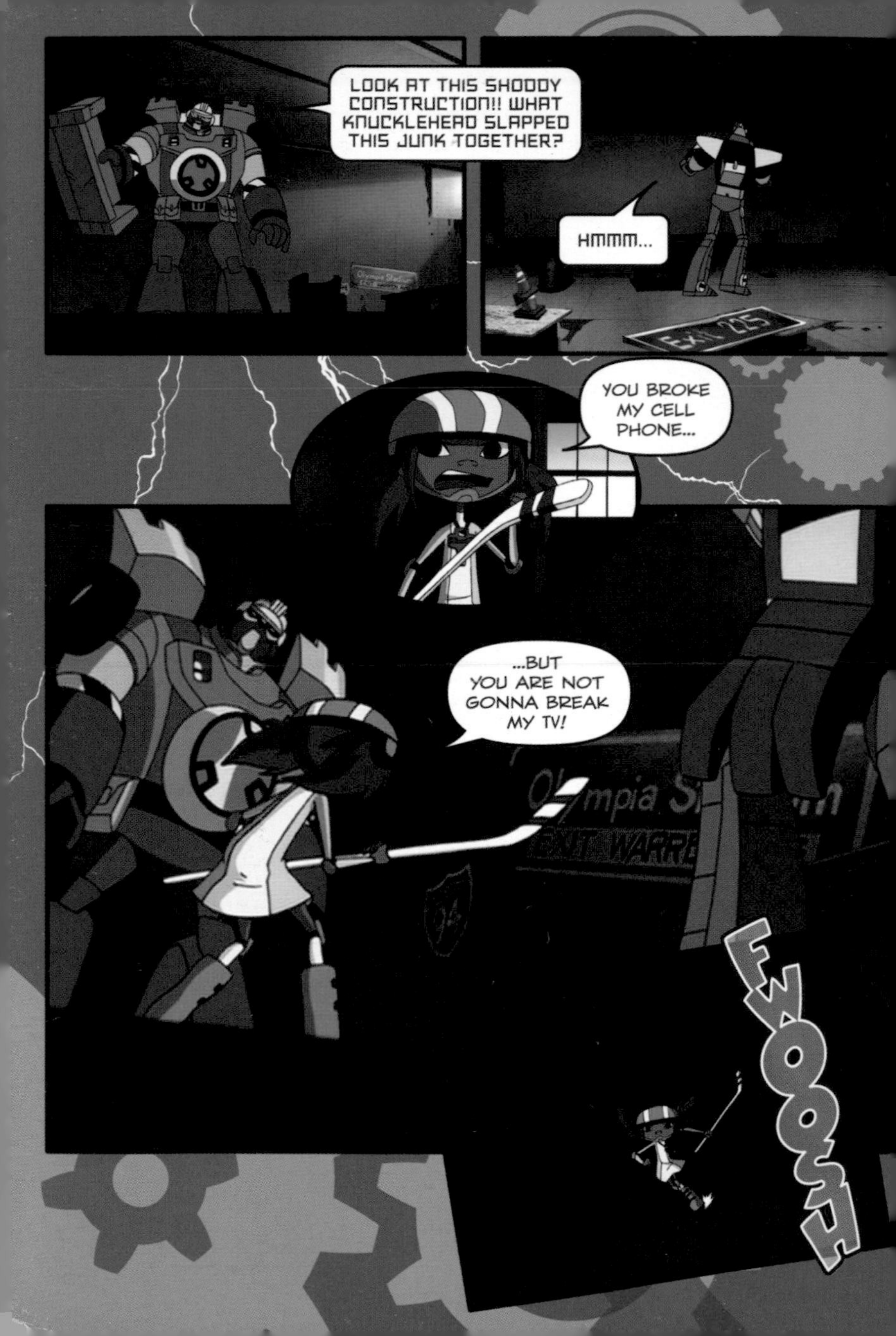
LOOK AT THIS SHODDY CONSTRUCTION!! WHAT KNUCKLEHEAD SLAPPED THIS JUNK TOGETHER?
HMMM...
EXIT 225
YOU BROKE MY CELL PHONE...
...BUT YOU ARE NOT GONNA BREAK MY TV!
FWOOSH

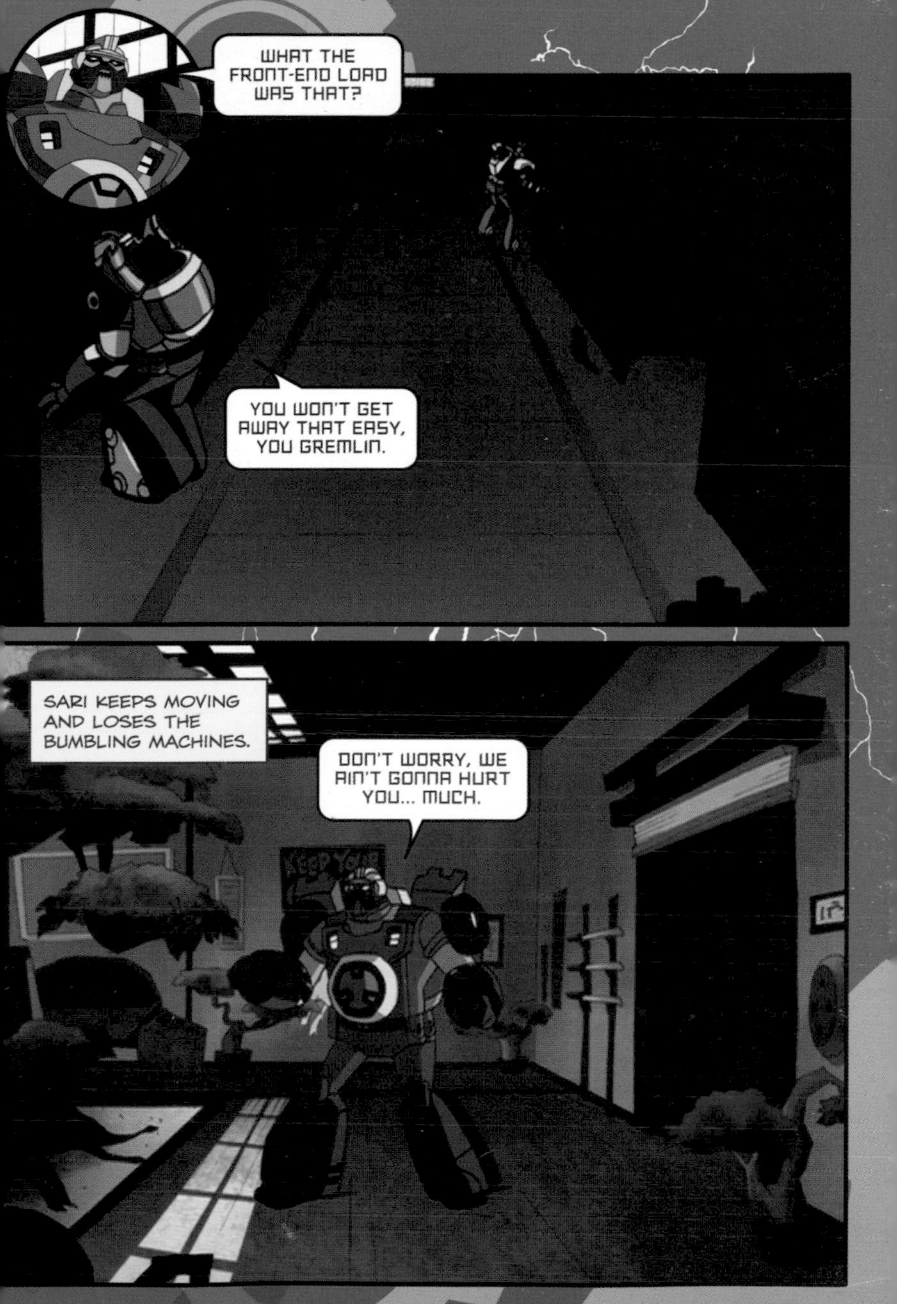
WHAT THE FRONT-END LOAD WAS THAT?
YOU WON'T GET AWAY THAT EASY, YOU GREMLIN.
SARI KEEPS MOVING AND LOSES THE BUMBLING MACHINES.
DON'T WORRY, WE AIN'T GONNA HURT YOU... MUCH.

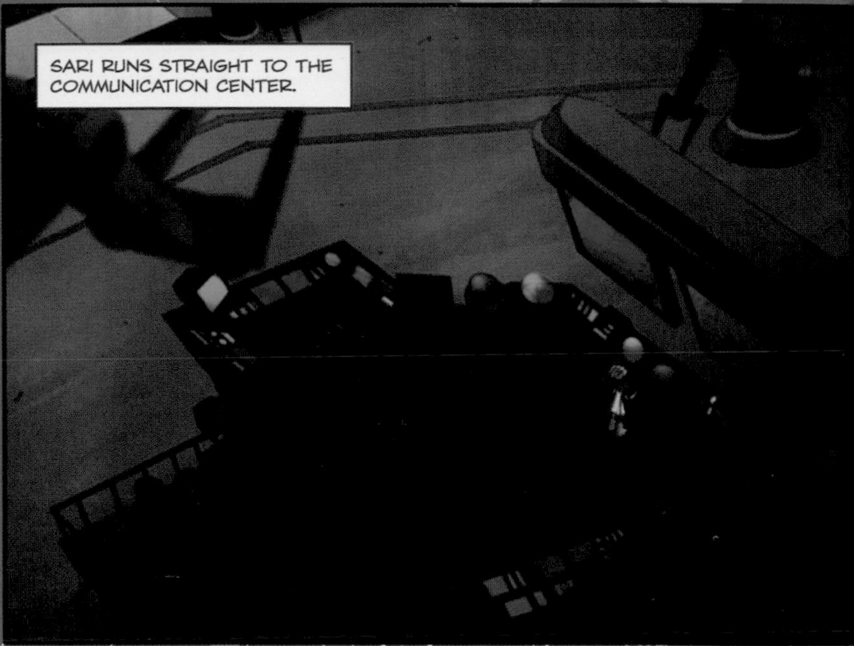
SARI RUNS STRAIGHT TO THE COMMUNICATION CENTER.

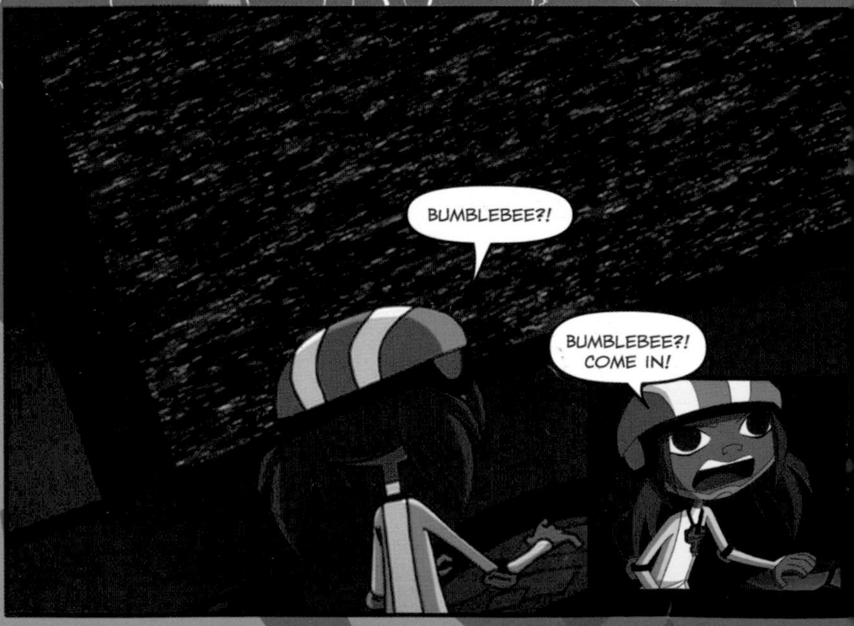
BUMBLEBEE?!
BUMBLEBEE?! COME IN!

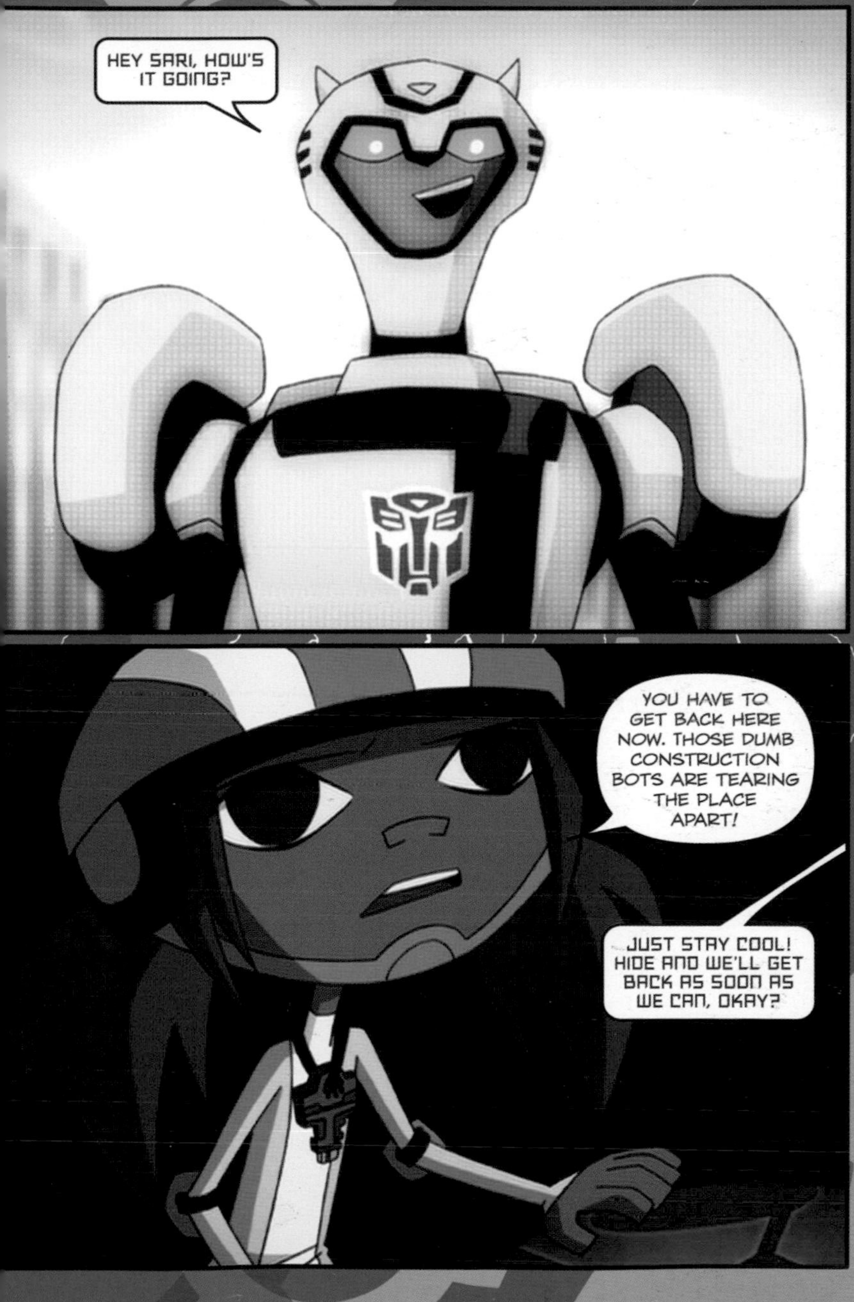
HEY SARI, HOW'S IT GOING?
YOU HAVE TO GET BACK HERE NOW. THOSE DUMB CONSTRUCTION BOTS ARE TEARING THE PLACE APART!
JUST STAY COOL! HIDE AND WE'LL GET BACK AS SOON AS WE CAN, OKAY?

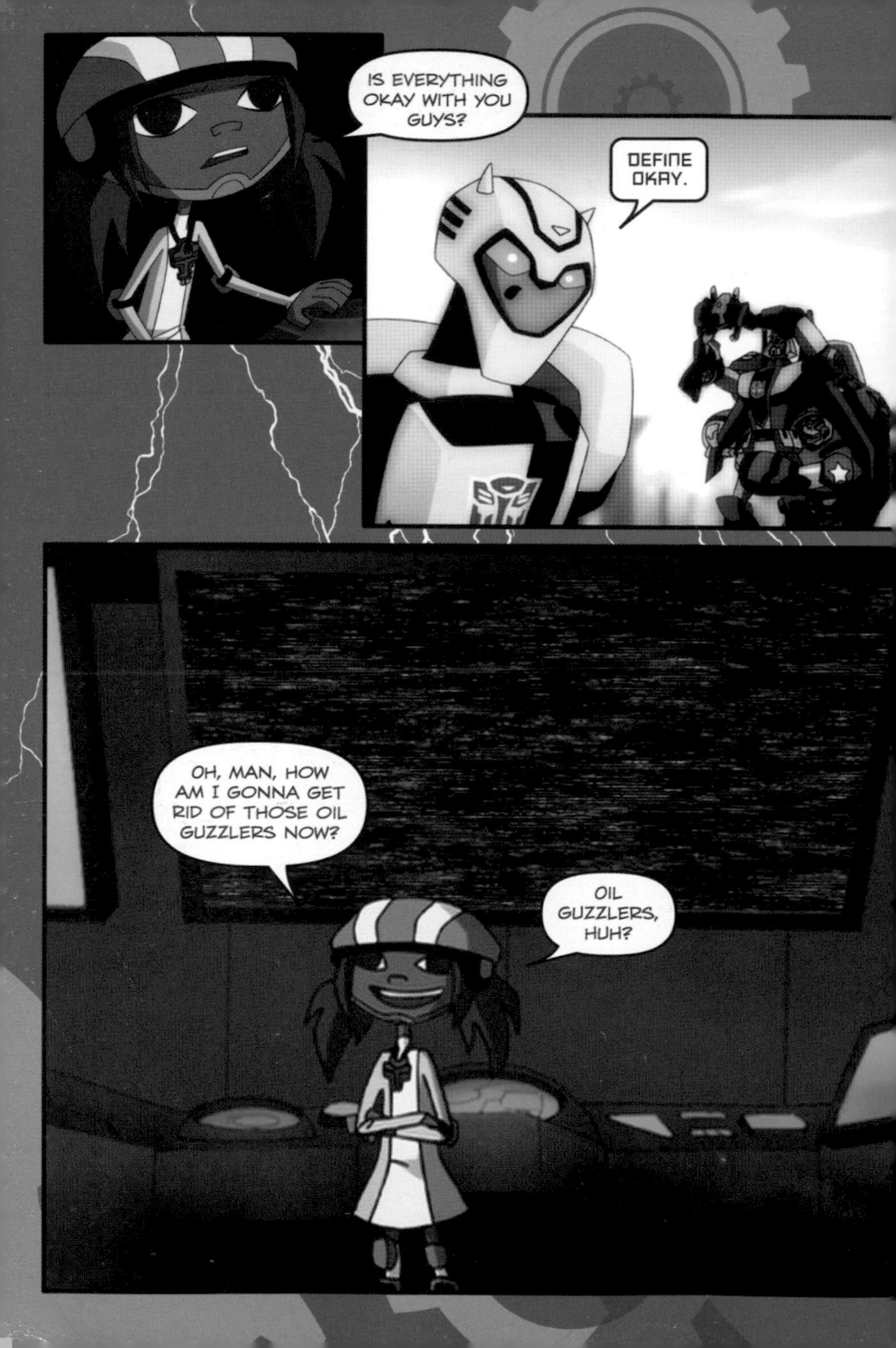
IS EVERYTHING OKAY WITH YOU GUYS?
DEFINE OKAY.
OH, MAN, HOW AM I GONNA GET RID OF THOSE OIL GUZZLERS NOW?
OIL GUZZLERS, HUH?

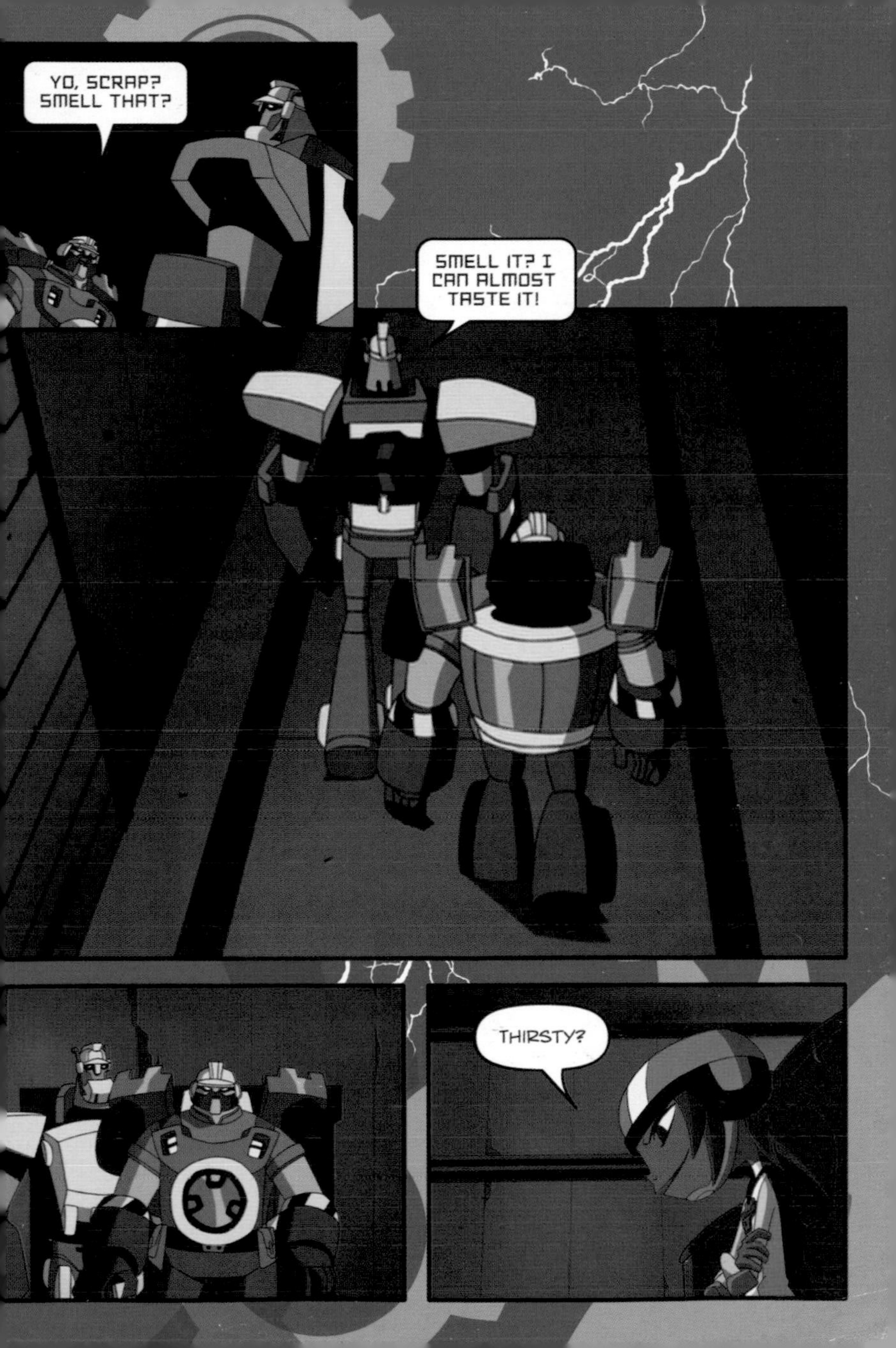
YO, SCRAP? SMELL THAT?
SMELL IT? I CAN ALMOST TASTE IT!
THIRSTY?

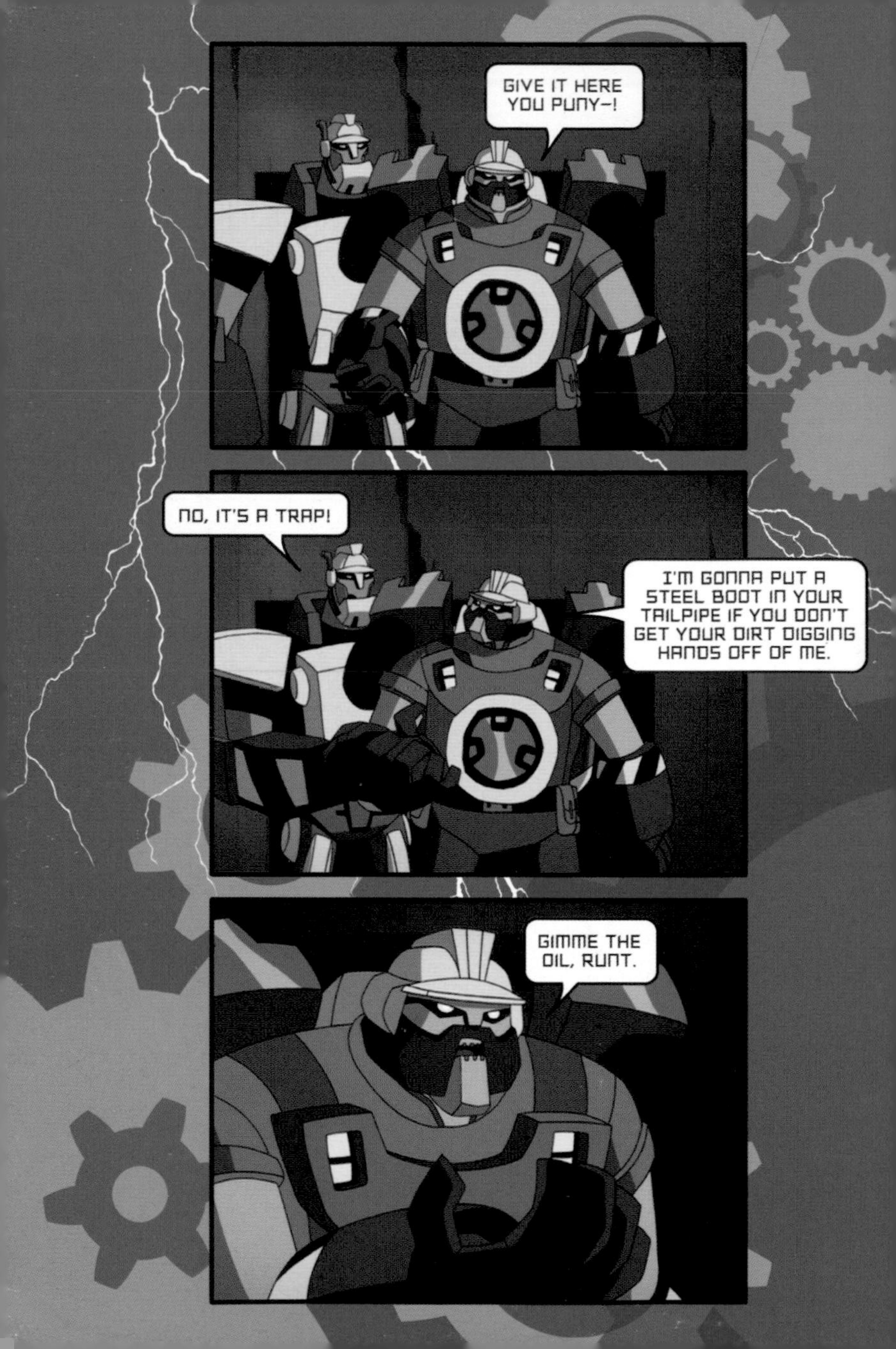
GIVE IT HERE YOU PUNY–!
NO, IT'S A TRAP!
I'M GONNA PUT A STEEL BOOT IN YOUR TAILPIPE IF YOU DON'T GET YOUR DIRT DIGGING HANDS OFF OF ME.
GIMME THE OIL, RUNT.

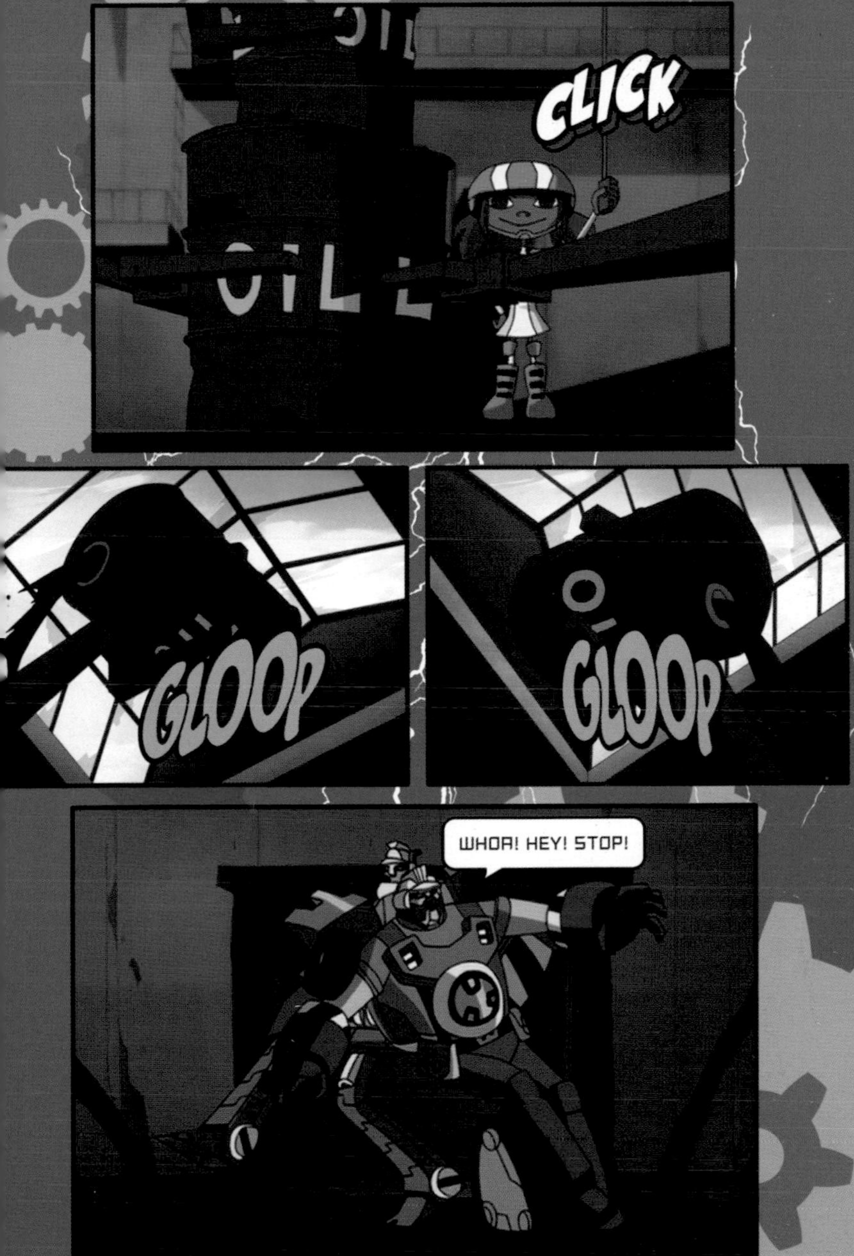
CLICK
GLOOP
GLOOP
WHOA! HEY! STOP!

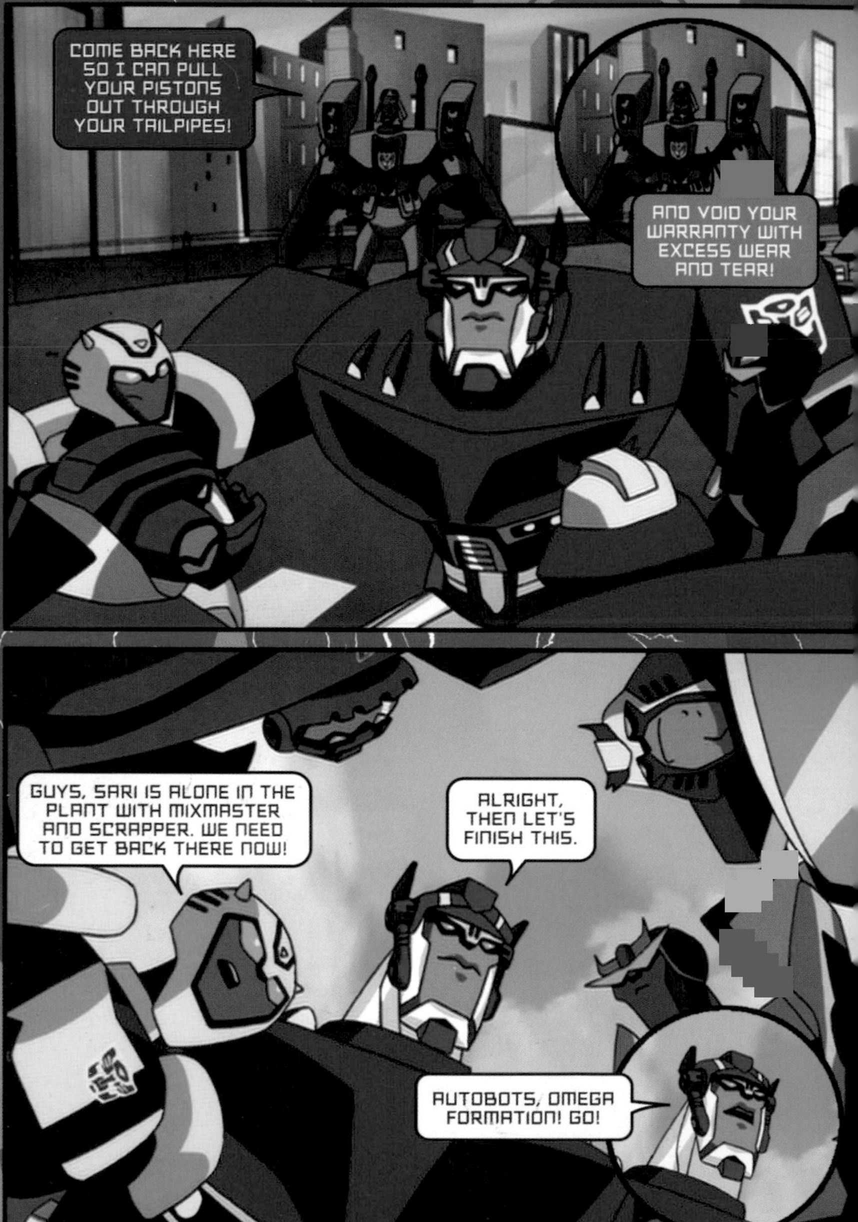
COME BACK HERE SO I CAN PULL YOUR PISTONS OUT THROUGH YOUR TAILPIPES!
AND VOID YOUR WARRANTY WITH EXCESS WEAR AND TEAR!
GUYS, SARI IS ALONE IN THE PLANT WITH MIXMASTER AND SCRAPPER. WE NEED TO GET BACK THERE NOW!
ALRIGHT, THEN LET'S FINISH THIS.
AUTOBOTS, OMEGA FORMATION! GO!

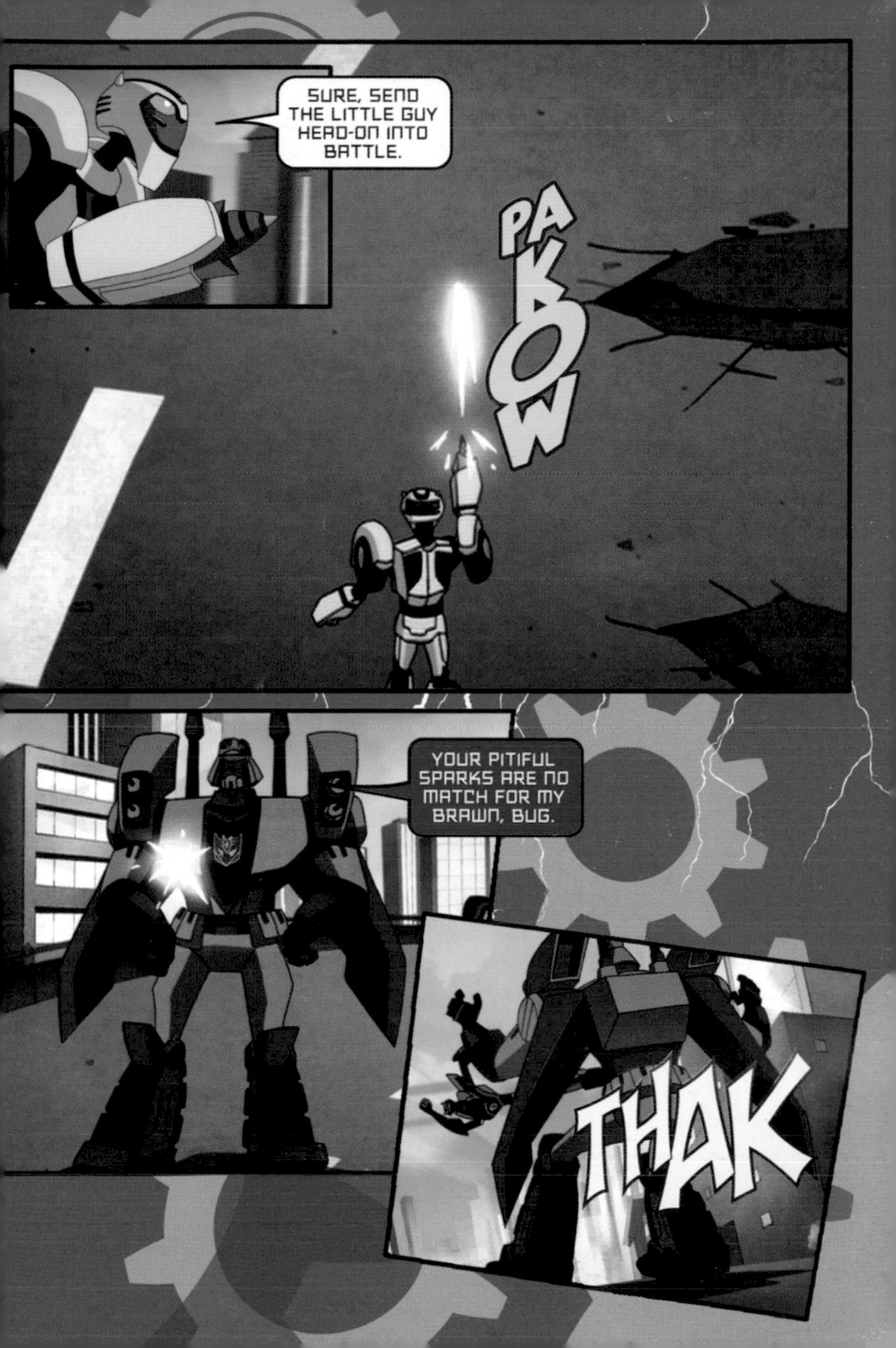
SURE, SEND THE LITTLE GUY HEAD-ON INTO BATTLE.
PAKOW
YOUR PITIFUL SPARKS ARE NO MATCH FOR MY BRAWN, BUG.
THAK

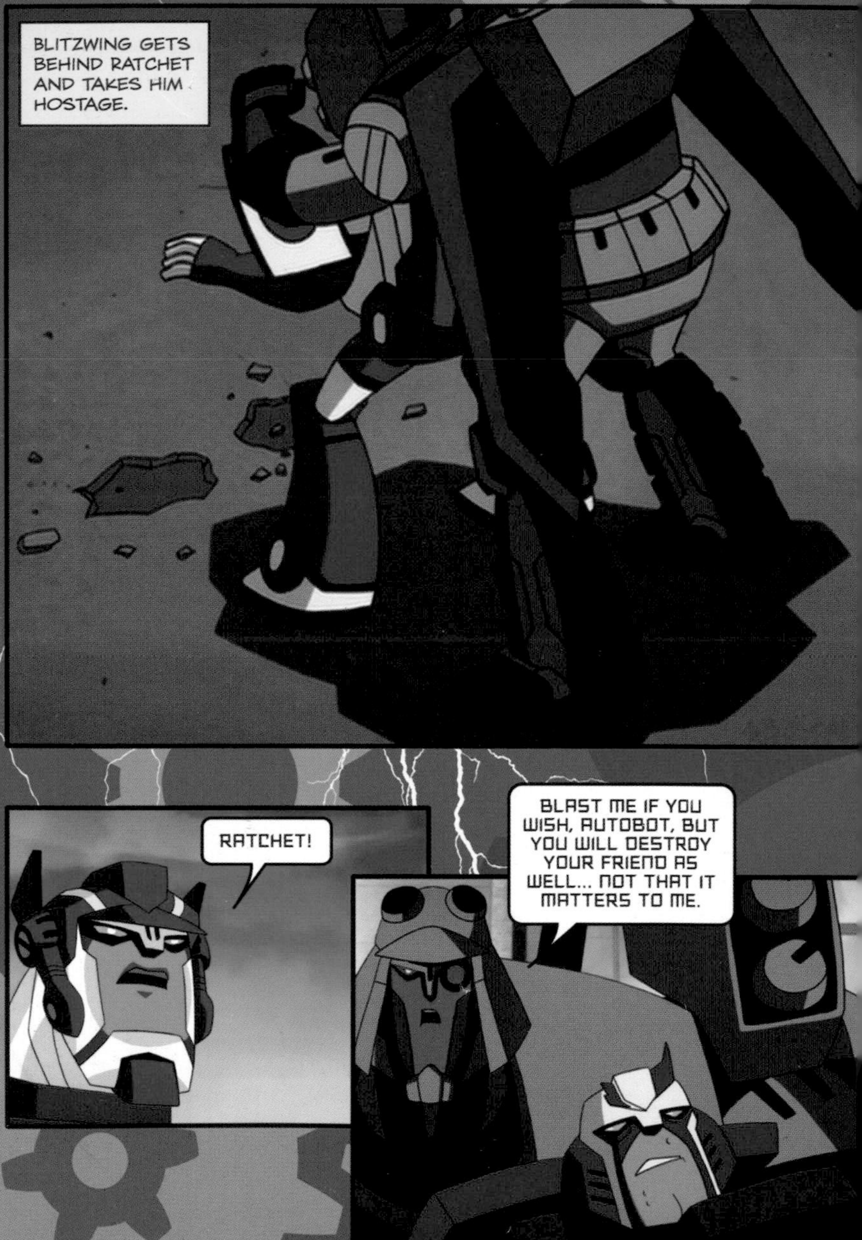
BLITZWING GETS BEHIND RATCHET AND TAKES HIM HOSTAGE.
RATCHET!
BLAST ME IF YOU WISH, AUTOBOT, BUT YOU WILL DESTROY YOUR FRIEND AS WELL... NOT THAT IT MATTERS TO ME.

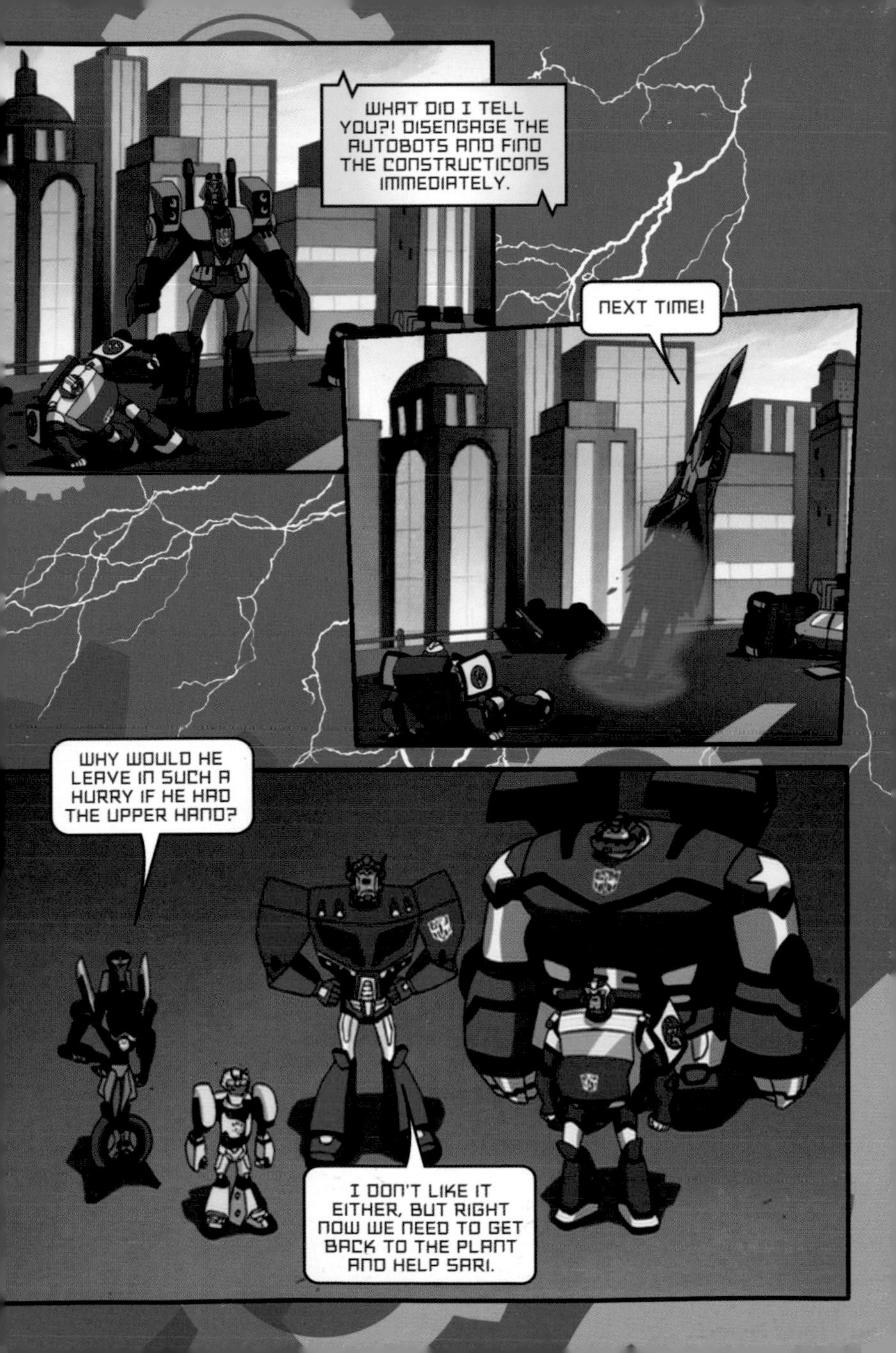
WHAT DID I TELL YOU?! DISENGAGE THE AUTOBOTS AND FIND THE CONSTRUCTICONS IMMEDIATELY.
NEXT TIME!
WHY WOULD HE LEAVE IN SUCH A HURRY IF HE HAD THE UPPER HAND?
I DON'T LIKE IT EITHER, BUT RIGHT NOW WE NEED TO GET BACK TO THE PLANT AND HELP SARI.

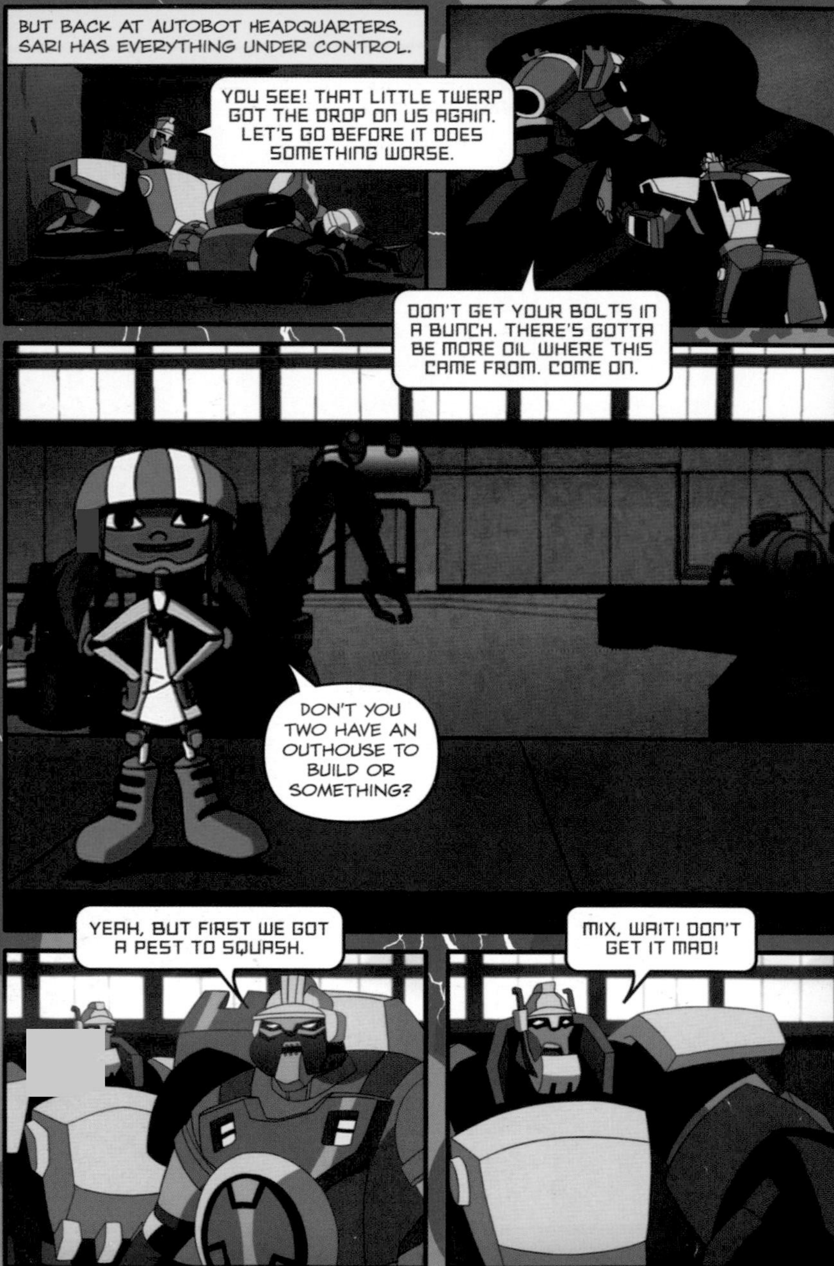
BUT BACK AT AUTOBOT HEADQUARTERS, SARI HAS EVERYTHING UNDER CONTROL.
YOU SEE! THAT LITTLE TWERP GOT THE DROP ON US AGAIN. LET'S GO BEFORE IT DOES SOMETHING WORSE.
DON'T GET YOUR BOLTS IN A BUNCH. THERE'S GOTTA BE MORE OIL WHERE THIS CAME FROM. COME ON.
DON'T YOU TWO HAVE AN OUTHOUSE TO BUILD OR SOMETHING?
YEAH, BUT FIRST WE GOT A PEST TO SQUASH.
MIX, WAIT! DON'T GET IT MAD!

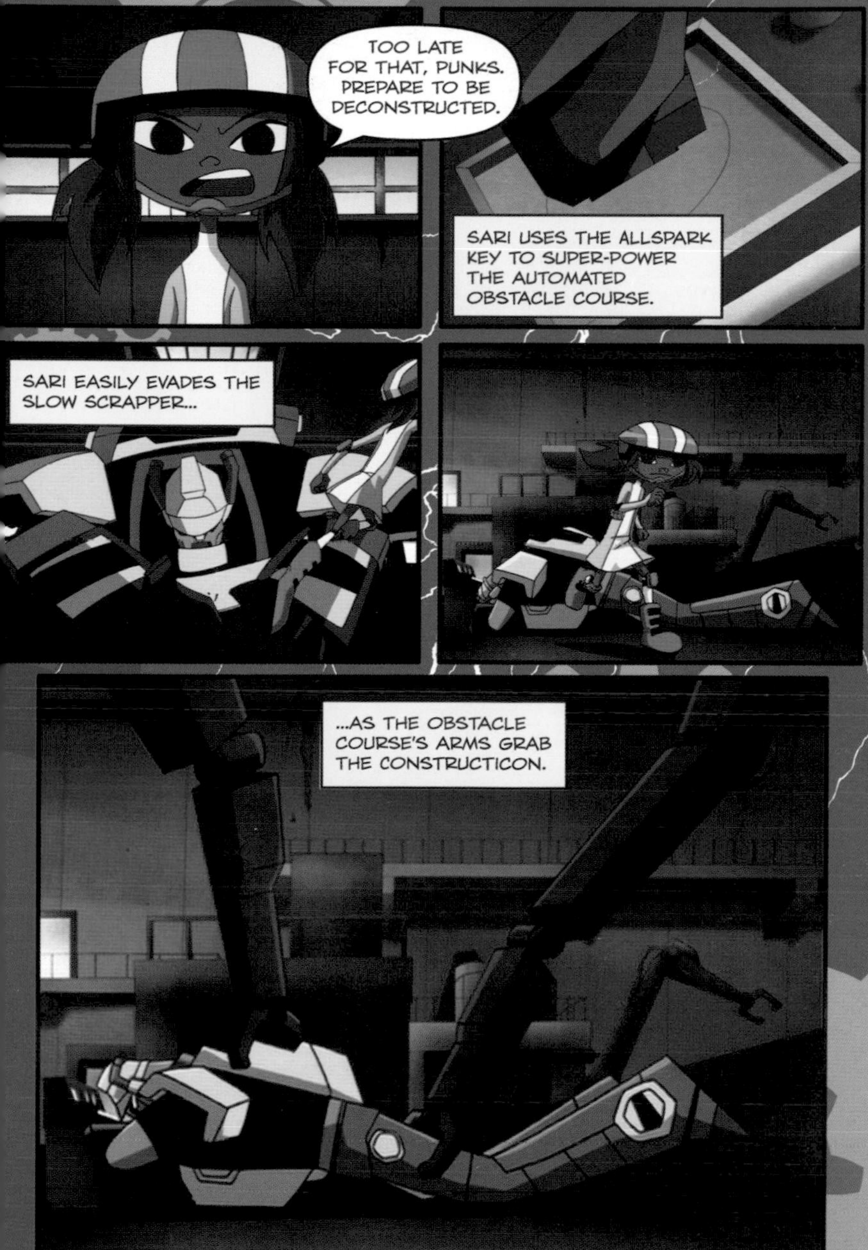
TOO LATE FOR THAT, PUNKS. PREPARE TO BE DECONSTRUCTED.
SARI USES THE ALLSPARK KEY TO SUPER-POWER THE AUTOMATED OBSTACLE COURSE.
SARI EASILY EVADES THE SLOW SCRAPPER...
...AS THE OBSTACLE COURSE'S ARMS GRAB THE CONSTRUCTICON.

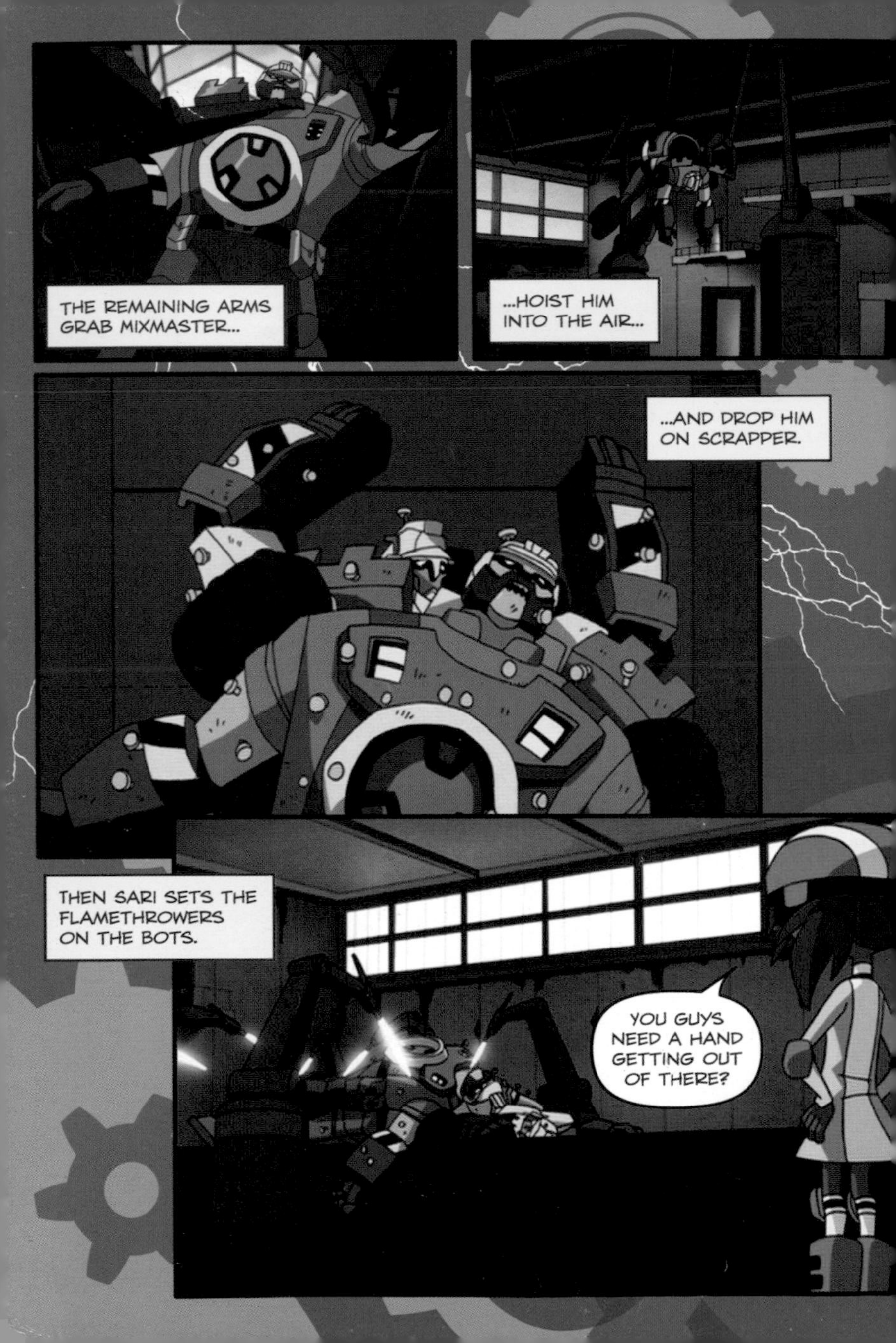

THE REMAINING ARMS GRAB MIXMASTER...
...HOIST HIM INTO THE AIR...
...AND DROP HIM ON SCRAPPER.
THEN SARI SETS THE FLAMETHROWERS ON THE BOTS.
YOU GUYS NEED A HAND GETTING OUT OF THERE?

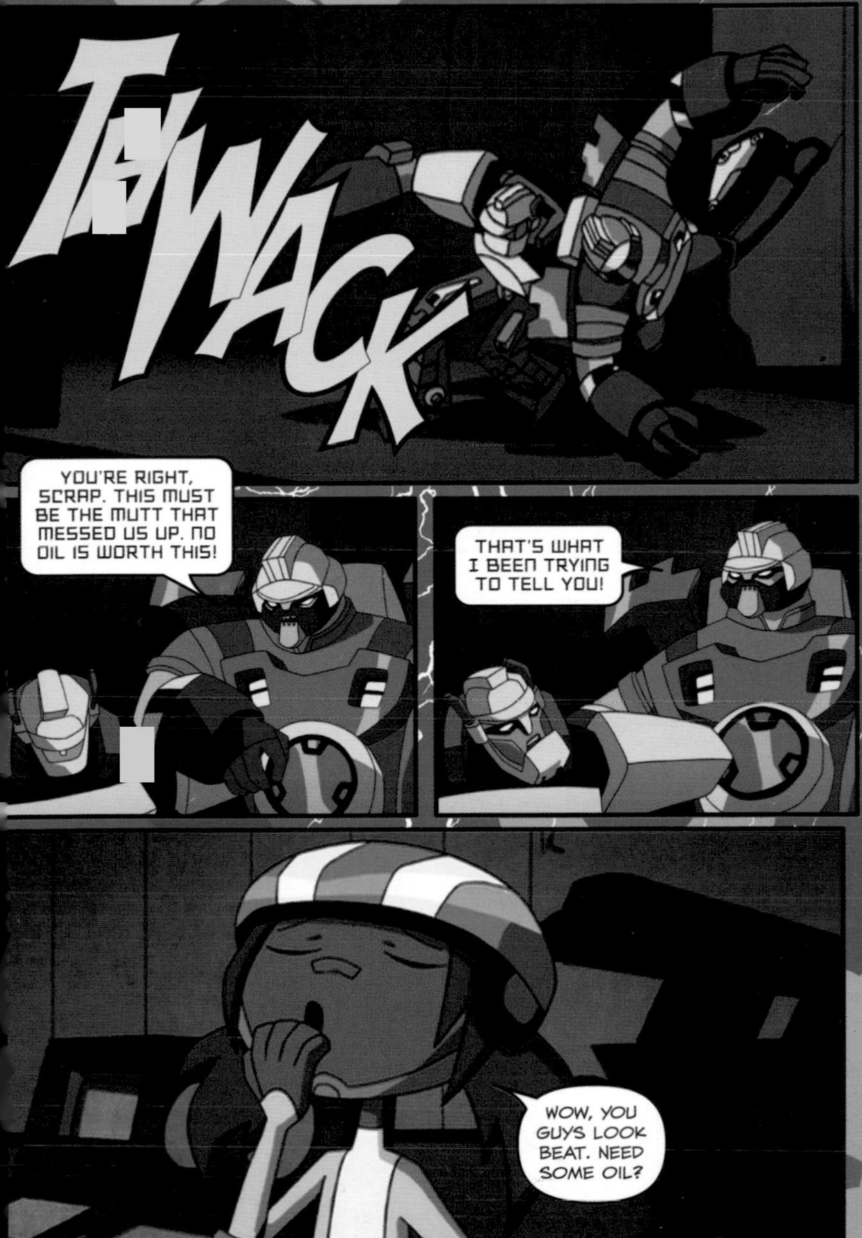
THWACK
YOU'RE RIGHT, SCRAP. THIS MUST BE THE MUTT THAT MESSED US UP. NO OIL IS WORTH THIS!
THAT'S WHAT I BEEN TRYING TO TELL YOU!
WOW, YOU GUYS LOOK BEAT. NEED SOME OIL?

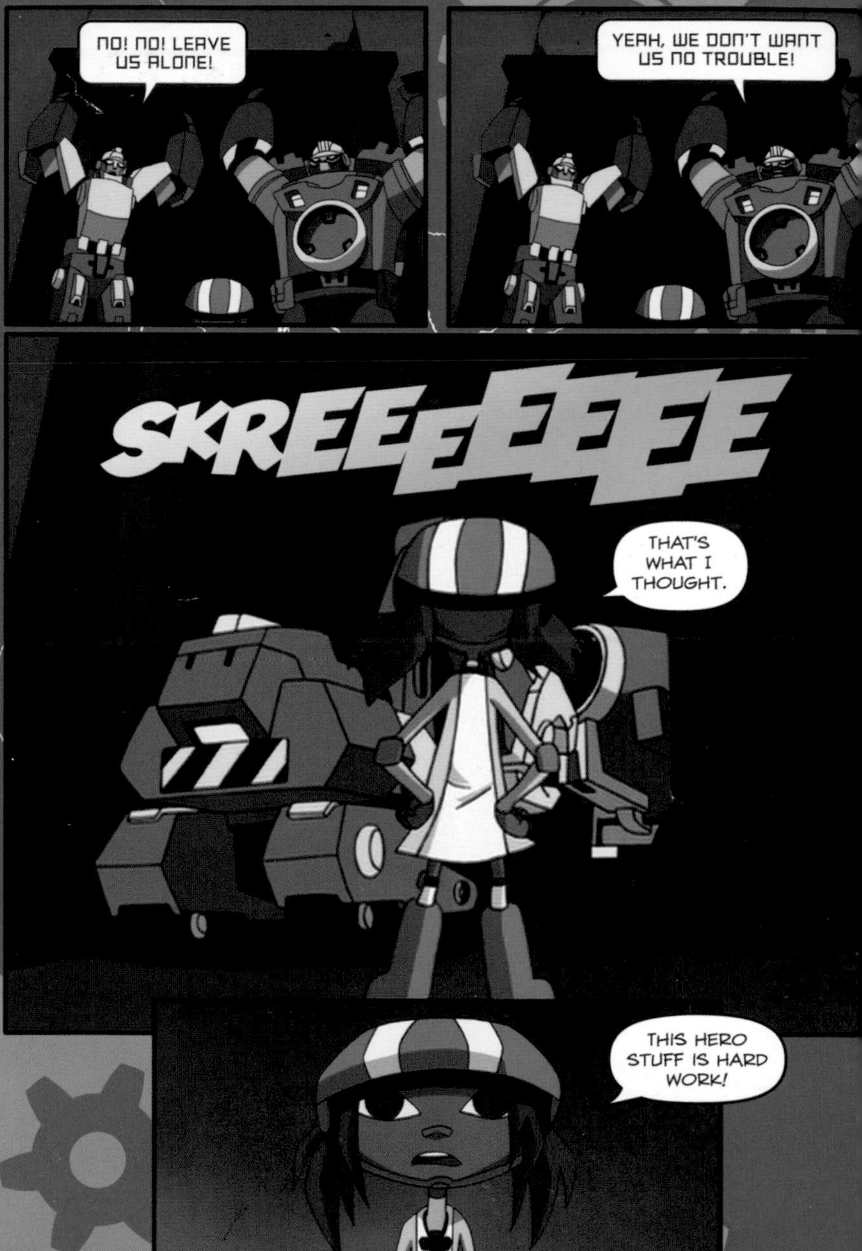
NO! NO! LEAVE US ALONE!
YEAH, WE DON'T WANT US NO TROUBLE!
SKREEEEEEE
THAT'S WHAT I THOUGHT.
THIS HERO STUFF IS HARD WORK!

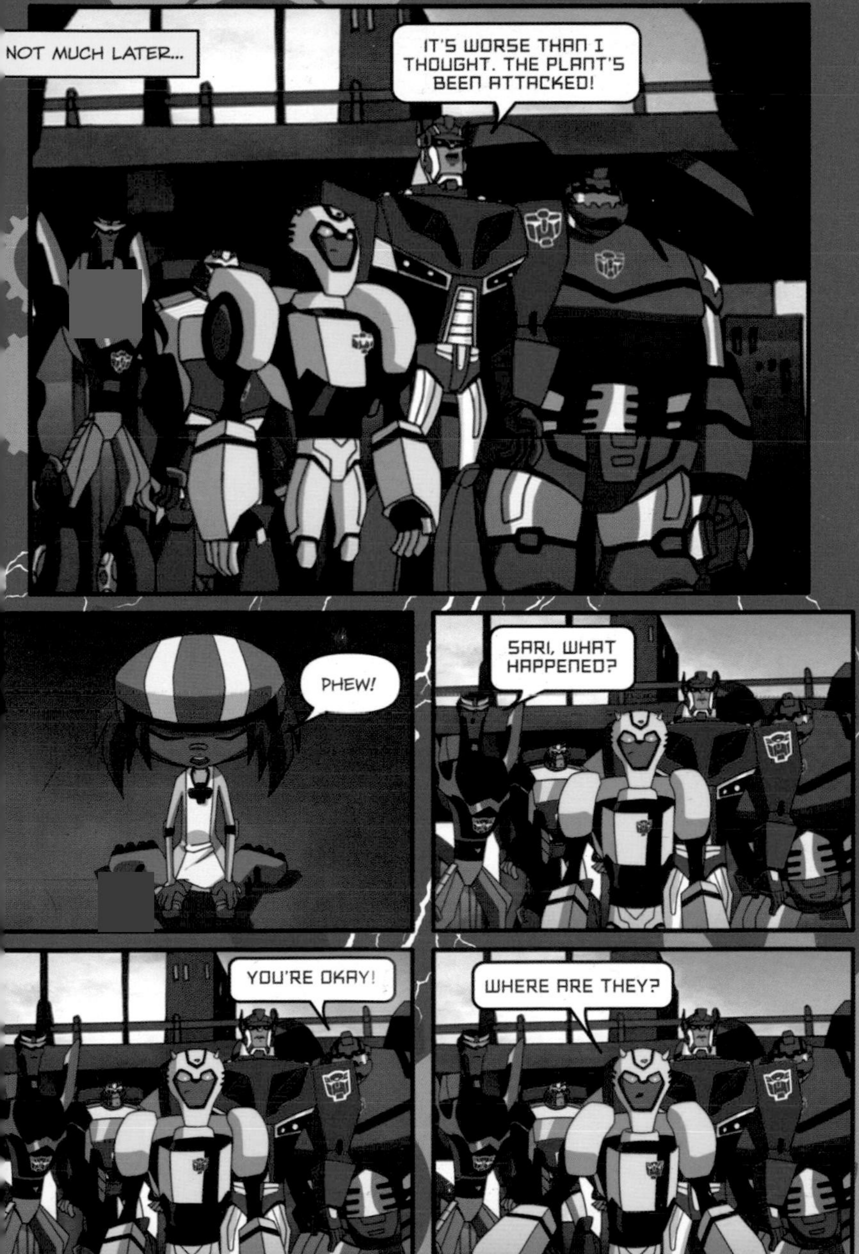
NOT MUCH LATER...
IT'S WORSE THAN I THOUGHT. THE PLANT'S BEEN ATTACKED!
PHEW!
SARI, WHAT HAPPENED?
YOU'RE OKAY!
WHERE ARE THEY?

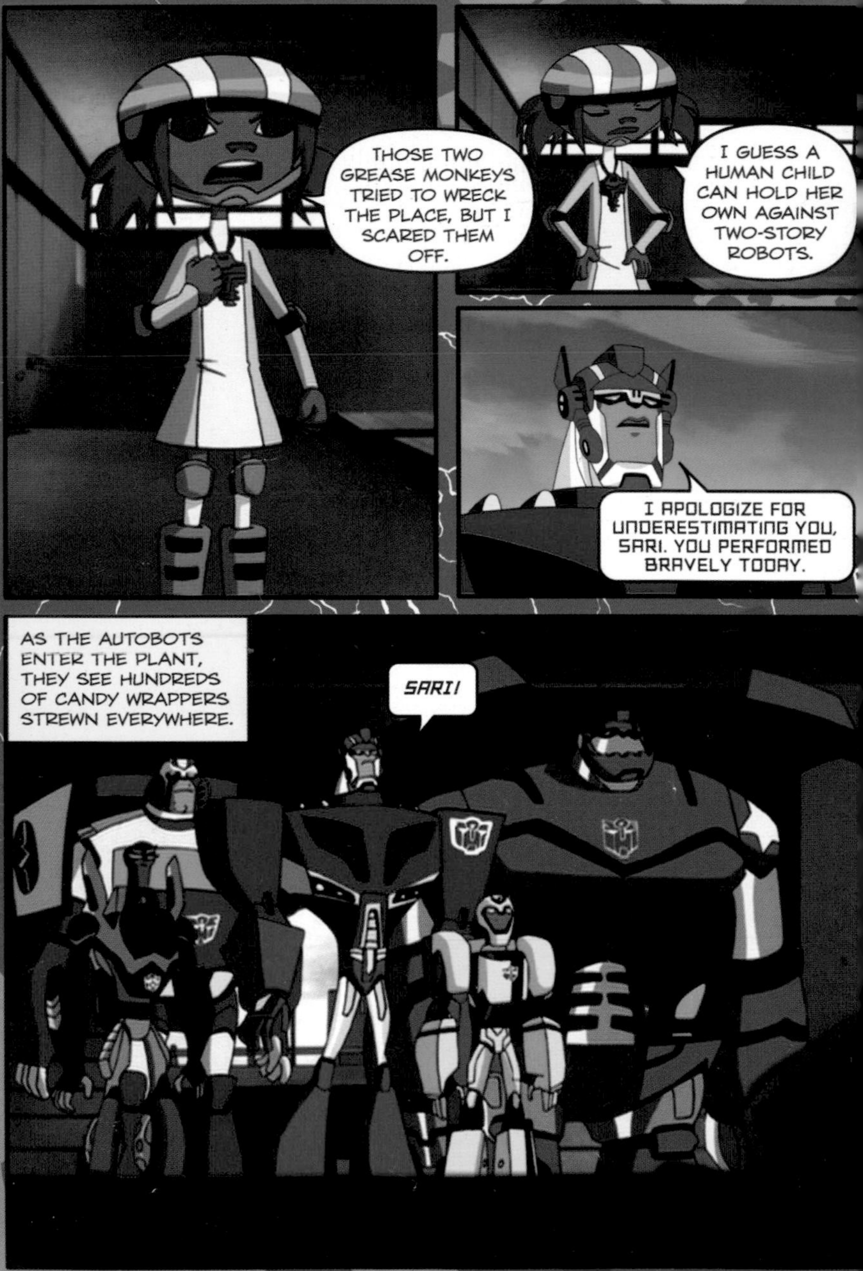
THOSE TWO GREASE MONKEYS TRIED TO WRECK THE PLACE, BUT I SCARED THEM OFF.
I GUESS A HUMAN CHILD CAN HOLD HER OWN AGAINST TWO-STORY ROBOTS.
I APOLOGIZE FOR UNDERESTIMATING YOU, SARI. YOU PERFORMED BRAVELY TODAY.
AS THE AUTOBOTS ENTER THE PLANT, THEY SEE HUNDREDS OF CANDY WRAPPERS STREWN EVERYWHERE.
SARI!

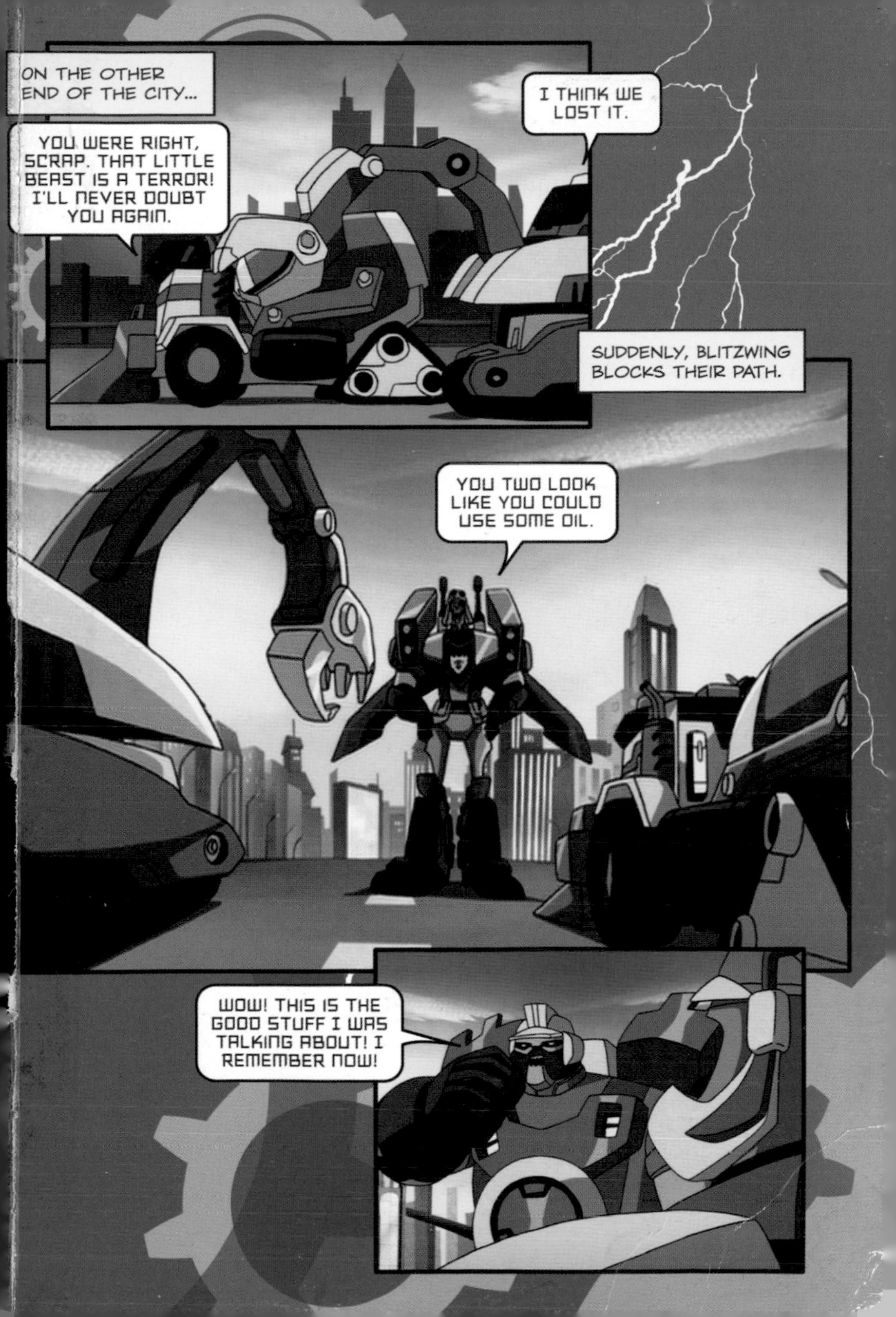
ON THE OTHER END OF THE CITY...
YOU WERE RIGHT, SCRAP. THAT LITTLE BEAST IS A TERROR! I'LL NEVER DOUBT YOU AGAIN.
I THINK WE LOST IT.
SUDDENLY, BLITZWING BLOCKS THEIR PATH.
YOU TWO LOOK LIKE YOU COULD USE SOME OIL.
WOW! THIS IS THE GOOD STUFF I WAS TALKING ABOUT! I REMEMBER NOW!

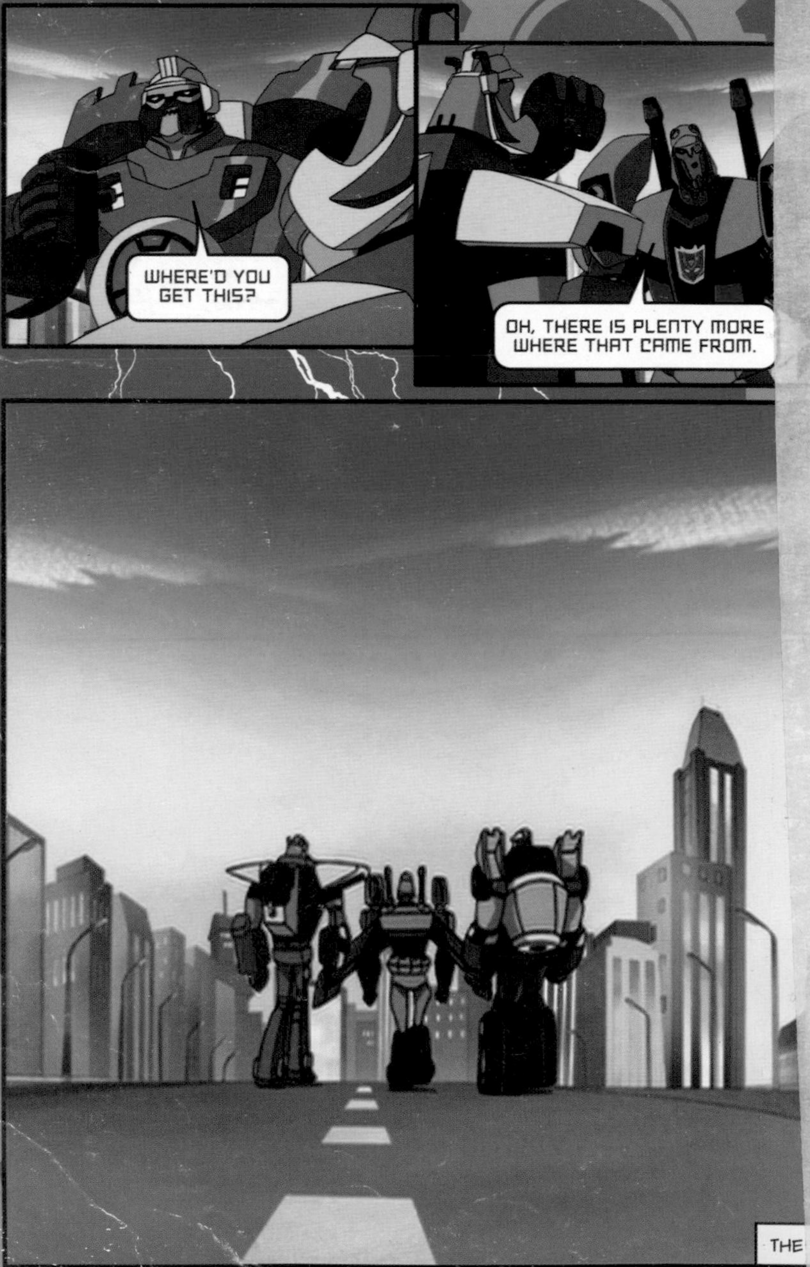
WHERE'D YOU GET THIS?
OH, THERE IS PLENTY MORE WHERE THAT CAME FROM.
THE END.